The World's Most Mysterious People

Lionel and
Patricia Fanthorpe

The World's Most Mysterious People

HOUNSLOW PRESS
A MEMBER OF THE DUNDURN GROUP
TORONTO · OXFORD

Hounslow Press
A Member of the Dundurn Group

Publisher: Anthony Hawke
Editors: Kathy Lim and Barry Jowett
Design: Scott Reid
Printer: Transcontinental Printing Inc.
Photographs: Lionel and Patricia Fanthorpe
Portrait Sketches: Theo. W. Fanthorpe

Canadian Cataloguing in Publication Data

Fanthorpe, R. Lionel
The world's most mysterious people

ISBN 0-88882-202-2
I. Biography. I. Fanthorpe, Patricia. II. Title

CT9990.F26 1998   920.02   C98-931582-7

1   2   3   4   5   02   01   00   99   98

We acknowledge the support of the **Canada Council for the Arts** for our publishing program. We also acknowledge the support of the **Ontario Arts Council** and the **Book Publishing Industry Development Program** of the **Department of Canadian Heritage**.

Printed and bound in Canada.

 Printed on recycled paper.

Hounslow Press
8 Market Street
Suite 200
Toronto, Ontario, Canada
M5E 1M6

Hounslow Press
73 Lime Walk
Headington, Oxford,
England
OX3 7AD

Hounslow Press
2250 Military Road
Tonawanda NY
U.S.A 14150

CONTENTS

<u>Dedication</u>

This book is dedicated to our friend
Robert "Slick" Phillips
of Pentyrch, near Cardiff,
in warm appreciation of the generous help he gave
to the Infinity Science Fiction Convention
at a time when it was most needed.

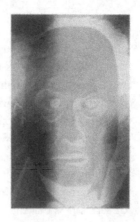

Foreword

by Canon Stanley Mogford, MA

Some of us who are now well on in years will be aware of these lines:

Lives of great men all remind us
We can make our lives sublime
And departing leave behind us
Footprints on the sands of time.

We remember them because they were printed on many of the exercise books once issued in schools. It was only very much later on in life that I, for one, realized that they came from the pen of one of America's greatest poets, H.W. Longfellow. Printed where it was, the verse was intended to inspire us to do well with our work and our lives. Later adult reflection might lead one to question the imagery chosen. Footprints will have to do well to survive in sand. The moment the sands dry and the winds blow, they are covered and gone forever. Only the very exceptional, the rarest of individuals, in any event, can hope to leave footprints showing, forever, where they have passed, and what they have achieved. Most of us have unpretentious lives and are more in tune with the words of Shakespeare. As he once put it, each of us tends to be "A poor player that struts and frets his hour upon the stage / And then is heard no more."

Some, however, are exceptions. They survive in others' memory and affection and will continue to do so forever and a day. Their immortality has been achieved through sheer goodness and holiness of life. Many admire the passive life, with its refusal to retaliate, its resolve never to hate and hurt in response to the malice of others: what Jesus meant when he spoke of "turning the other cheek." But few are capable of doing it. Mahatma Gandhi, however, was one who could, and did — and for his life of resigned submission, he will never be forgotten. Francis of Assisi will also always be revered as long as there are compassionate and idealistic people in the world who long to emulate one who was able to give, as they never seem to be able to do, surrender to poverty, in a way they find beyond them, and lead a life of selflessness that they can only admire from a distance. Those who long to serve the poor, the outcast, and the sick will also never lose sight of the leper saint, Damien, who, as a fit man, offered to serve within an isolated island leper colony, where, at that time, all would have been condemned by the disease to certain disfigurement and death. The opening words of one of his sermons to his lepers, after some years of service there, stand as his memorial: "My beloved fellow lepers...."

Footprints in the sands of time have been left by such men of rare quality, and all the winds, down all the centuries, will never erase what they have achieved. The author of this book, my friend of many years, could have been persuaded to write of them; perhaps, one day soon, he will.

Others, in marked contrast, have set cloven footprints on the sands of time. The way they have lived has been brutal and sadistic. Evil has been revealed through discovery of their concentration camps, their ethnic cleansing, their rampaging quest, at all costs, for power over the lives of others. The damage they have inflicted on humankind will always assure them of a place in any chamber of horrors, but they will have an immortality we lesser mortals will gladly forswear. They have scarred the world into which they were born, and the scars remain. The author of this book could also have made such people the subject of his research. Who knows? He may do so one of these days.

What the author has done is to look, not to the good or to the evil of this world, but, instead, to the great eccentrics of the generations — the odd, the strange, the unmanageable, the daring: those he calls men and women of mystery. With his wife, Patricia, Lionel has researched the lives of many such men and women, and has described for us the powers that drove them — their complex characters, the vagaries of their behaviour, the worst and the best of the instincts that competed to take control of their lives — and the fates that befell them. Most of us who read this book are ordinary, and we are glad of it. We are cut from a mould and differ little from one another. We are capable of flashes of goodness, a little genuine love and self-giving; we are also capable of a measure of hatred and other baser emotions. But with us, everything is more or less under control. We are average in all our ways, and our lives reflect it. Whereas we are average and all much of a pattern, the writer has uncovered those who are very *unaverage*. In some cases, people whom one would rather read about, perhaps, than meet. We can warm to them on paper, but we would never care to share our lives with some of the characters he has described for us here.

It has been my privilege to write the foreword for many, if not all, of Lionel Fanthorpe's recent books. This one, in particular, has fascinated me. All of my working life, I have been a Priest of the Church, as is Lionel, and a fellow religious like Rasputin seems to me from another planet. Like many of us living on a small income or on an even smaller pension, I warm to the good fortune of Bérenger Saunière, who somehow, somewhere, found money enough to do anything he liked for himself and his parishioners, but took the secret of his discovery with him to the grave. A reader all my life, my travels have mainly been on paper or in my head. And so those who actually penetrate the mysteries and share the privations of undiscovered areas, as Colonel Fawcett did, have my admiration, but not my wish to join them in their travels.

The Reverend Lionel Fanthorpe, with his wife as his researcher, has collected for us a rum grouping of people: flamboyant, mysterious, a few almost beyond our comprehension. He has drawn them from many generations, and from different countries and social groupings. As is his way, he has dealt with all of them fairly, showing neither prejudice nor dislike. I commend the book, with all its disturbing, fascinating characters, and hope and believe it will draw many readers over the coming years. Always remember, these mysterious men and women are not figments of the imagination. They are real. They once existed. We would do well not to forget both the good and the harm they have done.

Canon Stanley Mogford, MA
Cardiff, Wales, UK, 1998

Footnote
The authors are deeply grateful to their friend, Canon Mogford, whose great scholarship is widely recognized. It is a real privilege to have his support.

Introduction

People are mysterious. Human life is a great enigma. Science cannot tell us with any certainty what we are, where we came from, or where we're going. Neither can it tell us why we are here. Various mystics, religious leaders, psychologists, and philosophers have accepted the challenge, and come up with a wide variety of answers.

One of the riddles of the human mind and of its strange decision-making processes is that some of us accept one or another of the theories of such "authorities" while some of us don't. However, the human tragedy is that far too many of those who accept one explanation exclusively and enthusiastically, then spend most of their energy ridiculing, persecuting, or killing those who disagree.

In examining this sample of the world's most mysterious people in depth, we have tried to be as objective as possible, to stand away from our own personal religious and philosophical beliefs, and to do our best to treat the people we have studied with the tolerance and respect we think they deserve. The paradox inherent in that approach is, of course, that believing that people deserve tolerance and respect is in itself part of our own inescapable belief system!

We have learnt a great deal about our mysterious subjects in the course of our research into their unusual lives. In looking at such people in depth, it may be possible to pick up a few helpful hints about how to make the most of our own lives.

We thank all these men and women of mystery for what our studies of them have taught us about the Greater Mystery of life itself — and from that perspective, we commend them whole-heartedly to our readers.

Lionel and Patricia Fanthorpe
Cardiff, Wales, UK, 1998

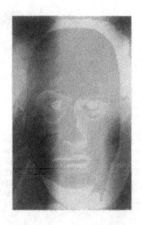

Chapter 1

Was Aleister Crowley a Genuine Black Magician?

Aleister Crowley's full name was originally Edward Alexander Crowley. The Aleister modification came later. He was born in Leamington Spa, England, on October 12, 1875. His parents belonged to a very strict fundamentalist Christian sect, usually referred to as the Plymouth Brethren. His childhood education, therefore, both at home and at a Brethren school, was heavily Bible-centred and puritanical. In consequence, young Aleister knew more about that type of Christianity than most people do, and, from all accounts, he hated and despised what he regarded as its narrow and restrictive teachings.

Psychologists often suspect that traumatic experiences in childhood can lead to violent reactions against the accepted household culture and the norms and mores associated with those childhood experiences. Crowley's reactions against fundamentalist Christianity would seem to support that view.

In Bernard Shaw's play *The Devil's Disciple*, the hero — whose real moral code is that of generosity and altruism, although he would be the last to suspect it himself — was raised in a grim, puritanical, New England community, in which he saw Satan as the only supernatural being who didn't seem to rejoice in human misery. The God preached by the puritanical fundamentalists seemed to him to be concerned only with sin, stern judgement, and rigorous punishment.

Aleister Crowley, the magician, who saw himself as 666, the Great Beast of the Book of Revelation in the Bible.

Crowley's nauseating behaviour reached an early peak when he killed the family cat, using several revolting methods (each of which would have been fatal on its own) on the pretext that he was testing the old adage about cats having nine lives.

His prodigious sexual appetite was already in evidence in his early teens, when he seduced one of the housemaids while the rest of the family was out attending a religious service. His prowess was legendary throughout his entire lifetime, and it was claimed that he had had sex with literally thousands of prostitutes and mistresses, as well as with his various wives and regular partners. His most famous case of instant sexual conquest was with a girl who saw his reflection in a shop window in Piccadilly and spent the next ten days in his hotel bedroom. She said that it was the power in Crowley's *eyes* that was overwhelming. He, himself, attributed his sex appeal to a peculiar "magical" perfume containing musk, ambergris, and civet, which he massaged into his scalp. Those who were not impressed by Crowley described it as sweet-smelling and faintly nauseating, but it was alleged to have upset any horses that got a whiff of it. They invariably whinnied as he passed.

Aleister's father died in 1887, and from then onwards, his mother turned against him. Her religious fanaticism was little short of venomous. She frequently referred to her son as the "Great Beast" bearing the magical number 666 as featured in the Book of Revelation, chapter thirteen, verse eighteen.

Many psychologists also suspect that labelling is a vital part of character formation. Again, Aleister's case seems to have provided an ideal reinforcement for those psychological theories. Whether it was his mother's hostile influence or something deeper, darker, and more mysterious, young Aleister became increasingly convinced of his identification with the beast.

In October of 1895, when he was 21, Aleister inherited a fortune of £30,000 — a very significant sum in those days — and went off to Trinity College, Cambridge. He left the university before completing his degree. During his years at Cambridge, however, he spent happy vacations climbing in the Alps, collecting rare books, writing poetry, and studying the occult.

These occult studies brought him into contact with a member of the Hermetic Order of the Golden Dawn, George Cecil Jones. Other famous members included S.L. MacGregor Mathers, its leader at that time, A.E. Waite, Dion Fortune, and W.B. Yeats, the poet. The Order saw itself as an occult society that studied the tarot, alchemy, magic, the cabbala, and astrology. Crowley joined them in 1898 and rose rapidly through the ranks. Despite not bothering to finish his Cambridge degree, he was a man of remarkably high intelligence, who could absorb knowledge like a gigantic sponge and process it faster than a Pentium chip.

During his time with the Golden Dawn, Crowley became friendly with Allan Bennett, who seemed to Crowley to have genuine magical abilities. One of their experiments involved charging a charm or talisman with supernatural energy in order to cure Lady Hall, who was seriously ill at the time. It didn't work. Instead of the hoped-for cure, it seems to have brought on a series of severe tremors, which were almost fatal to the frail old lady.

In the apartments that Crowley and Bennett shared there were two weird rooms they referred to as the "White Temple" and the "Black Temple." The White Temple was lined with mirrors, and in it, Crowley and Bennett experimented more or less harmlessly with what they regarded as "white magic." Their Black Temple was altogether more sinister. Its centrepiece was a skeleton, which Crowley claimed he fed with birds and other small living sacrifices, with the aim of eventually bringing it to life.

How real Crowley's supposed magic was is anybody's guess, but certain odd and inexplicable things seemed to happen in that atmospheric apartment. One evening in 1899, Crowley and a fellow magician returned to the flat after dinner to find that the White Temple had been vandalized. Its furniture and ornaments were in chaotic disarray, and many of the White Magic symbols were upside down. As Crowley and his companion put things back into their proper places they both thought they could see a throng of strange cloudy shapes that seemed to be moving round and round the room like some sort of quasi-religious procession. They described this "seeing" as a clairvoyant experience rather than as a purely optical one.

Like many similar organizations, the Golden Dawn split into various quarrelling factions: Crowley didn't seem to fit in with any of them and went off to study eastern mysteries, including yoga and oriental mysticism.

Crowley married Rose Kelly in 1903, and they spent their honeymoon in Egypt. Early the following year, they returned to Cairo, where Rose began going into trances and insisting that the Egyptian god Horus was trying to get in touch with Aleister. Prior to this, Rose hadn't shown much interest in magical phenomena, and Crowley, uncertain of the genuineness of her recent trance messages, took her to the Boulak Museum, where he asked her to point Horus out to him. Rose passed several depictions and statues of Horus without paying them any attention, then stopped decisively in front of a painted wooden funerary stele dating from the twenty-sixth dynasty. It showed a dead priest named Ankh-efen-Khonsu making an offering to Horus. What really impressed Crowley was the catalogue number of the exhibit: it was 666. Ever since his desperately disturbed and unhappy childhood, and his widowed mother's venomous treatment of him, Crowley had identified himself with that eldritch number, and called himself the Great Beast of the Book of Revelation. Another of his many self-appointed titles was "Master Therion" — "Therion" also meaning "Great Wild Beast."

Crowley was so impressed by this Horus exhibit number in the Boulak Museum (which is statistically far more probable than winning a $10-million jackpot in the lottery) that he began to pay serious attention to Rose's psychic advice. She directed him to go to his room at midday on April 8, 9, and 10, and write what was dictated to him by a nebulous, ethereal figure, which Crowley thought seemed to speak from inside his mind or even over his shoulder as he wrote. The result of this unearthly dictation was a book called *The Book of the Law*. The central theme was the philosophical doctrine of "thelema," a Greek word which Crowley used to indicate "will," "volition," or "determination," although it can also signify "new epoch," "new aeon," or "new age."

Finding our true selves and then living in accordance with our true wills is no bad thing. In *Hamlet*, Shakespeare makes Polonius say: "To thine own self be true, / And it must follow as the night the day, / Thou canst not then be false to any man." But the most subtle and dangerous thing about evil is its ability to twist and pervert goodness and truth. The fanatics who tortured and then burned innocent people at the stake had the virtue of enthusiasm and of ostensibly good intentions, but without their essential partners: humane common sense and tolerance. The scribes and Pharisees of first-century Palestine did everything they could to keep the letter of the

Sacred Law — but totally missed its true spirit: that the finest form of worship is loving kindness and mercy shown to others.

Crowley was absolutely right to argue that every individual human being who deserved to be called such should be free, independent, and autonomous. Many a courageous warrior has died worthily defending that liberty, preferring death to surrender.

But this essentially noble and honourable principle of fighting for individual liberty and independence went grotesquely pear-shaped in Crowley's case, because of his total blindness to the moral limits of all that is in the name of personal freedom.

"Do what thou wilt is the whole of the law," said Crowley. If only he had added, "But my freedom ends at the point where it causes pain or unhappiness to someone else. My freedom ends at the point where it interferes with yours. I am free to do anything provided, always, that it causes no harm to others or to myself." His emphasis on thelema and following one's own will would then have done very little harm and, possibly, a great deal of good.

Crowley's downfall was the classic tragedy of a brilliantly intelligent, energetic, and determined personality cursed with the fatal flaw of selfishness. He mistakenly thought that morality and altruistic concern for others were an unwarranted restriction on his right to do as he willed, and to seek his own pleasure at any cost. He failed to see that only by genuinely loving others, and by unselfishly seeking the happiness of those we love, can we ever hope to achieve real and lasting happiness for ourselves.

Crowley rejoined George Cecil Jones, formerly of Golden Dawn fame, and in 1906, they tried to organize a new magical order to continue where the original Golden Dawn had practically petered out. They called their new group "AA," which stood for "Astron Argon," meaning "the Silver Star." It soon became the main channel for Crowley's thelema teachings.

Four years later, Crowley met Theodore Reuss, head of OTO (*Ordo Templi Orientis*) in Germany. Reuss's group had once been that of very senior Freemasons, but they broke away from the Craft and became an independent organization. When Reuss had a stroke in 1921, Crowley became head of the OTO, and it, too, then became a major vehicle for his thelema teachings.

The original OTO claimed that it had mastered the greatest secrets of ancient magic, which turned out to be surprisingly close to Crowley's thelema ideas. The old wizard Paracelsus, among others, had believed that this true magical secret lay in being able to imagine what it was that you wanted to achieve with such power, and in such detail, that your thoughts were able to influence — even to control — the simple physical reality around you — just as a skillful potter shapes clay on her wheel. Take the analogy of painting: given a blank canvas and a palette full of colour, an artist can create images of great beauty and realism. In the hands of a person with little or no artistic talent, only crude, imperfect and simplistic images will appear. The talented sculptor can turn a block of marble into a horse, or a girl on a dolphin, and make them appear so lifelike, they seem able to gallop or swim. Without that skill, the aspiring amateur stone-cutter can produce nothing better than a few barely recognizable caricatures. So it is with magic, argued Paracelsus, Crowley, and his thelema school. Failure to achieve comes from the neophyte magician's inability to envisage his aims and objectives in sufficient depth and detail. The ancient Amerindian wisdom, which the English Archie Belaney embraced when he became the Canadian Indian Grey Owl, also teaches that the greatest dreamers acquire the power to turn their dreams into reality.

Biblical teachings on the nature of that omnipotent faith — faith that can move mountains, heal the sick, raise the dead, walk on water, feed a huge crowd with a meagre handful of bread and fish, or change water into wine, point in a parallel direction. "Ask and ye shall receive. Knock and it shall be opened unto you. Only believe...."

Some aspects of modern physics — especially those of a quasi-philosophical or semi-metaphysical nature, which question the role of the observer in understanding causality — seem to be verging on the indistinct borders of what both Paracelsus and Crowley would have thought of as classical magic.

Heisenberg's famous uncertainty principle states that the more accurately a scientist determines the position of an object, the less certain he or she is of its momentum; and the more accurately the scientist determines its momentum, the less certain he or she is of its position.

Erwin Schrodinger's famous imaginary cat is also relevant here. He put the idea forward more than half a century ago, to highlight what he saw as an absurdity in quantum physics. In Schrodinger's day, the quantum theory postulated that the outcome of a quantum experiment could not be considered as "real" until it had been measured or observed by an intelligent observer. Schrodinger's imaginary cat was left in a state of half-and-half superposition of states, so that, in terms of quantum theory observation and measurement, it was paradoxically dead and alive at the same time.

Much more recently, Dipankar Home and Rajagopal Chattapadya, working in the Bose Institute in Calcutta, developed a practical version of Schrodinger's imaginary cat-in-the-box experiment. Working on something that Alastair Rae said about DNA in *Quantum Physics* (1986), the Bose Institute scientists substituted real DNA for the imaginary cat, and tried to resolve the paradox of whether a DNA molecule was damaged, or undamaged, depending upon whether it was struck, or not struck, by a single ultraviolet photon. So-called common sense suggests that the DNA molecule would "know" whether it was damaged or not, quite independently of whether a human observer looked at it and "told" it. The Bose scientists themselves favoured this common sense argument, but Schrodinger's intriguing quantum paradox still waits patiently to be fully resolved.

Mind magic of the thelema type has its parallels in artistic creation, biblical miracle faith, and the riddles and paradoxes of the quantum theory, as well as in management science. Projects have to be planned before they can be executed successfully: the better, the deeper, the more extensive and the more detailed the planning, the greater the likelihood of achieving practical success in the physical world. So, the Crowleian-Paracelsian magician would argue, the stronger the will and the clearer its vision of the desired magical objective, the greater is the likelihood of magical success.

Prior to the First World War, Crowley and his companions spent a fortune on promoting thelema, but with scant success. In 1914, he went to the USA, where he was even less successful. Not surprisingly, his editorship of a pro-German news sheet led to accusations of treachery to the UK. He went back to Europe in 1920 and founded his Abbey of Thelema in Sicily. For a time, it attracted a few disciples, including Raoul Loveday, a brilliant Oxford student who subsequently died there of gastroenteritis, probably as a result of weird magical experiments involving the drinking of blood, or possibly as a result of drinking contaminated water.

Loveday's widow worked tirelessly to bring Crowley down with a virulent press campaign, and finally succeeded. The Abbey of Thelema was closed, and Sicily deported Crowley.

All in all, he was never really a deliberate deceiver, charlatan, or cheat, except insofar as he also deceived, cheated, and deluded himself. He certainly seemed to believe in what he wrote and taught, and at times, he appeared to be able to exercise a few interesting paranormal powers.

Despite having devoted his life to his magical thelema mysteries, Crowley's road was rough and mainly downhill after leaving Sicily. He died in poverty and in poor health on December 1, 1947, in a low-cost boarding house in Hastings, Sussex, England, unsure, at the end, whether any of the ideas to which he had devoted his high intelligence, his dynamic energy, and his entire life had had any significance at all. His last few pathetic words were said to have been along the lines of: "I feel so puzzled and perplexed by it all."

Chapter 2

Who were King Arthur and the Wizard Merlin?

In a strange old Welsh document known as *The Gododdin of Aneurin* which goes back to the sixth century, or even earlier, there is a reference to a hero who fought well, "although he was no Arthur." It would be tantamount to complimenting a great athlete on his or her excellent performance today by saying he or she did well "although it wasn't quite up to Superman's standard." We all understand that Superman is a fictional character, but that doesn't prevent us from using his performance as a yardstick for others. Was the writer of Gododdin comparing his admired warrior to a fictional Arthur or to a historical character, or even to someone who had a foot in both worlds? In a Hollywood epic about King David, the old King is asked by a wide-eyed boy whether Goliath was really as big as people said he was, to which question David replied, "I think he grows a little every year." Arthur, although real enough, may well have gradually increased in stature in much the same way as that Hollywood Goliath.

But allowing that Aneurin, the *Gododdin* author, was talking about a historical Arthur, whose prowess on many a battlefield was still recalled with awe a century or two later, we are still left with the question, "who was he?"

Gildas, a monk who wrote during the sixth century, recounts a great battle at Mount Badon, which apparently halted the westward thrust of the Saxon invaders for a few years. Gildas himself doesn't mention Arthur by

Arthur of the Britons, the Once and Future King. Celtic or Romano-British War Lord — or someone far stranger and more mysterious than that?

name in connection with the Badon victory, but the Welsh Annals do, and although they were a few centuries later than Gildas, they do not hesitate to link Arthur with a great victory over the Saxons on Mount Badon. These Welsh Annals also contain a sombre reference to the "strife of Camlann in which both Arthur and Medraut perished."

So the search for Camlann may well have started the quest for similar-sounding Camelot, and Medraut would seem to have been Arthur's fatal kinsman Mordred, born, according to some accounts, of an incestuous relationship with Arthur's evil and treacherous kinswoman, the enchantress Morgana.

Another interesting early source of Arthurian information is Nennius, who was busy translating old Welsh stories into Latin during the early ninth century. In Nennius's *History of the Britons*, Arthur was involved in at least a dozen great conflicts, of which Badon was only one. Nennius also refers to Arthur as a sort of war lord or field marshall, rather than as a king, using the Latin phrase *dux bellorum*.

A romantic adventure poem, *The Spoils of Annwn*, which appeared in the 900s, has Arthur performing all kinds of strange, magical, heroic deeds, as well as winning ordinary battles against mortal foes. Giants are slain; dragons and monsters are defeated; witches and wizards are overcome. The quest motif features here as well: Arthur, like the classical warrior heroes centuries before him, goes to the Land of the Dead to search for the magic cauldron. Is this, perhaps, a foreshadowing of all the Christianized Holy Grail stories that accumulated later around Arthur and the knights of Camelot? Gwalchmai (Galahad?) and Llenlleawc (Lancelot?) also appear in these earliest Welsh versions of Arthur's adventures. The beautiful but unhappy Gwenhwyfar (Guinevere?), Arthur's wife, also features prominently in these early tales. After these first, fragmentary, semi-mythical records had played their pioneering part, the medieval writers began to dominate the Arthurian scenario.

In 1125, William of Malmesbury, an early historian, wanted as complete an account of Arthur's life, exploits, and death, as possible. He got one from Geoffrey of Monmouth's *History of the Kings of Britain* in 1135. Geoffrey possessed a vivid imagination, a fine sense of narrative, and a curiously muddy reservoir of miscellaneous data, in which myths, legends, folktales, and oral traditions were partially dissolved, while a few historical facts bobbed about rather uncertainly on its brackish surface.

In 1155, Robert Wace made a free translation of Geoffrey's work into French, and added a few nice touches of his own. Robert de Borron wrote *Merlin* in the early thirteenth century and introduced the sword in the stone theme. French author Chretien de Troyes embroidered the tales still more delicately, and Sir Thomas Malory drew down the medieval curtain in the fifteenth century with his tragic *Morte d'Arthur*, set in Glastonbury, and featuring the return of Arthur's magic blade Excalibur to the Lady of the Lake.

What then was this medieval legend of Arthur, Merlin, Guinevere, and the knights at its fullest extent? As Merlin is usually regarded as the agent by whom Arthur reached the throne, via the sword in the stone, it is with Merlin's legend that the story really begins.

In the Arthurian legend of Merlin, King Constans, who drove Hengist from Britain, died leaving three sons: Constantine, Uther, and Pendragon. Constantine, the eldest, succeeded his father, and appointed Vortigern as his chief minister. Hengist invaded again; Vortigern betrayed Constantine, and the young king was slain. Vortigern then took the throne despite the existence of the dead Constantine's younger brothers.

Vortigern, aware that his throne was precarious, prudently decided to build a fortress on Salisbury Plain. Each morning, however, according to the legend, the masons found that the walls they had built the day before had collapsed during the night.

Wise men, soothsayers, and astrologers were duly consulted. They told Vortigern that the walls would continue falling until the ground had been sprinkled with the blood of a child without a human father.

At this point in the story there is a dynamic confrontation between the wise and powerful St. Blaise and Satan himself. Satan was plotting to introduce his offspring through a pious and innocent virgin, who came regularly to St. Blaise as her confessor. Because she told him her every thought and action, Blaise was able to frustrate the satanic incarnation plot.

Merlin the Magician: who was his mysterious father? What weird powers did he possess? Where is he now?

The pregnant girl was locked in a tower until the baby was born. The unfailingly vigilant Blaise beat Satan's minions to it, rushed in before they could, and baptized the babe, naming him Merlin: thus delivering him from becoming a satanic agent. Although Christian baptism — especially by a saint — saved the child and neutralized what would otherwise have become the satanic aspect of Merlin's character, he still retained various superhuman powers because of his parentage. After all, according to Christian tradition, Satan, or Lucifer, had once been a bright and holy angel.

Merlin's beautiful and innocent young mother was due to be condemned to death for bearing Satan's child, but that same miraculous child started talking at two or three days old and told her that he would save her. When the trial began, he sat upright in her arms and argued the case for her innocence so effectively that she was acquitted.

As a child of five, he met some of Vortigern's men, whom he knew were looking for him, and fearlessly accompanied them to the usurping king's palace. On the way, they passed a youth buying a pair of shoes. Merlin laughed. Vortigern's men asked what he was laughing about. Merlin said that the unfortunate young man's purchase was a waste, as he would die that day — and he did. Vortigern's men were impressed. He gave them several more grim examples of his prophetic powers before they reached Vortigern's throne room.

Once in the king's presence, Merlin told him boldly that the wise men had deliberately misled him about the reason for the walls collapsing, as they were jealous of Merlin's greater wisdom and greater powers, and wanted the King to kill him. Vortigern asked what the real reason for the collapsing was. Merlin explained that a white and red dragon were fighting to the death below ground. Their mortal combat was renewed each night, and that was what threw the walls down. Vortigern gave orders that the beasts must be found and stopped.

Everyone duly assembled to watch the fight as soon as the dragons were uncovered. After an earth-shattering contest, the white dragon won the battle, but then, seeing all the king's warriors assembled, it shuffled away as though afraid, and was never seen again. The walls of Vortigern's fortress on Salisbury Plain could now be built.

Merlin made another prophecy: the dragons, he declared, were symbols of the struggle between the usurping Vortigern and the sons of King Constans, who would soon land in Britain with a great army and defeat Vortigern. They did. The usurper was burnt to death in his newly completed castle on Salisbury Plain.

Merlin was now appointed adviser and chief minister to Uther and Pendragon. Hengist was preparing another attack with his vast Saxon army. Merlin prophesied that Uther and Pendragon would win, but that one of them would die fighting for Britain. His words came true. Pendragon died in the battle in which Hengist was defeated yet again. Uther, to honour his brother, added Pendragon's name to his own, and asked Merlin to construct a fitting monument to the dead King.

Merlin complied with the king's wishes by bringing from Ireland, in a single night, the stones with which he erected Stonehenge.

Merlin's legend next involves him with the Round Table. He went to Carlisle (then known as Carduel) and constructed a magnificent castle for Uther Pendragon. A superb round table became its main feature. Merlin said that this circular table was made in the tradition of a similar one that had once been the property of Joseph of Arimathea, who had once had a following like that of Uther Pendragon's knights.

When the table was completed and ready for guests to feast at, the medieval equivalent of a housewarming was held at Carduel, to which all the knights and nobles, with their wives, were invited. The most beautiful woman in the land was Yguerne, wife of Gorlois, the ruler of Tintagel in Cornwall. Tragically, Uther Pendragon fell passionately in love with Yguerne, and Gorlois couldn't help but notice it. The situation was grimly parallel to that of David and Bathsheba in the Old Testament, when Bathsheba's loyal and loving husband, Uriah, was murdered on David's orders, so that David could have Bathsheba. Gorlois stormed out of

Carduel, locked Yguerne in the formidable, sea-girt fortress of Tintagel, and went to war against Uther Pendragon.

In this version, the legendary Merlin was always Uther Pendragon's man through thick and thin, irrespective of the ethics of the situation. He changed Uther into the likeness of Gorlois — who was away fighting Pendragon's men elsewhere on the battlefield — and changed himself and his companion, Ulfin, into facsimiles of two of Gorlois's squires. Then the three of them presented themselves at Tintagel, where the completely unsuspecting Yguerne opened the gates to admit them. Uther's night of passion in the guise of Gorlois left Yguerne pregnant with Arthur, who was always understandably thought to be Gorlois's son.

The hapless Gorlois, however, was killed in battle next day, and Uther Pendragon lost no time in marrying the beautiful Yguerne. When Arthur was born, he was generally regarded as the posthumous child of Gorlois, and was given to Merlin to be raised. The magician entrusted him to the care of Sir Hector, and he grew up for all intents and purposes as the younger brother of Hector's son, Kay.

When Uther Pendragon finally died, there was apparently no heir. Only Merlin knew the truth, and he bided his time, prophesying that in due course, the true king would be revealed by magic.

Arthur became king through the sword in the stone miracle, and Merlin, showing no apparent signs of age — like the equally mysterious Count of Saint-Germain — became King Arthur's loyal and trusted adviser and chief minister, as he had once been to Uther Pendragon.

In this version of the legend, it was thanks to Merlin that Arthur was always successful in battle, overcoming twelve kings and acquiring an international reputation rivalling that of Charlemagne or Ghengis Khan.

Merlin's ability as a shape-shifter also figures prominently in his legend. On one occasion he was supposed to have turned into a stag and to have delivered a challenge from Arthur to Oberon's father.

Apart from the great funeral monument at Stonehenge, which he allegedly raised by magic to honour the dead Pendragon, Merlin had a great reputation as an architect and builder. He built Camelot for Arthur, and designed and created several magical fountains.

There is also a connection made between Merlin and the Grail, or rather, one of the earlier, pre-Christian drinking vessels or cauldrons that became blurred together in the Holy Grail legends. He is given credit in one of the stories for making a drinking vessel that could detect character. When an evil or treacherous person attempted to drink from Merlin's Cup, it always overflowed. His other magical artefacts included Arthur's impenetrable armour, and a magic mirror that reflected whatever the user asked to see.

Tolkien portrays a similar one in *Lord of the Rings*, which Galadriel uses. The wicked queen in *Snow White* has another.

Just as Arthur had problems with Guinevere and Uther Pendragon had had difficulties with Yguerne, so Merlin's life was overshadowed by his relationship with his beautiful mistress, Vivian, the Lady of the Lake. Anxious to learn all of his magical secrets, Vivian followed him everywhere, and finally, having stolen the spell from him, she imprisoned him forever in a hawthorn bush deep in the forest of Broceliande in Brittany. There are many Breton legends telling how Merlin's voice can still be heard shouting for help there. Curious, but relatively recent, carvings in the Forest of Tay in Scotland may be artists' impressions of this tree-entrapment magic: one appears to represent the prisoner's wide open and silently screaming mouth; another shows a fierce dragon desperately attempting to claw his way out of the encircling wood.

Another version of the legend, which shows Vivian in a better light, relates how she imprisoned him in an underground palace to protect him, a palace to which she alone could gain access. How does this square with the legendary idea that Merlin, like Arthur and the knights, lies sleeping somewhere, waiting to be called? Legends of sleeping knights in a hidden chamber below Roslyn Castle in Scotland, or in a secret tomb beneath its neighbouring chapel, also echo the legend of a Merlin who waits there while the centuries roll past.

There can be little doubt that those great friends and formidable scholars, J.R.R. Tolkien and C.S. Lewis, had professional access over the years to some very curious old manuscripts, some of which undoubtedly influenced their brilliant writings. Every now and then, the judicious Lewis and Tolkien reader comes across tantalizing hints, glimpses of things in their work, which seem to owe more to myth and legend than to pure, imaginative fiction. One such glimpse relates to Merlin. In *That Hideous Strength*, which completes Lewis's science fiction trilogy, the forces of evil discover Merlin lying in suspended animation in a secret tomb not far from what sounds remarkably like Durham University. Lewis actually disguises the fictional university in his story, but its scenic resemblance to the real Durham is striking. When revived, Merlin brings about the downfall of the evil forces that disturbed his long rest.

Most interesting of all, in this connection, is Lewis's suggestion that the Merlin of Arthurian legend is one of the last of Tolkien's ancient Men of the West. If, as some scholars have suggested, Tolkien's entire mythology of Middle Earth, with its wizards, elves, dwarfs, orcs, ents, and strange semi-human races, is not based solely on the professor's brilliant imagination, but on certain ancient manuscripts that came his way, then the strong possibility

Does this strange carving represent Merlin trapped in the tree and screaming for help?

Does this struggling dragon represent Merlin, the great Welsh Wizard, in dragon form fighting his way out of the tree?

Do these ancient Pictish carvings represent the unfortunate Guinevere being torn to pieces by wolves?

exists that his powerful and long-lived Men of the West may have had some basis in fact.

Is Lewis's tantalizing reference to Merlin a carefully disguised clue, just as his "imaginary" university bears an uncanny resemblance to Durham? Biblical references to patriarchs who enjoyed great longevity abound; were they also, in some way, an echo of Tolkien's Men of the West, and of Lewis's Merlin?

Some of the strangest Arthurian evidence is to be found in the Pictish stones of Meigle in Scotland. When we closely examined and photographed these recently, it became apparent that the strange old designs on them were open to various conflicting interpretations.

One explanation of the indistinct figure surrounded by stylized lions or wolves is that it represents the death of the unfaithful Guinevere. This version of the story was told to us by a local expert in Meigle. During a period of imprisonment, Guinevere had agreed to sleep with the warden of the castle where she was being held to ransom, in return for not being passed around the rest of his castle garrison. When Arthur's men finally stormed the castle, the King unsympathetically ordered her to be thrown to the wolves for accepting the warden's offer with such alacrity, when most of us would have found it perfectly understandable, given the alternative.

Another traditional interpretation of this particular carving was that it represented Daniel in the lions' den, and the beasts surrounding the central figure were powerless to cause harm.

This same ancient Pictish stone at Meigle also contains carvings of a centaur, warriors on horseback, and a child. Other stones in the same collection depict mysterious aquatic beasts and strange, unidentifiable, cryptozoological creatures.

A more elaborate version of the sword in the stone phenomenon that started Arthur's reign concerns an assembly of British nobles at St.

Stephen's Church in London on Christmas Day. After Mass had been celebrated, a large stone appeared mysteriously in the churchyard. Above the stone was an anvil, and in the anvil, the magic sword was lodged. An inscription declared that only the man who was able to withdraw the sword was the rightful king.

It has been suggested by some researchers that the whole sword and stone episode was historically factual, but that there was a trick to withdrawing the sword. One of the jewels on the hilt was cunningly attached to a system of thin levers and a gear or two inside the blade. Part of the way down the slot in the anvil was a recess into which a bolt sprang from the side of the blade. This bolt, like a mortise lock, slid into its secret socket deep inside the anvil and kept the sword in place. The theory goes on to suggest that Merlin had either engineered the whole thing himself, or had it constructed to his design by a skillful armourer or blacksmith. There were fifth- and sixth-century artisans who would have been capable of carrying out such work.

According to one version of the legend, Arthur handed the sword to his adopted brother, Kay, Hector's son, to use in the tournament. Sir Hector, who had brought up Arthur on Merlin's instructions, saw this happen, and recognized the blade as the one from the anvil of destiny on the stone. The whole company was summoned, and Arthur replaced the sword and then withdrew it again. He was then warmly acclaimed as the rightful king.

This honeymoon period of ready and joyful acceptance at the start of Arthur's reign was short-lived, however. Dark rumours began to spread.

Some now said that he was *not* the pre-wedlock son of Uther Pendragon and the voluptuous Yguerne — as Merlin had declared him to be after the episode with the sword in the stone — but that he had been cast up as a miraculous babe from the depth of the Atlantic on the crest of a huge ninth wave, and had landed at Merlin's feet.

This mysterious sea-babe aspect of the Arthurian story links in with the donation of the sword Excalibur from the equally mysterious and aquatic Lady of the Lake. If he was a strange aquatic child, was she — his real mother — guarding the magical blade for him until he came of age to use it? It also ties in with the strange history of King Mérovée, founder of the early French Merovingian dynasty, and sometimes referred to as "Mérovée the Twice Born." According to this legend, his mother, while already pregnant with him, was swimming in the Mediterranean, when she was either raped or seduced by an intelligent aquatic being referred to as a Quinotaur. In some inexplicable way, part of the Quinotaur's genetic material was infused with that of the embryonic Mérovée. From this, according to legend, came the magical powers associated with the Merovingian dynasty, often referred to as the "Thaumaturgical Kings."

Who were King Arthur and the Wizard Merlin?

The remarkable Dogon people of Bandiagara in Africa have a puzzling ancient tradition, which includes frequent references to a race of highly intelligent — and technologically advanced — amphibian extra-terrestrials, whom they call Nommos, meaning "associated with water" in the Dogon language. Their tradition asserts that the Nommos landed somewhere northeast of Bandiagara, and looked like a fish-anthropoid hybrid. Like the Oannes of the ancient Babylonian records, and the Sumerian Enki, these amphibian demigods of the Dogon tradition acted as helpers and teachers to the terrestrial people they visited.

The third century BC Chaldean priest and astronomer, Berosus, described something that rose from the Erythraean Sea to teach and heal the Babylonians: "The entire body of the creature resembled a fish, but had a second head below its fish's head. It also had feet attached to its fish's tail."

If only a small fraction of these amphibian super-being legends is taken at face value, the possibility exists that benign, water-dependent extra-terrestrials were visiting the Earth in those same romantic Dark Ages from which Arthur and Merlin sprang. If Arthur, like Mérovée, had unusual genetic material, some of the traditional Arthurian stories are open to interesting reinterpretations. Was the submerged Lost Land of Lyonesse somewhere off the rugged Cornish peninsula, west of Gorlois and Yguerne's Tintagel? Was it merely the terrestrial human, Uther Pendragon, whom Merlin contrived to bring to the beautiful Yguerne's bed that night? Or did the wily old magician have other masters, stronger and stranger than Uther, living beneath the waves?

This area of conjecture raises the old and unanswerable question as to which legends cloak the truth, and which myths mask the hidden facts.

Folklore and mythology have proved time and time again to be more than fiction and fable. There is almost always an intense fire behind their smoke. The stronger and more persistent the mythology and legend, the more interesting that true, historical fire turns out to be. The final, irrefutable evidence vindicating the historical reality of both Arthur and Merlin has yet to be discovered: when that evidence is unearthed, it may reveal a mystery greater than any other in the medieval legends.

Chapter 3

Who was the Count of Saint-Germain?

Guiseppe Balsamo, otherwise known as the Count of Cagliostro, was born in Palermo, in Sicily, on June 2, 1743. History tends to depict him as a suspected charlatan, a possible magician, and a wildly popular adventurer, who was warmly acclaimed by Parisian society in the late eighteenth century. He reportedly died an ignominious prisoner in the Apennine fortress of St. Leo on August 26, 1795.

His many claims to fame included seances, soothsaying, alchemy, miraculous healing, and the production of aphrodisiacs and elixirs of youth. He also claimed that he knew the elusive Comte de Saint-Germain, who had initiated him into a Masonic order. If Cagliostro was telling the truth for once, his evidence about Saint-Germain is significant.

Saint-Germain was widely known as the "Wonderman," and nothing reliable is known of his parents or of his real place of origin. One of the wilder speculations about his origins identifies him with Cartaphilus, the Wandering Jew of legend.

In outline, that legend refers to a Jewish collaborator working as a door-keeper for Pontius Pilate and his Roman forces of occupation, during the first century AD. In another version, Cartaphilus is a bystander who spits on Christ as he journeys to Calvary. Either way, the heart of the legend is that Cartaphilus told Christ to hurry on, when he had stopped for a brief rest.

The Count of Saint-Germain. Did he have the alchemists' secrets of longevity and transmutation?

The strange Cagliostro, friend of the enigmatic Count of Saint-Germain. It is hard to tell which man was the more mysterious of the two.

Jesus looked steadily at him and said: "I will continue my journey — but you shall tarry in this world until I return."

The legend goes on to suggest that Cartaphilus had no idea what Jesus meant, until he noticed that all his friends and acquaintances were aging and dying, while he, himself, looked and felt no older than he had done on the day he had spoken so unsympathetically to Christ.

The Cartaphilus legend had become obscured and half-forgotten by the dawn of the thirteenth century, but it was suddenly revived by European travellers coming home with odd stories about their encounters with a curious-looking stranger who confessed to being Cartaphilus. In 1228, when an Armenian bishop visited St. Alban's in England, he claimed to have had a recent meal with Cartaphilus.

There was a surprisingly consistent general pattern to these reported sightings by European travellers: Cartaphilus seemed to be moving steadily westwards. Was he the same man who called himself the Count of Saint-Germain?

He turned up in Vienna in 1740, where contemporaries described him as a powerful and good-looking man apparently in his thirties. The main topic of conversation was his clothes. When all of fashion-conscious eighteenth-century society was wearing bright, almost gaudy, colours, Saint-Germain always wore Hamletesque black, with white lace at his neck and cuffs. If his clothes were plain and sombre, his jewels compensated for their drabness. His fingers were encrusted with brilliant diamond rings and his shoe buckles were also decorated with diamonds. In addition, he had yet more diamonds studded all over his fob and snuffbox. If the seemingly more exaggerated versions of his arrival in Vienna are to be believed, he even carried tiny diamonds in his pockets to use instead of money.

During his time in Vienna, he made the acquaintance of Count Lobkowitz and Count Zabor, who were friends of the massively influential French Marshal de Belle Isle. The eminent Frenchman was far from well at the time, but Saint-Germain used his mysterious powers to heal him. Overwhelmed with gratitude, de Belle Isle took Saint-Germain to Paris as his protégé and provided him with luxurious living quarters and a lavishly equipped laboratory.

Doing the social round in Paris, Saint-Germain attended a soiree arranged by the elderly Countess von Georgy. In the 1670s, her now-deceased husband had been an ambassador in Venice. She asked Saint-Germain if his father had been there then. "No, Madame," he replied gallantly. "It was I, myself, who met you there, and I recall you most vividly as a very beautiful young girl."

"Utterly impossible!" the old countess retorted. "The Count Saint-

Germain whom I met was thirty or forty years old then. He could not possibly still be alive!"

"Gracious Lady," replied Saint-Germain, with an inscrutable smile, "I must confess that I am very old." He went on to tell her so many details of the Venetian society of the time that he convinced her that he really had been there in the 1670s.

"You're a most extraordinary man, a devil perhaps," she said, aghast. Her mention of the devil apparently had an electrifying effect on Saint-Germain. According to the story, he began to shake as if he was having a spasm, winced with pain, made his excuses, and hurriedly left the soiree.

As tales of the Count apparently grew with the telling, it was rumoured that he claimed to have met the Holy Family, that he had a particular respect and affection for St. Anne, mother of the Virgin Mary, and that he had been the one who proposed that she should be made a saint during the deliberations of the Council of Nicaea in AD 325. Saint-Germain also claimed to have been a guest at the wedding in Cana of Galilee where Jesus turned the water into wine. But his claims went back further than the Christian era: he said that he had known King Solomon and had met the Queen of Sheba.

His claims to have the secret of great longevity — the legendary Elixir of Life — were substantiated by his valet, who was alleged to have been given it by his grateful master. Challenged by one of Saint-Germain's guests to say whether or not the Count really had known Solomon and Sheba, the valet replied gravely: "I'm afraid I cannot comment, sir. You see, I have been in the Count's service only for the past century."

Jeanne Antoinette de Pompadour, mistress of Louis XV, was very impressed by Saint-Germain, and so was Louis himself. Whether or not Saint-Germain had any paranormal powers, he was certainly blessed with an above-average level of human skill and intelligence. In 1760, he was Louis's trusted messenger to Austria.

His fortunes began to decline, however, when he made two powerful and energetic enemies: Casanova and the Duc de Choiseul. Choiseul was Louis's foreign minister at the time, and he managed to persuade the King that Saint-Germain was betraying him to the English. In consequence, Saint-Germain had to leave France in a hurry. He went first to England, then to Holland, where he took the title of Count Surmont. For a time, he appears to have busied himself as an industrialist, setting up factories, laboratories, and plants to process pigments and to manufacture paints and dyes.

He left Holland as a wealthy man and established himself next in Tournai, where he changed his name again to the Marquis de Monferrat. In 1768, he turned up in Russia, where he came to the attention of Catherine the Great. Assisting his new patron against the Turks, Saint-Germain employed his diplomatic skills once more, and soon became chief adviser to Count Alexei Orlov, chief of the Russian imperial forces. Things went so well for Saint-Germain in this context that he was promoted to a very high position in the Russian army, where he adopted the British style of the time by calling himself General Welldone. At the Battle of Chesne, the Turks were resoundingly defeated, and, his duty in Russia done, Saint-Germain set off on his travels again.

In 1774, he turned up in Nuremberg. Is there the remotest possibility that he was connected in any way with Kaspar Hauser, the mysterious boy with no history who appeared in Nuremberg without explanation a few years later? Hauser caused some consternation and embarrassment by claiming to recognize a portrait in the Vienna Art Gallery: it had been painted in 1628. If old Countess Georgy really had seen Saint-Germain in Venice many years before, was the bewildered Hauser telling the strange but simple truth when he claimed to have known a woman who had been dead for a century? If there was a connection between Hauser and Saint-Germain's earlier visit to Nuremberg, might Saint-Germain also have been the mysterious stranger who killed Hauser in the Hofgarten in Ansbach, because the boy knew too much — that same mysterious assassin who left no traces in the snow?

Saint-Germain's 1774 visit to Nuremberg took him into the orbit of the margrave of Brandenburg, Charles Alexander. Saint-Germain asked the margrave for funds to establish a laboratory. This time he was using the name Prince Rakoczy. There were three Rakoczy brothers from Transylvania (at one time the haunt of the notorious Vlad Dracul, the impaler, who was turned into Count Dracula, the vampire, in Bram Stoker's novel) but, unknown to the worthy Margrave Alexander, all three were dead when Saint-Germain arrived in Nuremberg. Count Orlov paid a visit while Saint-Germain was there, embraced him warmly, and thereby enhanced his status for some time with the unsuspecting margrave. However, information about the deaths of all three Rakoczys finally reached Alexander. Saint-Germain admitted his true identity, then prudently left Nuremberg rather rapidly.

Saint-Germain's most powerful enemy in the French court, the Duc de Choiseul, had accused him of being a double agent working for Frederick the Great as well as for the British, but when Saint-Germain begged Frederick for help, his appeal went unanswered. Choiseul may have been wrong, of course, or Frederick may have employed Saint-Germain on an "if-anything-goes-wrong-I've-never-heard-of-you" contract — said to be a popular device with politically astute potentates in turbulent times.

There is some evidence that Saint-Germain's next stop was Leipzig, where he told Frederick Augustus, Prince of Brunswick, that he was a high-ranking freemason, which links closely with Cagliostro's evidence. Frederick himself was the Prussian grand master, and Saint-Germain may not have been aware of this when he made his claims. Frederick refused to recognize Saint-Germain as a genuine mason. The secret signs Saint-Germain used were not those used by the Prussian lodges Frederick supervised. But was Frederick correct in his rejection? Is it possible that Saint-Germain had learnt his ritual long before Frederick? Was it freemasonry of an older and altogether more arcane type that Saint-Germain had learnt, something that had been largely lost and forgotten before the relatively new European lodges were founded in the eighteenth century, and presided over by aristocrats of Frederick's generation?

The records of Saint-Germain become cloudier over the next few years. He was cared for by the generous Prince Charles of Hesse-Cassel, and some of those who believed in Saint-Germain's paranormal powers may have suspected a conspiracy between him and his patron, to allow the former Saint-Germain to assume a new identity. Many espionage stories use the device of a supposed death to enable an agent to take on a whole new character.

Is that what Saint-Germain and Charles did? According to the parish records and to the stone Charles erected for Saint-Germain, the Count died at Charles's castle on February 27, 1784. His monument reads: "The man who was known as the Comte de Saint-Germain and as Welldone, and of whom nothing else is known, lies buried in this church."

The inscription is remarkably similar to the one raised for Kaspar Hauser half a century later: "Here lies the Enigma of our time: his birth unknown — his death a mystery."

Whatever may have happened in the Prince's castle, or whatever may lie buried in Saint-Germain's coffin in the church at Eckenforde, the mystery did not die in 1784.

For some reason best known to himself — or perhaps with Saint-Germain's connivance — Prince Charles burnt all the Count's papers in 1784, giving his reason as " ... lest they be misinterpreted."

Grimm, co-author with his brother of the famous *Fairy Tales*, described Saint-Germain as the most able man he had ever met. Horace Walpole wrote of him when he was in London in 1743: "He is called an Italian, a Spaniard, a Pole, a somebody who married a great fortune in Mexico and ran away with her jewels to Constantinople, a Priest, a fiddler, a vast nobleman."

While in the UK in the 1740s, Saint-Germain was arrested as a Jacobite spy, but released shortly afterwards.

Stories of the Count's appearances well into the nineteenth century and beyond fascinated Napoleon III, who organized a special enquiry team to investigate Saint-Germain. Their report was destroyed by a mysterious fire at the Hotel de Ville in Paris in 1871. Those who believed that the Count was still alive and as powerful as ever maintained that the fire had not been accidental. There were secrets in the report that he wished to conceal.

Just as there is a faintly possible link between Saint-Germain and Kaspar Hauser of Nuremberg, so there is a far stronger link between Saint-Germain and the mysterious treasure of Rennes-le-Château.

Bérenger Saunière, the enigmatic priest of Rennes-le-Château, became suddenly and unaccountably rich towards the end of the nineteenth century — not too many years after Napoleon III's report on Saint-Germain vanished in the fire. Father Saunière seems to have spent money like water between the time he acquired his mysterious wealth in 1885 and his death in 1917. There are many and varied accounts of his life, and numerous theories abound as to the source of his wealth. Some of the wilder suppositions suggest that he acquired the secret of alchemical transmutation from somewhere, or that he possessed some other arcane method of *creating* wealth. There was talk of black magic, grave robbing, and murder. Some researchers believe that Saunière found an ancient Templar treasure, or even a Visigothic one, hidden below his ancient church. According to some chroniclers, the most intriguing part of his story is that he had an illicit relationship with Emma Calvé, the famous French opera star, who was also reported to be involved in the magic and mystery that intrigued Parisian society at the time. There is an 1897 photograph in existence which Emma autographed to: "The Count of St Germain, the Great Chiromancer who has told me many truths."

Another curious mystery attributed to Saint-Germain after his supposed death was his appearance in Paris shortly before the French Revolution, where he warned Marie Antoinette of its dangers. According to some accounts, she recorded in her diaries that she deeply regretted her failure to heed his warnings.

The Count apparently turned up again in Sweden in 1789, where he tried to warn King Gustavus III of impending trouble. Saint-Germain also told his friend, Mme. d'Adhemar, that he would see her on five more occasions. She also noted that he seemed always to be in his mid-forties. According to her account, these five meetings took place as he had prophesied, and she was always totally surprised by them. The last of them was in 1820, on the night before the Duc de Berri was murdered.

In the 1970s, a French alchemist named Richard Chanfray gave a demonstration on TV, during which he appeared to be able to turn lead into gold. Chanfray also claimed that he was the Count of Saint-Germain.

Our good friend, Elisabeth van Buren, who has been a student of the

Rennes-le-Château mystery and has lived in the vicinity of Rennes for many years, is convinced that Saint-Germain is still very much alive, and actively engaged in occultism and mysticism today. She believes that she has actually received messages from him.

The Count of Saint-Germain may be no more than a relatively recent and singularly vivid example of the undying hero myth, a variation of the "sleeper in the cave" legends. But there are enough intriguing shreds of evidence and mysterious clues to suggest that he might just be more than that. If people like him with strange, time-defying powers, and other paranormal abilities, people such as the so-called gods of the ancient Greek, Roman, and Egyptian pantheons, are more than myth and legend, where did they come from originally, and what is their purpose here today? Could they be extra-terrestrial beings? Or survivors of an ancient and powerful quasi-human race that once occupied Atlantis, Lemuria, or the mysterious continent of Antarctica beneath its mile-thick shield of ice?

Chapter 4

What Really Happened to Colonel Fawcett?

Percy Harrison Fawcett was born in Torquay in 1867. He disappeared in Amazonia in 1925 while searching for a mysterious Lost City. Fawcett was convinced that it existed. Whether he was right or wrong — and the balance of such evidence as exists lies more with him than with his critics — Colonel Fawcett was one of the bravest, most exciting, and most interesting men ever to stamp his powerfully adventurous personality across Amazonia.

Tragically, he never returned from his last hazardous quest, but his unmistakable gold signet ring did. Somehow, it made its way back to Britain and is now safely in the keeping of his vivacious and talented granddaughter, Rolette. She actually showed it to us, and allowed us to photograph it when we called to interview her about her famous grandfather.

Fawcett's unique signet ring could provide an important clue to his disappearance, and to his ultimate fate. The lady from whom Brian Ridout obtained it a few years ago was the widow of the Amazonian to whom Fawcett had allegedly given it, and he had been very reluctant to say how it had come into his possession. All he would admit was that Colonel Fawcett had given it to him "for services rendered." Percy's daughter, Joan, unhesitatingly identified it as her father's, and it certainly bears the Fawcett family motto *"Nec Aspira Terrent."* The family is absolutely certain that the Colonel would never have parted with it except in the most extreme circumstances.

Colonel Percy Fawcett, the heroic explorer, who disappeared in Amazonia in 1925.

Rolette's information comes directly from her mother, Fawcett's daughter Joan, who was born in 1910, and was barely 15 when her father vanished on his last known expedition to Cuyaba in the Matto Grosso. Joan remembers him as a kind, gentle, enlightened, and liberal man — an assessment that is especially impressive when Fawcett's style is compared with the harsh and repressive behaviour of many more conventional military officers of that period who were his colleagues and contemporaries.

Joan, for example, was very fond of animals, and her famous father supported and encouraged her in this.

To try to understand Fawcett's compulsive motivations, we can find no better clue than in Rudyard Kipling's poem *The Explorer*, which contains the line, "Something hidden. Go and find it."

Kipling and Percy Fawcett were kindred spirits. They would have understood each other well. They were both mental explorers, as well as globe-trotting adventurers. Fawcett's open-minded curiosity and his interest in metaphysics led him into both Freemasonry and the Theosophical Society, where he met Annie Besant.

Annie, born in 1847, was the daughter of Emily Morris and William Wood, a doctor, who died tragically young, and left Emily more or less destitute when Annie was only 5. Emily was able to get a job caring for the boarders at Harrow School, but wasn't able to look after young Annie at the same time. Emily's friend, Ellen Marryat, raised Annie for her, and became largely responsible for her upbringing.

In 1866, when she was 19, Annie met a pathetically narrow-minded and strictly traditionalist young clergyman named Frank Besant, and made the major mistake of marrying him. Two children in three years, combined with her husband's restrictive views, led to inevitable domestic conflict for an independent, imaginative, and freedom-loving woman like Annie. She started to re-examine her religious beliefs, and refused to attend communion services: Frank ordered her out of the house. They had a legal separation, and their son, Digby, stayed with his cantankerous father, while their daughter, Mabel, went to London with Annie.

As well as being a close friend and collaborator of Charles Bradlaugh, the publisher and social reformer, Annie knew Edward Aveling and George Bernard Shaw, the dramatist.

Understandably, it was in this kind of progressive, adventurous, and imaginative company that Fawcett felt most at home.

In the 1890s, Annie became a supporter of Helena Petrovna Blavatsky, the founder of theosophy. Fawcett was also deeply interested in it.

At 17, Helena Hahn, as she then was, married Nikifor Blavatsky, an army officer who was also a provincial vice-governor in Tsarist Russia. Like Annie and Frank Besant, Helena and her husband soon parted, and Helena developed an interest in spiritualism and occultism in general, which took her on extensive tours of Europe, Asia, and the USA. She was also said to have studied various forms of eastern mysticism under the guidance of numerous Hindu mahatmas. She, herself, believed that she had strange occult powers.

Together with H.S. Olcott and others, she founded the Theosophical Society in 1875. Her book, *Isis Unveiled*, was published in 1877, and deservedly attracted considerable attention. Her main thesis was a criticism of contemporary science and religion, together with a plea for mystical experience and spiritual ideas as the best route to real insight and authority.

These were views to which Fawcett was thoroughly sympathetic.

Fawcett's talents went a long way beyond those of a successful soldier, a fearless explorer, and an uninhibited and innovative thinker: he was also a talented descriptive writer. His account of his mystical out-of-body experiences in Trincomalee, and of the legendary treasure said to lie hidden in the labyrinth below the old fortress there, make compelling reading. (*Blackwood's Magazine* no. 1720, vol. 285, February, 1959.) So does his intriguing account of another ancient Sri Lankan treasure hidden beneath a curious stone construction known as Galla-pita-Galla (literally "rock-upon-rock" in the Sinhalese language), which is situated not far from the city of

Badulla. Fawcett's discovery there of a few bricks of solid gold hinted at the presence of far greater treasure concealed farther down. (*Blackwood's Magazine* no. 1793, vol. 297, March, 1965.)

According to Fawcett's own intriguing account, the events leading up to the tragedy of his mysterious disappearance may, in one sense, have begun with the shipwreck of the Portuguese adventurer, Diego Alvarez, barely a quarter of a century after Columbus reached America. Diego's life was saved by the timely intervention of a beautiful Native girl named Paraguassu, whom Fawcett himself described as "the Pocahontas of South America." Through his attractive young wife, Alvarez established friendly relations with her people and subsequently invited a number of his Portuguese friends and family to join them. Paraguassu's sister married another Portuguese adventurer, and their son, Muribeca, discovered (or was shown?) many local mines, from which he extracted gold, silver, and gemstones.

Muribeca had a son named Roberio Dias, who also knew the locations of his father's mines. In the early seventeenth century, Roberio visited the king of Portugal, Dom Pedro II, and attempted to do a deal with him: the secret of the mines in exchange for the title of a marquis. Neither trusted the other, and as a result, Roberio was imprisoned. He died in 1622, and the secret of the mines died with him.

Over the years, many expeditions set out to find them and failed dismally, with great suffering and loss of life. Fawcett ultimately discovered an ancient document in Rio de Janeiro telling the story of one such expedition led by a nameless adventurer from Minas Gerais.

After months of struggle and suffering, this searcher and his small party reached a mountain range that seemed impossible to scale, but two of the expedition who were gathering fuel for the campfire found the way up accidentally. When the Minas Gerais party reached the top, they saw the ancient ruins of an enormous city in the valley beyond the mountains, not more than five miles away.

When they reached these ruins and explored them at close quarters, the men from Minas Gerais were particularly impressed by a vast square in which a column of black stone occupied the central position. At the top of this column stood the well-preserved statue of a man, one of his hands rested at waist level, the other pointed north. These early explorers were even more impressed when one of their number, Joao Antonio, discovered a gold coin among the ruins. This bore the image of a young man on one side; a bow, a crown, and a musical instrument were depicted on the other.

Fawcett also records an episode in 1913, when the then British consul was shown a similar ruined city hidden deep in the rain forest. Together with the Minas Gerais discoveries, this incident convinced Fawcett that there must be further fascinating ruins of great historical importance waiting to be discovered in the depths of Amazonia.

His contact with Annie Besant, Helena Blavatsky, their theosophist friends, and several other equally uninhibited and imaginative speculative thinkers, tended to strengthen Fawcett's own hypothesis that the ancient, culturally advanced civilizations of South America might well have originated in Atlantis.

If mysterious Atlantean secrets had lain hidden somewhere beneath those jungle-shrouded Amazonian ruins, what impact might they have had on the science and technology of the 1920s, as well as on the philosophy and religion of the period — if only Fawcett had succeeded in bringing them back?

Another significant factor is that Colonel Fawcett was descended from the ancient and mysterious O'Sulivan-Mors family. Mors was the original Norse name of the noble House of Sinclair, rulers of the kingdom of Orkney, those same fearless Sinclairs who befriended the surviving Knights Templar after they were treacherously attacked by Philip IV of France in 1307.

Fawcett's Mors/Sinclair ancestors were great seafarers and explorers, just as the Colonel himself was. It was Prince Henry Sinclair of Orkney who almost certainly reached Newfoundland and Nova Scotia with the aid of the Venetian Zeno brothers, long before Columbus crossed the Atlantic. There is every likelihood that Henry Sinclair took refugee Templars with him on that epic, pioneering voyage, and that those same fearless and determined warrior-priests were responsible for constructing the strange subterranean treasure store and labyrinth for which Oak Island in Mahone Bay, off the coast of Nova Scotia, is famous.

Perhaps the most significant factor of all in Fawcett's unusual lineage is the legendary family claim that the O'Sulivan-Mors included a mermaid among their remote ancestors. The mysterious Merovingian French dynasty was reputed to have been in possession of magical powers; the themselves claimed that their founder, Mérovée, was the son of a strange, aquatic demigod, a Quinotaur, and of a human mother. In this, there is a parallel to King Arthur of the Britons, who was also said by some of his contemporaries to have had a mysterious aquatic origin; according to one persistent account of Arthur's origin, Merlin had plucked him as a babe from a huge wave.

So there are legends of an aquatic Mérovée, an aquatic Arthur, and an aquatic ancestor for the O'Sulivan-Mors, from whose lineage the adventurous Colonel Fawcett eventually sprang. Could it be that those remarkably similar legends are partially obscured symbols providing a link with Atlantis?

If a handful of gifted survivors of a great lost Atlantean culture managed to reach South America in the remote past, did their learning inspire and guide the builders of those ancient lost cities that Diego Alvarez found, and Percy Fawcett sought?

Did he ever find his esoteric metropolis? If not, what really became of him?

Fawcett's son, Brian, was working on the Peruvian railways in 1927, when he met a French civil engineer named Roger Courteville. He claimed that he had met a gaunt, elderly Englishman who was far from well, and who had said his name was Fawcett. Courteville's description of this sick and confused old man did not tally very closely with Fawcett, but it was remotely possible that years of illness and hardship had changed the Colonel almost beyond recognition.

Commander George Dyott led a big, well -equipped search party to look for Fawcett in 1928. On the far side of the Kuliseu River, Dyott met the chief of a Nafaqua Indian village. In the chief's hut lay a metal uniform case that had once undoubtedly belonged to Fawcett: the chief's son even wore the maker's label on a string around his neck. But this didn't help the searchers: the case was one that Fawcett had disposed of in 1920, at least five years before disappearing during his last quest.

Journalist Albert de Winton led another search party in 1930. He reached the Kalapalo village, where he thought Fawcett's party might have been killed — but then de Winton himself failed to return.

Stefan Rattin, a Swiss trapper, believed that he had seen Fawcett alive in 1931, but the elderly Englishman whom he described as being held prisoner by tribesmen living north of the River Bomfin was unlike the Colonel in several significant ways — especially in his height. It was greatly to Rattin's credit that he returned to try to bring the mysterious white captive back with him, but tragically, just like de Winton, the courageous Swiss rescuer never made it home again.

Fawcett's theodolite-compass reached Britain in 1935. It was still in good condition and appeared to have been looked after by someone who understood it. A note in the lid of the compass case recorded that it had been found near a Bacairy Indian camp.

Yet another report suggested that Fawcett was safe with the Aravudu tribe, but that they would not allow him to leave.

Finally the reports of this kind dwindled and died away altogether. Three-quarters of a century have passed since Fawcett's disappearance, and at this point in time, it is highly unlikely that any more concrete or definitive evidence about his last adventure will emerge from the Matto Grosso.

But the weight of evidence suggests that there are many strange mysteries

Colonel Fawcett's talented and vivacious granddaughter, Rolette de Montet-Guerin, who now guards the miraculous signet ring.

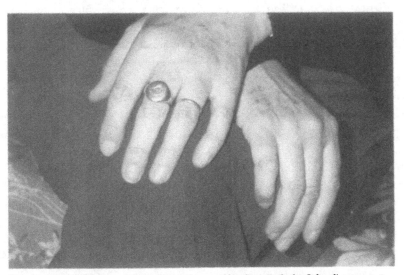

Rolette de Montet-Guerin, Colonel Fawcett's granddaughter, with the Colonel's signet ring on her hand.

hidden there — including lost cities that may well have owed their existence to arcane Atlantean culture. Whether Fawcett found one before he finally ended his Amazonian quest is impossible to say, but such was the man's great character, courage, and determination, that he may well have succeeded. If he did, and if his record of that final quest still miraculously survives, it will be among the most exciting reading of the century.

As an epilogue to this research on Fawcett, we arranged a special meeting for his granddaughter, Rolette, and two gifted psychometrists, the talented artist Pamela Willson and author Rosie Malone. Each psychometrist examined the signet ring sensitively and carefully. Rosie's first impression was one of pain and surprise. The ring seemed to cut or stab her hand sufficiently to make her cry out. This was so pronounced that she was unable to pick it up again, and asked Pamela to retrieve it for her. Pamela said that it gave off a feeling of intense cold, which ran up her spine and made her shudder. She was certain that the wearer had been in a very unhappy state of mind when he had last worn the ring. She also got the strong impression that something painful was digging into the centre of her spine. In her own words, she felt as if she was "trapped in ice cold water."

Rosie tried again and added that there was persistent pain associated with the ring, and a sensation of being trapped. She sensed the nightmare experience often described as "wading through treacle" which might have referred to struggling through deep mud, or, perhaps, through an Amazonian swamp. Rosie again strongly emphasized the association of pain and other negative feelings with this mysterious ring, and showed the researchers some marks on her hand where she had been holding it. Pamela was strongly aware of sensations of pressure, restriction, and confinement, as if a steel band was being drawn tightly around her brow. Both psychometrists felt that there had been a great deal of suffering associated with the ring.

What Pamela also saw in connection with the ring was a large house in beautiful scenery, and a white dog, of which the Colonel had been very fond. Rolette confirmed the accuracy of both these pre-Amazonian associations.

Sadly, it looks from this psychometric evidence gleaned from the Colonel's signet ring that his final days in Amazonia may have been clouded by great pain, close confinement, and deep unhappiness.

Chapter 5

Nikola Tesla: Electrical Engineering Genius

Nikola Tesla was born on July 9, 1856, in Smiljan, which was then part of the province of Lika in the old Austro-Hungarian Habsburg Empire. It later became part of Yugoslavia. Nikola was the second son of the Reverend Milutin Tesla and his brilliantly gifted wife, Djouka. Milutin was a poet and philosopher, as well as a priest. He was a deeply sensitive man who was easily offended, and who tended to bear grudges afterwards. His first profession before turning to the church was as an army officer, but the toughness of military life did not fit well with his sensitive character, and he resigned his commission after only a short period of service. Milutin was as keenly interested in politics, economics, and social justice as he was in theology and religious history, and his sermons often had social or commercial themes.

Nikola's strange electrical engineering inventive genius seems more likely to have come down to him through Djouka's genes than through Milutin's. His mother had an exceptional, almost photographic memory. Amazingly, despite her brilliance and inventiveness, she was illiterate: perhaps her incredibly efficient powers of recall made literacy superfluous. She could recite all the old sagas, together with entire books of the Bible. She created many labour-saving household gadgets, including her own loom. Her weaving and needlework were legendary, and she could tie three knots in an

49

eyelash, using nothing but her hands, when she was well over 60. Djouka's phenomenal mind-powers, inventiveness, and dexterity were clearly evident in her second son. Her first son, Dane, had had them as well, but he had died in a tragic accident when he was only 12. The innate love of experimentation and discovery almost killed Nikola as well. As a child, he was very interested in birds, and especially in the mechanics of flight, and the effects of air and wind resistance. Once, taking a large umbrella in both hands, the young Tesla leapt from the roof of a barn. Landing with a bone-jarring crash, he spent the next six weeks recovering. One day, in the town of Gospic, Nikola was one of a large, happy crowd celebrating the inauguration of the new Gospic and district fire brigade and the first public demonstration of all their new technical equipment consisting of the latest pumps, reels, and hoses. Music played. Speeches were made. Brawny firemen then heaved away at the pumps, nothing came out of the hose. Young Nikola shouted, "Please keep pumping," and raced down to the river, where he found that there was a kink in the hose. Heaving and straining at the heavy tubing, the lad finally managed to straighten it out: water gushed and spurted from the other end, to the delight of the sweating firemen and the onlookers. On that day, the ingenious young scientist became one of the heroes of Gospic.

At school, young Nikola's mathematical ability was phenomenal. He seems to have had the same powers as Trachtenberg, the brilliant mental mathematician who used his ability to calculate as a psychological escape route from the horrors of a Nazi concentration camp, and who later founded the Trachtenberg Institute. Tesla himself described the process by

Nikola Tesla, brilliant but unorthodox electrical inventor.

which he reached the answers to mathematical problems as something that just unfolded by itself without any conscious effort on his part, other than that of reading and understanding the nature of the problems. He actually *saw* the answers, which seemed somehow to have sprung from his subconscious, and for him, they had the same clarity, solidity, and definition as the print in the textbook or his math teacher's writing on the blackboard. Tesla's strange ability to create these visible forms and symbols — so real that he could walk round them and view them from other angles — was to play a vital part in his future career as an outstanding inventor in the field of electrical engineering.

In Edgar Allan Poe's "Fall of the House of Usher," there is a vivid description of the hypersensitivity and hyperacuity suffered by one of the major characters. The slightest noise sounds like an explosion to him; the lightest touch feels like an agonizing blow delivered by a heavyweight boxer. When Tesla was working in Budapest for the Central Telegraph Office, he was taken ill because of overexertion and long hours without sleep. He suffered exactly the same symptoms as the Poe character. Tesla complained that he could hear a watch ticking loudly in a distant room well away from where he was lying in bed. A friend or nurse speaking quietly sounded like thunder, or an avalanche, to him. Traffic in the street outside his home vibrated him so violently and painfully that rubber pads were placed beneath his bed: it was almost like the fairy tale of the real princess who could feel one hard, dried pea underneath six mattresses. Direct sunlight through the bedroom windows hurt his eyes, but in the dark, he could locate objects on the far side of the room.

Another example of Tesla's strange mental powers was provided in Budapest in 1882, as he walked through the city with his friend Szigeti. Tesla seems to have switched into that special alternative reality mode for which he later became so famous. He saw a vision — for want of a better word — which showed him clearly how the alternating current electric motor could be constructed and made to function. Szigeti had to lead his excited friend out of the way of the city traffic. In H.G. Wells's short story *The Strange Case of Davidson's Eyes*, a man has lost the ability to see what's close to him in his normal environment, but is able to view a strange scene on an island on the other side of the world. As he ascends or descends the slopes in Britain, so his strange visions of the unknown island ascend and descend as well, as though he is watching the scenes through a remote TV camera. When Tesla went into his alternative reality, it was very similar to Davidson's unnerving experiences in Wells's story.

Disappointed because he couldn't persuade European manufacturers to take up his new ideas for an alternating current motor, Tesla went to the

USA in 1884 and joined Thomas Edison for a short while. The two brilliant inventors were poles apart in terms of personality, and a serious quarrel between them was almost inevitable. When it came, Tesla left Edison and set up on his own. Much of his laboratory work was aimed at demonstrating the superiority of alternating current.

One of the inventions for which he is best remembered is the Tesla coil, still frequently used in TV and radio circuitry today. Tesla patented it in 1891. Basically, it consists of a central cylindrical core of soft iron, with an induction coil around it. There is an inner, primary coil of just a few turns of copper wire, and an outer, secondary coil of many turns. The current in the primary coil is automatically stopped and started again by an interrupter. The current produced magnetizes the soft iron core and sets up a wide magnetic field in the induction coil. One of Tesla's many experiments with this coil provided the ancestor of the modern fluorescent tube.

Tesla worked with the Westinghouse company for a while, where his motors were developed and used extensively in mining, printing, and ventilation.

A magazine interview in August 1894, included an interesting physical description of Tesla, who was typical of the tall, slim, hyper-energetic, brilliantly intellectual, ectomorphic body type of a Sherlock Holmes. The interviewer described Tesla as: "very thin ... more than six feet tall ... less than 140 lbs. ... He has very big hands ... His thumbs are remarkably big

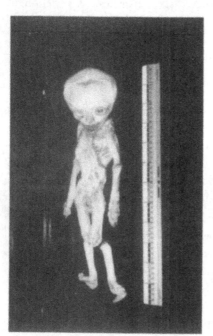

Could this tiny, weird, mummified creature possibly be an *alien*? The authors examined it closely in White's City, New Mexico. It bears a striking resemblance to the alleged Roswell aliens less than 150 miles away.

even for such big hands." The journalist went on to argue, somewhat quaintly, that big thumbs were a sign of extra high intelligence because apes had relatively small thumbs. His description of Tesla's head is particularly interesting. The eyes were deep-set and lighter than the interviewer had expected. He described Tesla's head as "spreading out at the top like a fan … shaped like a wedge."

The miniature, mummified, humanoid body we examined and photographed in the White's City Museum in New Mexico, USA, had a similarly shaped head, as did the aliens who were alleged to have crashed at Roswell — not far from White's City — in 1947. The late Hughie Green, at one time a very well known British and Canadian radio and TV entertainer, was a flight lieutenant (later promoted to major) in the RCAF at the time of the Roswell crash. He was driving through New Mexico when the crash happened, and heard the original local radio station broadcasts. He later expressed surprise at the speed with which the story had been dropped — as though some kind of official cover-up was in action.

Unlike his friend and contemporary Marconi, the distinguished radio pioneer, Tesla was not interested solely in transmitting radio waves. His great interest was in finding ways to transmit huge amounts of electrical power. In 1899, using a huge coil generating millions of volts, he managed to pump millions of watts into the air before the generator burned out. This amazing achievement took place in Colorado Springs. A copper ball about a metre in

Hughie Green, the famous broadcaster, was serving with the Royal Canadian Air Force at the time of the Roswell crash, and was surprised by the speed with which the story was dropped.

diameter was mounted at the top of a two-hundred-foot tower. Below this, Tesla had erected a square building containing two enormous coils, a primary and a secondary one. His theory was that a resonating electrical and radio system would be created so that it would go on reinforcing itself and drawing current from the earth. Resonance can destroy a bridge, or keep a child's garden swing going, provided that the auxiliary push is applied in exactly the right place, at exactly the right time. In the briefest possible outline, the heart of Tesla's brilliant theory was that high frequency radio waves would travel across the world and then return. Provided he had tuned them correctly to the natural frequency of the oscillation of the earth's own electrical currents, he reckoned that they would reinforce the voltage pushes in his two-hundred-foot mast, and so increase the current being drawn from the earth.

It worked only too well. Lightning bolts over 130 feet long crackled out of the copper ball surmounting Tesla's tower. It was undeniably spectacular. Then, just as suddenly and successfully as it had begun, the vast electrical firework display stopped. Tesla checked with his assistant, Czito, to discover what had gone wrong. They soon found out. The Colorado Springs Generating Company's generator was burnt out. There was simply no more power available for activating Tesla's great tower, coil, and copper ball experiment. It was fortunate that Tesla himself had designed the Colorado Springs generator. He had it up and running again in a matter of days.

One of the greatest mysteries associated with Tesla and his globally effective electrical experiments concerns the great Siberian explosion that rocked Tunguska like a twenty megaton nuclear bomb on June 30, 1908. Some researchers accept that it was a meteorite, albeit an unusual one. Others suggest that a nuclear-powered alien spacecraft crashed there and exploded. A third theory concerns Nikola Tesla himself.

In 1935, Tesla, commenting on a mysterious secret electrical weapon he had designed, said "it will destroy anything, men or machines, approaching within a radius of two hundred miles." What had he invented? Would it really work in practice? There can be no doubt that his great electrical machine at Colorado Springs worked amazingly well. Is it remotely possible that Tesla, fascinated by the idea of transmitting vast amounts of power over huge distances, had caused the enormous Tunguska explosion of 1908 during some of his earlier experiments?

Tesla described the basic principles of a prototype laser, which would also have been applicable to a particle gun, as far back as 1900. Such beams consist essentially of wave energy in bundles or packets, which are produced at precisely their own inherent frequency. This gives rise to a coherent emission, more or less equivalent to Tesla's ideas about standing waves in the paper he published at the turn of the century.

There were some serious speculations in the London *Evening Standard* in the 1970s referring to severe electrical storms over Canada, indirectly involving Tesla's last surviving assistant, Arthur Matthews, who, it was said, had been interviewed about Tesla's work by a mysterious Russian electrical engineer. The *Evening Standard* later reported that Major-General George Keegan, one-time chief of US Air Force Intelligence, suspected that the Russians might have developed a particle gun to destroy intercontinental ballistic missiles. Were experiments with that device based on Matthews' recollections of Tesla's work, and could experiments from inside the former USSR have caused the severe electrical storms over Canada?

Andrew Michrowski, one of the top scientists working in eastern Canada at the time, was convinced that Russian experiments with Tesla's original ideas had produced traumatic meteorological effects. Watson Scott, who was then working in Ottawa with the Canadian Department of Communications, made several interesting suggestions. He wondered whether what the Russians might have been doing with a Tesla-type particle beam had been responsible for the abnormal UK drought in 1976, the surprisingly warm weather in Greenland, and the great rarity of snow in Miami.

Kit Pedler, writing in Colin Wilson's superb collection *Men of Mystery* (W.H. Allen, London, 1977), describes his interesting theory of an alternative framework of science, one in which the individual scientist is part of an integrated system in which he or she has a vital creative or formative role. This is remarkably close to the so-called "magical" theories put forward by Paracelsus and Crowley's "thelema" school of thought. To what extent is the observer and measurer of phenomena an essential part of the phenomena themselves? Did Tesla create a purely internal type of alternative mental reality that was all his own, which, although useful to him as an inventor and experimenter, had no tangible existence outside his head? Or was there much more to it than that? Did he not so much invent something as get in touch with something that had an independent existence of its own? Just what are thought forms, or "tulpas" of the kind Madame Blavatsky believed she had made? Is there some alternative explanation, perhaps? Can powerful thinkers like Paracelsus, Crowley, Blavatsky, and Tesla create something inside their minds, which then, in some mysterious way, goes on to acquire an objective, external existence?

St. Paul's letters strongly advised his readers in the early Church to think about things that were pure, good, and lovely. Was he hinting at the possibility that thoughts can acquire an objective reality and, in that form, can work more good or evil than the thinker dreams possible?

Tesla's inventions are far too numerous to list. Some were practical, readily applicable, and almost mundane; others were much more advanced than the science fiction of Tesla's day. He patented an electric arc lamp, a commutator for dynamos, various electromagnetic motors, electrical distribution systems and regulators, generators and alternators, control mechanisms for moving vessels or vehicles, a tele-automaton boat, a VTAL aircraft, and a machine he believed could photograph thoughts. He also believed that he was receiving messages from intelligent beings on other planets — and perhaps he was.

He also seems to have possessed some of the prophetic abilities of Mother Shipton, Nostradamus, and Coinneach Odhar, the Brahan Seer. At one of his parties, for example, Tesla was almost obsessively determined that several of his friends should stay the night. They were the same guests who would otherwise have travelled on a train that crashed later that night.

Other fascinating possibilities connect both Tesla and Einstein with the highly controversial Philadelphia Experiment, in which a ship and its crew were alleged to have travelled through the fourth dimension.

It was also rumoured that the FBI and CIA took a keen interest in the many scientific papers left in Tesla's home when he died. Were those officers, perhaps, looking for details of the formidable weaponry that Tesla claimed he could produce?

Surely, the truly great Nikola Tesla deserves a far more distinguished place in the hall of fame than history has yet granted him. His brilliant, innovative theories and inventions deserve further serious scientific investigation today: there is much conceptual gold still left in Tesla's deep intellectual mine.

If his alternative reality was not just a unique personal possession, a creation of his magnificent but eccentric mind; if, rather, it was reached via a doorway that he discovered and used, there is no reason why others cannot locate and use that doorway as well.

Chapter 6

Maria Marten and the Red Barn of Polstead, Suffolk, and John Chapman, the Pedlar of Swaffham, Norfolk

Farmer John Corder was a prosperous man by the standards of the early nineteenth century. He owned and farmed three hundred good fertile acres, and three of his sons — John, Thomas, and James — seemed likely to follow in his agricultural footsteps. It was his fourth son, William, of whom Farmer Corder despaired.

Literature and learning were both suspect in the minds of many early nineteenth century farmers like old John Corder. They tended to have a solid, practical approach·to life. Young William had aspirations to become a man of letters, but Corder, Senior made it abundantly clear that his youngest son was going to stay on the farm and work for a living. William's father also let him know unequivocally that when the time came, he would be working as a hired help for his elder brothers and not as a profit-sharing partner.

Locked inside a small, pale, short-sighted body, William Corder's mind brooded darkly on thoughts of escape and revenge. His school life had never been pleasant for him. The rough and ready country children in the Polstead village school laughed at his literary aspirations and nicknamed him "Foxy."

Perhaps revenge, resentment, and a desire to level the score against society, and against his family, in particular, were among the motives that led William to steal from his father and indulge in minor confidence tricks. There is evidence that he stole and sold a pig or two from the farm, and

William "Foxy" Corder, hanged for the murder of Maria Marten in the Red Barn: but was he really guilty?

William Corder's house still stands in the Village of Polstead in Suffolk, England, scene of the Red Barn tragedy.

that he borrowed money in his father's name for his own use. On the rare occasions when such opportunities arose, William would sneak off to London without his father's knowledge, using money he had stolen or "borrowed." During these London visits he met Thomas Griffiths Wainewright (1794–1847) who wrote articles and reviews for the *London Magazine* during the 1820s. In addition to his literary talents, Wainewright was also an accomplished artist, a highly skilled draughtsman, an expert forger, and a ruthless poisoner. From the privileged and luxurious life of a dandy in Georgian London, he died as a convict in the wilds of Tasmania. How much influence did the charismatic Wainewright exert over the weak and impressionable Corder, and did he pass on any of his arcane knowledge of poisons to that young man?

Far from being the handsome, wealthy, confident, and sophisticated seducer of innocent teenage country girls — as he was portrayed in several of the contemporary melodramas and musicals written about him — William Corder was an undersized, physically weak, and mentally self-deluded petty criminal who made Napoleonic gestures and who was generally ridiculed.

The real Maria Marten, daughter of Thomas Marten, was an equally long way from her popular portrayal in those same Georgian theatrical entertainments, which invariably cast her as an innocent, dewy-eyed, teenage heroine. Far from being an ingenuous young country girl seduced by an experienced and unscrupulous man of the world far older than herself, Maria was actually two years older than William, and had already had three children by different lovers, including William's elder brother, Thomas.

Maria Marten of Polstead, Suffolk, England, whose body was discovered in the Red Barn after her stepmother dreamed it was there.

Long before she became the youngest Corder boy's mistress, Maria was well known in the Polstead area as a girl who was happy to oblige anyone who could produce the necessary money. Wealthy Peter Matthews, for example, was one client who allegedly gave her an allowance of twenty pounds a year following his affair with her. Not surprisingly, Maria was on the police wanted list on an immorality charge. When she ceased to be seen around Polstead — following her murder and the concealment of her body under the floor of the Red Barn, the general opinion among the villagers was that she'd probably gone to London to work as a prostitute full time.

As far as Maria was concerned, therefore, the four Corder brothers and their wealthy father were of considerable interest as prospective customers, or even, in the case of the four young men, as potential husbands, if she was very lucky indeed.

Perhaps her hopes in that direction began to evaporate when Thomas, who had fathered one of her children, was drowned in an accident when the ice gave way on Polstead village pond. The next two brothers, James and John, died young from typhus and tuberculosis. Life in early nineteenth-century Suffolk was infinitely healthier than life in London, or in any other major city of that period, but infectious diseases were major hazards even there. John Corder, William's father, also died, which left the unprepossessing William as Maria's sole surviving target for matrimony.

With his father and brothers gone, William was now a wealthy man. Living at the farm with his widowed mother, he had come unexpectedly into an inheritance that most men would have greatly enjoyed, but the literary bug constantly tormented him. He didn't enjoy farming at all, and thought of nothing except how to get to London as often as he could, and live among the literary society he so much admired, especially that sector of it revolving around the sinister but charismatic Wainewright.

In spite of the lure of literary life in London, William found himself involved in a relationship with Maria, which had almost certainly come about at her instigation. He was the father of her next child: a poor, sickly little thing, which died in infancy in suspicious circumstances. Was William's possible knowledge of poisons involved here, too?

The early death and informal, irregular burial of that baby lead on to darker speculations about whether the seemingly inadequate and ineffectual William might have been a great deal more sinister than was previously supposed. Was he, after all, a much more dangerous and purposeful character than historical criminologists usually give him credit for? His father and elder brothers had made his life a misery, and had offered him no prospects. A man with nothing to live for and nothing to look forward to can become extremely dangerous.

In the normal course of events, the simple passage of time would have released him from his father's unwelcome restrictions, but with three elder brothers between him and his inheritance, freedom must have seemed remote. Was Thomas's death in the pond entirely the tragic accident that it seemed? It certainly would have been convenient for William. And did his extensive reading, under Wainewright's guidance, include morbid subjects, such as toxicology? Did he learn from Wainewright of any slow poisons that might appear to mimic the symptoms of typhus or tuberculosis? Or had he, perhaps, read enough about the spread of those and similar fatal diseases to know how to encourage infection?

Even the least medically educated mediaeval soldier knew that flinging a few dead animals over the walls of an enemy's castle often helped to spread disease among the defenders. Such basic knowledge would not have been outside Corder's scope, and his brooding, vengeful mind might well have adjusted it to a small enough scale to infect two brothers, rather than a whole garrison.

If Corder and Maria could callously dispose of the body of their sickly infant son, whom neither of them seemed to have wanted, would either or both have been capable of actually poisoning that child, as well as poisoning James and John, or deliberately infecting them?

What if the original scenario had been something like this? Maria and her stepmother Anne ("Mole-Catcher" Marten's second wife) realized that although the three elder boys might be good paying customers on a casual basis, only William was weak and malleable enough to be persuaded to marry her. Either by plotting the plans for these deaths herself, with William's connivance, or by working as his willing accomplice, was Maria able to clear the way for William to inherit the farm?

Now comes the fatal quarrel between the two of them in the Red Barn. Was Maria threatening to tell what she knew about William's part in his brothers' deaths? Or was she threatening William that he would go the same way that she'd already sent James and John, if he didn't soon marry her? Knowing her to be ruthless and dangerous from their murderous work together, which would have included the death of their baby son, did William suddenly realize that if he didn't quickly dispose of her, she may sooner or later dispose of him?

This conjecture and speculation seems to provide a strong and tenable motive for the fatal quarrel between William and Maria in the Red Barn. The usual theory was that she wanted to get married quickly, whereas Corder was unwilling to be trapped then — if ever — by a wife who didn't share his all-consuming enthusiasm for London and its literary life. On balance, it seems more likely that William shot Maria because he was afraid

The meadow where the Red Barn once stood. Maria's body was found here after her stepmother's persistent nightmares.

of what she might reveal about his role in his brothers' deaths, or because of what she had threatened to do to him, rather than because of a trivial disagreement about marriage.

The most intriguing part of the Red Barn mystery is the role that Mrs. Anne Marten, Maria's stepmother, played in the whole strange and sordid enigma. After Maria's disappearance — ostensibly, she had gone down to Ipswich with Corder so that they could get married there, well out of the way of the outstanding immorality charge against her — her stepmother claimed that she was plagued by nightmares and visions centring on the Red Barn.

These disturbing phenomena had one central message: Maria had been murdered by William Corder and her body lay concealed in a shallow grave in the floor of the barn.

Anne claimed after the nightmares that she knew *exactly where* in the barn Maria lay buried: under the right-hand bay as you entered.

Anne's husband, Thomas, the Polstead mole-catcher, did his best to comfort her when these recurrent nightmares woke her. Sobbing, the second Mrs. Marten told him repeatedly that in her dream, she had seen the earth opening to reveal Maria's body buried under that highly significant spot in the Red Barn.

Finally, as it seemed to be the only way of allaying his new wife's fears about Maria, Thomas Marten agreed to investigate the matter.

The Martens' cottage in Polstead, where Maria was born. It was here that her stepmother had the strange dream.

Accordingly, he called on Pryke, who acted as bailiff for William Corder, and had the necessary authority to admit him to the Red Barn. Even then, although Pryke was perfectly helpful and co-operative, Marten felt that he had to justify his unusual request. He told the bailiff that he thought Maria might have left some of her things there when she had gone away with William Corder.

Once inside the Red Barn, Marten went straight to the right-hand bay and began to examine the floor below the loose hay that lay almost everywhere. He poked a stick into surprisingly soft earth and then began to dig.

He found Maria's badly decomposed body barely a foot down, almost naked and wrapped in an old sack. It was her earrings that her father recognized, and by these, he identified her rotting corpse. He and the bailiff then set out grimly together to notify the village constable of their gruesome discovery.

Corder, by this time, had gone to London, where, in St. Andrew's Church in Holborn, he had married a demure and well-educated young schoolmistress named Kathleen Moore, who was more or less financially independent. They set up a school together in Ealing, with William Corder as headmaster. He adjusted to the new role with alacrity. He acquired a scholarly pair of glasses, and delighted in carrying books with him wherever he went.

It was here that a painstakingly diligent police constable named Jonas

Lea succeeded in tracking him down. Corder was halfway through his breakfast that April morning in 1828, when Lea arrived at their door.

Corder attempted at first to deny all knowledge of anyone called Maria Marten, but three months later, he found himself facing a murder charge at Bury St. Edmunds Assizes, where Anne, the dead girl's stepmother, was the most effective witness against him.

Mrs. Marten noticed things. She had a phenomenal eye for detail, and an amazing memory for dates and places, as far as the murder was concerned. On one occasion, as she said in evidence, she distinctly recalled seeing Corder at a local Polstead funeral, carrying a large green umbrella that Anne knew to be Maria's.

William's defence was transparently flimsy. He and Maria had quarrelled in the Red Barn, and she'd either shot herself using one of his pistols, or been shot accidentally when his pistol went off. He later confessed that he had shot her during a struggle in the Red Barn, but what their quarrel had been about never really emerged during the trial. The jury reached their verdict in well under an hour. Corder was found guilty and hanged in front of Bury Jail with a crowd of thousands who had gathered to watch him go. His last words were: "I deserve this fate."

At the heart of the Red Barn mystery is stepmother Anne Marten's nightmare. Is it possible to glimpse hidden truth by paranormal means in nightmares, visions, and dreams? Are such visions merely meaningless products of the human mind? Are they strange, psychic glimpses of an inevitable and immutable future, or do they only reveal possibilities? Some psychologists would suggest that when presented with data indicating very unwelcome possibilities, the human mind may suppress the unacceptable conclusions at a conscious level; instead, they filter out in symbolic form through the subconscious as dreams and nightmares.

Let us go along with this theory for a moment for the sake of the argument. Anne Marten was a keen observer of detail. What she saw and heard led her to believe in the strong probability that Corder had killed her stepdaughter, Maria, and had hidden her body in the Red Barn. This data, together with her acute anxiety over Maria, may have manipulated her subconscious to produce the nightmare of Maria lying below the barn's right-hand bay, where Thomas Marten and Pryke the bailiff duly discovered it.

It is remotely possible, of course, that there were more than two conspirators in the hypothetical plot to destroy the older Corder brothers, leaving the way clear for William to inherit the property and marry Maria. Was Anne Marten in on that plan too? Had she been aware that Corder and Maria had disposed of Corder's brothers and shortened the life of their own sickly and unwanted baby son? On the fateful day when Maria was shot, had Mrs. Marten suspected that Corder was responsible, but had not known what to do about it?

Purely for the sake of argument, we can start from a position in which we presuppose that hunches, dreams, nightmares, and psychic visions do not exist, and cannot be *allowed* to exist because of the damage they could inflict on widely accepted philosophic and theological paradigms. So there has to be another reason why Maria's stepmother, Anne, suddenly began to demand that the right-hand bay of the Red Barn should be excavated. Such knowledge could only have come about — omitting the possibility of psychic interventions — if Anne had seen either the murder being committed, or Corder digging frantically to conceal Maria's corpse. In that case, she would have known perfectly well just where Maria lay. Why didn't she speak out then, instead of playing along with Corder's myriad excuses?

In the early nineteenth century, it was death, and not divorce, that was the great despoiler of family life. Widowers generally tended to take on much younger women as second wives. If Mrs. Anne Marten was a lot younger than her mole-catcher husband, might the amoral William Corder have made a pass at her as well as at Maria?

What if the reason for the furious quarrel between Maria and William in the Red Barn was that Maria had just discovered that William was having an affair with her stepmother as well? Corder was weak and undersized. Maria was a sturdily built country girl. If she had attacked him physically in her anger, Corder might well have drawn his pistol to defend himself. As Maria falls dead or dying, Anne, attracted by the noise, enters the Red Barn. With her young rival out of the way, Anne makes a deal with Corder. As soon as old Tom, the mole-catcher, is out of the way as well, Corder must marry Anne in return for her silence about Maria's murder and the concealment of the body. To save his skin, Corder readily agrees.

For several months, Anne goes along with the various prevarications which attempt to explain Maria's absence. Then she learns that despite his promise to her, Corder has married a young schoolmistress in London. Anne's fury knows no bounds. She cannot now go to the police and say: "I know that William Corder killed Maria because I saw him burying her body in the Red Barn."

The first question that a good detective like Jonas Lea would have asked would surely have been: "Why didn't you call us then?"

But people were still very superstitious in the first half of the nineteenth century. Dreams and visions, omens, and portents were often taken seriously. Anne's convenient nightmares tightened the noose around Corder's slender neck.

Theories abound, but the mystery of Anne Marten's curiously accurate nightmares remains.

In this context, another strange East Anglian dream adds to the mystery: the weird adventures of John Chapman, the Pedlar of Swaffham in Norfolk, England, not so very far from the Red Barn in Polstead, in Suffolk. One night, during the 1440s, John had a strangely compelling dream in which he was told that if he went to London Bridge, he would hear news that would make him wealthy. Despite his wife's advice to the contrary, John determined to go. After a long, tiring journey with his faithful dog, John stood on London Bridge for three days, chatting with passers-by, in the hope that the news foretold in his dream would come his way. He heard nothing of any significance. Tired and disappointed, he was about to set out for Swaffham, when a friendly stranger asked what he was doing there. John liked the man's kind, open face, and told him the outline of his strange dream. He did not give his name, nor the fact that he lived in Swaffham. The stranger laughed and said that if he, himself, was foolish enough to believe in strange dreams, he would already be visiting a town in Norfolk where, in one of his dreams, a fortune had lain buried beneath a tree in a pedlar's garden. John thanked him politely for his time, and set off for home as fast as he could. He dug beneath the tree in his garden and unearthed a box of coins with a strange inscription on the lid in Latin, which he could not read. But what John

Town sign from Swaffham in Norfolk, England, carved by Harry Carter, cousin of Howard Carter who went with Lord Carnarvon to find the Tomb of Tutankhamun. The sign shows John Chapman, the pedlar who discovered the treasure following a strange dream.

lacked in formal education, he made up for with native wit and shrewdness. He put the lid of the box in his window, like an ornament, and sure enough, two young Latin scholars strolled past and stopped to translate it: "Under me doth lie / Another much richer than I."

At the first quiet opportunity when he was sure he was unobserved, John dug deeper under the tree and found a huge earthenware pot full of coins and jewels. This second find made him a member of the truly wealthy gentry, and he was not ungenerous. He bestowed many gifts on the poor, and paid for repairs and extensions to Swaffham Parish Church, where his effigy, along with his faithful dog, is carved on the pew ends. He is also featured on the Swaffham town sign, carved and painted by Harry Carter, woodwork master at Hamond's Grammar School in Swaffham, which co-author Lionel attended as a boy. Interestingly enough, this same Harry Carter, the teacher, carpenter, and artist, was cousin to Howard Carter, who accompanied Lord Carnarvon when he discovered the tomb of Tutankhamun.

Chapter 7

Paracelsus — Alchemist, Physician, and Magician:
Alias Philippus Aureolus Theophrastus Bombastus von Hohenheim

Paracelsus took his name from a famous first-century Roman doctor named Celsus. He added the "para" to indicate that he surpassed the original Celsus in medical knowledge and healing skills. Paracelsus (his real name was Philippus Aureolus) was born on November 11, 1493, and died in suspicious circumstances on September 24, 1541. His untimely death was a great loss to both medicine and science.

Paracelsus's father was a doctor and pharmacist, although not a very successful or prosperous member of either profession. Paracelsus's mother died while he was still a child, and his father then moved away to southern Austria, to the town of Villach. The Fugger family, who were extremely wealthy merchant bankers from Augsburg, had founded the Bergschule in Villach, and Paracelsus's father got a job there as a chemistry teacher. That exceptional old Bergschule in Villach was roughly the equivalent of a modern technical college: it specialized in turning out bright young practical scientists who would be able to work as managers, foremen, and metallurgists in mining operations involving iron, tin, mercury, and gold.

As a youngster, Paracelsus met and talked with working miners. He learned all kinds of strange things from their folklore and heard weird accounts of metals that apparently grew in the earth like root vegetables.

In the early sixteenth-century there were large numbers of young students trekking across Europe and calling at one famous old university after another, in the hope of learning something valuable. Paracelsus joined this migratory band, and before his twentieth birthday he had attended colleges at Basle, Cologne, Heidelberg, Leipzig, Tubingen, Vienna, and Wittenberg.

Paracelsus, a rigorous young critic who did not suffer fools gladly, was not particularly impressed with any of them. He had a bitter, biting wit and referred to the staff of these so called "high universities" as no better than "high asses." Understandably, this attitude did not exactly endear him to the university authorities and teachers. He became even less popular with the establishment when his comment referring to other sources of information became widely known. Freely translated, it reads: "Not all wisdom is learnt in universities. Old wives' tales and the folklore of gypsies, beggars, bandits, wayside magicians, and wanderers also contains useful information. The travelling doctor is the one who learns most. Experience of the world increases our knowledge."

Paracelsus annoyed the academics still further by his acerbic comments about the language in which knowledge could best be expressed. In his opinion, the vernacular was clearer and more honest than the formal vocabulary of the debating chamber and the lecture room. In particular, he poured scorn on the scholasticism of Avicenna, Aristotle, and Galen, who were then the recognized and accepted pillars of Greek and Arabian medical science.

Paracelsus, physician and magician.

Some accounts of his life suggest that he graduated from the medical school in Vienna in 1510, when he was only 17. He, himself, always maintained that he had obtained his medical degree at Ferrara in 1516; however, the academic records for that year are lost. Was their mysterious disappearance due to Paracelsian magic, carelessness, a genuine accident, or the machinations of his many highly placed enemies? What Paracelsus enjoyed most in Ferrara was the powerful criticism there of Galen, Avicenna, and the other ancient authorities, whom Paracelsus himself ridiculed and despised.

Medicine and astrology were inseparable in Paracelsus's time, and this was yet another area in which he found himself diametrically opposed to the traditional received wisdom. He just could not fully accept that stars and planets controlled the health-destiny of every organ and limb in the human body.

As soon as he had taken his degree at Ferrara, Paracelsus set off on his many travels. The early sixteenth century was not a good era for travel. Shakespeare uses the interesting phrase "putters-out-of-five" to indicate a bizarre and primitive form of travel insurance. In effect, the traveller laid a bet at odds of five to one against his own safe return. If he was lucky enough to return safely against all the hazards of shipwreck, warfare, disease, and banditry, he could claim back from the underwriter — the putter-out-of-five — five times the amount he had deposited with him before setting out. Actuarial science wasn't as sophisticated in the fifteenth and sixteenth centuries as its computerized descendant is today, but the odds undoubtedly favoured the underwriter rather than the traveller.

Paracelsus visited almost every mainland European state, as well as England, Ireland, Scotland, and Wales. Enlisting as an army surgeon, he served in that capacity in Holland and in Italy. A Russian adventure led to his being taken prisoner and being held by the fierce Tartars, from whom he was very fortunate to escape with his life: or perhaps his magical skills had more to do with that escape than good fortune alone. His escape route took him into Lithuania, and from there, to Hungary.

When his persistent wanderings took him to the mystic East, Paracelsus visited Palestine, Egypt, Arabia, and Constantinople, the one-time capital of the Eastern Roman Empire. He, himself, regarded his extended travels as one huge series of educational visits. Everywhere he went, he studied medicine, alchemy, and magic. He often spoke and wrote of the latent forces of nature, which he always wanted to examine, investigate, understand, and ultimately control. The biblical Book of Revelation, with which Paracelsus was undoubtedly very familiar, speaks of a new Heaven and a new Earth, and for Paracelsus, these meant what he referred to as "the new star of imagination, in a new Heaven." It was in this metaphysical area, and in their view of imagination and will, especially, that Paracelsus, Tesla, and Crowley converged most closely. Alchemist-physician, electrical inventor, and black magician, all realized that a combination of imagination and determination was capable of achieving far-reaching results.

"Resolute imagination is the beginning of all magical operations," Paracelsus wrote. "Because men do not perfectly believe and imagine, the result is that arts are uncertain when they might be wholly certain."

In the middle of the 1520s, Paracelsus went back to his old home in Villach to find that his fame had run there well ahead of him. He was still only a young man in his early 30s when he was appointed as physician and medical lecturer at Basle. The great crowds of young, itinerant European students — to which Paracelsus, himself, had once belonged, now began beating a path to his doorstep in Basle.

Just as the belligerently challenging Martin Luther had pinned his ideas against indulgences on the church door almost a decade earlier, so the equally aggressive Paracelsus did the same, with his open invitation on June 5, 1527, on the doors of the university where he was lecturing. Paracelsus's unforgivable sin, in the eyes of the outraged authorities, was to throw his lectures open and invite anyone who wished to come to attend them, irrespective of whether they were members of the university or not. With the unfair advantage of hindsight, it is easy enough for the historian to accuse Paracelsus of being his own worst enemy, of inviting social and professional disaster with the alacrity of a bleeding pearl diver swimming across a shark-infested lagoon. Disaster duly accepted the invitation and came to Paracelsus's party — although it first allowed him a year or so of precarious success at Basle.

His fame spread to every corner of the known world. Crowds queued for his lectures. Medically, he talked a great deal of sense — an amazing amount of sense, considering all the superstition, misinformation, and bigotry pervading the century in which he lived. Much of what he said made fools of the orthodox practitioners of his time. Hatred and jealousy smouldered all around him. Yet, perhaps, there is such a thing as too much self-confidence. Shakespeare portrayed Julius Caesar as a man of towering strength and ability, but one who failed to heed a timely warning. Paracelsus suffered from the Caesar syndrome. When his enemies finally ganged up on him, he was lucky (perhaps, again, magically lucky) as he had been in Russia, to escape with his life, but that was about all he had left. For nearly ten years, he wandered disconsolately from place to place — including Colmar in Alsace — keeping just a few paces ahead of his vengeful enemies, and relying on the help and hospitality of loyal friends.

Just as the long Hebrew exile in Babylon gave priests, scholars, and scribes time to edit and re-edit their holy literature, so his decade of exile gave Paracelsus time to polish, revise, and think through all the knowledge he had acquired on his long and wide-ranging travels. When he published *Der grossen Wundartzney*, it became an amazing success, and restored his fortune, his professional reputation, and his social advantages.

Excellent as his writings were, and popular as his lectures were, Paracelsus's significant contributions to medicine and chemistry were by no means restricted to what he said in the lecture hall or to what he wrote in his books. He was also a hard-working, practising physician, to whom many of his patients owed their lives. Paracelsus became an expert on syphilis, and suggested that it could be cured by giving the patient carefully measured doses of mercury. This idea preceded, by four centuries, the Salvarsan mercury treatment for syphilis, which was developed in 1909.

In a sense, Paracelsus was also a pioneer of homeopathic medicine — the principle that minute doses of what causes illness can put it right. When Stertzing was overwhelmed with plague during 1534, Paracelsus allegedly cured many plague victims there by giving them bread pills in which he had wrapped a minute amount of their excreta, hygienically extracted on the point of a needle.

Paracelsus argued that the silicosis from which so many medieval miners suffered was not caused by witchcraft, the anger of the gods, or the vengeance of subterranean evil spirits disturbed by their digging. In his view, silicosis was caused by the simple inhalation of metal vapours. He also thought that certain undesirable elements in drinking water, especially lead, were the main contributory causes of goitre.

One of his more interesting magical medical devices was a curious trident, which Paracelsus, himself, designed as a cure for impotence and diseases of the genitals supposedly brought on by witchcraft. Paracelsus said that the trident should be made from an old horseshoe and engraved with various magical symbols. On the day of Venus and in the hour of Saturn, the magical therapeutic trident had to be concealed in the bed of a running brook. The victim would then be healed, and the infliction would bounce back and infect the witch or wizard who had performed the spell that had made the original victim ill. Eliphas Levi (1810–1875), widely regarded as an authority on ritual magic, had other interpretations of the famous Paracelsian trident. He suggested that it actually represented the Holy Trinity and the three major alchemical elements: salt, sulphur, and mercury. But the writing, the lecturing, and the practical healing work all came to a sudden and premature end.

Having gone to Salzburg to work for Duke Ernst of Bavaria, Paracelsus died there in the White Horse Inn in suspicious circumstances, at the age of 48. Either his luck had run out, or his magic had worn too thin to withstand any more attacks from his still-smouldering enemies.

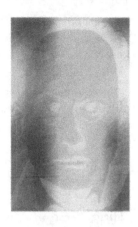

Chapter 8

Rasputin

Rasputin's real name was Grigory Yefimovich Novykh, and he was born in or around 1872, as far as can be ascertained. His nickname "Rasputin" was an offensive Russian epithet implying a character whose main interests were sex, alcohol, and debauchery. There was, however, a great deal more to Rasputin than this popular image of him as an unkempt, alcoholic sex maniac, cursed with weird religious obsessions, but strangely blessed with inexplicable healing and prophetic powers.

One way of considering Rasputin is through the metaphor of an intense Russian chess game, in which he is an important, but erratic, piece. Regard those relevant major political, historical, and social events that took place before the Communist Revolution and the bloody downfall of the Romanovs as that game's opening gambit. The deaths of the Tsar and his family at Ekaterinburg on July 16, 1918, then become the inevitable, fatal checkmate. Before that tragedy ended the match, Rasputin seemed to fly diagonally and unpredictably across the turbulent middle game like a demented white bishop: wielding great power and influence at one moment, and dying stubbornly and reluctantly beneath a frozen river the next.

One basic view of the four centuries of Russian history preceding the overthrow of the last tsar was that it was mainly a brutal cavalcade of tyrannous dictators and exploiters who ruled their long-suffering peasants with pain, fear, and the constant threat of execution. Ivan the Terrible, to quote just one example, enjoyed nothing more than torturing his people in droves over long periods.

That kind of seed produces bitter harvests. Exploit and tyrannize a strong, courageous race for long enough, and the people's leaders will begin to rise bitterly and remorselessly against you. Inevitably, the Russian people began to retaliate, to strike back at those they saw as their tormentors. Thus, in 1881, Alexander II succumbed to a glass globe full of nitroglycerine.

It was Russia's misfortune — and the world's — that Nicholas II was totally the wrong kind of character to hold the crumbling Russian Empire together. He was kind, charming, and gentle: he could have been a successful village priest or a lovable schoolmaster. In a situation that demanded strength, decisiveness, statesmanship, and ruthless determination, Nicholas II was of less use than a chocolate fireguard.

Some expert historians and psychologists who have studied Rasputin's convoluted character in depth have wondered whether his curious contradictory mixture of intense spirituality and debauchery might have been the result of abuse in his early life. The possibility certainly exists.

The young and impressionable Grigory came into contact with a fanatical religious sect known as the "Khlysty." Their interests included flagellation, and they embraced the morbid belief that persecution and martyrdom were, in some inexplicable way, good for people. Their rituals seem to have been designed to induce altered states of consciousness, and

Rasputin: what strange powers did he possess?

any kind of sexual contact was expressly forbidden. Despite this (or perhaps, more realistically, because of it), the Khlysty repudiated their own legal wives, and took on "spiritual wives" instead. These ladies shared their beds, but in theory at least, no sexual activity took place between them. Finding this difficult to believe, opponents and critics of the Khlysty spread the word that their so-called religious ceremonies were more like ancient Roman orgies.

Grigory's encounter with the Khlysty came about because he worked as a wagon driver when he was a teenager, and on one journey, he was asked to convey a young novice monk to the monastery at Verkhoture. On the long, slow, dull journey they discussed religion. As a result of that fateful discussion, Rasputin spent several weeks in the monastery, although, as far as is known, he never actually became a monk.

Rasputin's colourful, contradictory, and enigmatic character would present a challenge to the ablest and most experienced psychologist or psychiatrist. Where was the real Rasputin all this time? Were his religious urges, the desire to find spiritual purpose and meaning in life, stronger than his very powerful sexual instincts? Were there times when one aspect of his character was in the ascendancy, and then another? And what part did his desire to escape from the dead-end boredom of a Russian peasant's life in the late nineteenth-century play in his subsequent adventures?

Russia was still very close to being a medieval-style feudal state when Rasputin was a teenager. In feudal times, the only practical escape route for an ambitious young peasant was to try to enter the Church. Joining the army, doing well in battle, and so attracting the attention of some aristocratic commander who might bring your courage and skill to the king's attention, was another route, but it was less certain and more dangerous than joining the Church.

Psychological tests for natural dominance in a personality have suggested that roughly one person in twenty has a high dominance rating, a natural desire to organize or lead a group. This statistic has been tentatively explained by the suggestion that in prehistoric times, twenty was an optimum size for a successful, surviving group of hunter-gatherers. As cities and civilization overtook humanity with the passing of the millennia, very few of the 5 percent of natural dominants had much chance to dominate. To characters like Rasputin, being a headteacher, foreman, platoon commander, village priest, or football captain wouldn't seem quite as exciting or satisfying as being the undisputed leader of a hunting party seeking edible prey, while simultaneously avoiding sabre-toothed tigers.

When another natural dominant like Alexander the Great had the significant advantage of being born as the son of Philip of Macedon, his chances of success were hugely amplified. Grigory's family background, however, weighed heavily against him. To return to the chess analogy, he can be understood as a singularly ambitious pawn desperate to reach the far side of the board and so convert to a piece with royal power and authority.

Other traumas affected his early development. Under the stern old Russian penal system, he was flogged and imprisoned for relatively minor offences. He married one of the many local girls whom he was perpetually pursuing and had a son by her. As with his visit to the monastery at Verkhoture with the novice monk, this event seemed to change Rasputin's life. To everyone's great surprise, he settled down and became a devoted husband and father. Then his beloved baby son died at six months and Rasputin was devastated. Extreme and morbid religious urges flooded over him again, and he went back to the monastery at Verkhoture. He also read the Bible and various other religious books obsessively, then embarked upon a gruelling two-thousand-mile pilgrimage on foot, first to Mount Athos in Greece, and then on to Palestine.

The emperor Napoleon was said to have undergone a strange mystical experience alone in an awesome stone chamber deep inside the Great Pyramid during his Egyptian campaign. Those who knew him well claimed that he was never the same man afterwards. Something similar appears to have happened to Rasputin during his rigorous spiritual adventures on the pilgrimage to Mount Athos and to the Holy Land. When he came home to Pokrovskoe, he had acquired a great deal of additional nervous energy, undeniable charisma, and a hypnotic stare like that of du Maurier's fictional Svengali in *Trilby*.

Maurice Paleologue, the French ambassador, later said of Rasputin: "His gaze was at once penetrating and caressing ... direct and yet remote. ... When he was excited ... his pupils became magnetic." Another observant contemporary once said of him: " ... someone terrible and powerful looks out from behind those eyes ... enticing you into an impenetrable labyrinth." Comments made by the Countess Jukovskaya (one of the many aristocratic Russian women whom Rasputin seduced) may go some way towards resolving the paradox of his contradictory mixture of intense spirituality and unrestrained sexuality: she said that Rasputin had told her sin was necessary in order to experience true repentance and holiness afterwards.

During those early post-pilgrimage days at Pokrovskoe, he converted most of his back garden into a shrine or small chapel, and spent hours praying there.

As was the case with the rebelliously independent Father Bérenger Saunière in Rennes-le-Château in France at about the same date, the local church authorities took a dim view of Grigory's informal religious practices.

The village priest complained to the bishop at Tobolsk, who promptly came to investigate, but was disappointed to find no substantial evidence of heresy on Rasputin's part, although many of his enemies were accusing him of being a member of the hated Khlysty sect. The general attitude in the church seems to have been: "Find out what Grigory is up to — and stop him." As Yussopov and the other assassins discovered in 1916, stopping Rasputin was much easier said than done. There is even an account of a hard-boiled police interrogator who became one of Rasputin's many converts.

Rasputin did seem to exercise genuine powers of prophecy and some sort of second sight on several occasions; yet they apparently deserted him when he needed them most in Yussopov's palace. His daughter Maria gave evidence of an occasion in St. Petersburg when he was plainly aware that a woman was carrying a carefully concealed revolver. Rasputin struck it out of her hands before she could fire at him.

Among his prophecies was that of the birth of a son and heir to Nicholas and the tsarina, Alexandria, whose love for each other went back a long way: Nicholas had first met the twelve-year-old Alexandria, or Alix, of Hesse-Darmstadt when he was the sixteen-year-old Crown Prince of Russia, and they had married in 1894, shortly after the death of Nicholas's father. On his journey from Pokrovskoe to St. Petersburg, Rasputin stopped off at Sarov to pray specifically for a son and heir for the Romanovs — a son and heir on whom the future of the dynasty and the stability of Russia might well depend. He also prophesied that a son would be born to Alexandria within the year.

There is an interesting link here between Rasputin's prayer for an event and his prophecy that it would come to pass, and the Christian teaching: "When you pray for something, believe that you have already received it — and you will receive it." This effective kind of faith ties in yet again with Paracelsian magical mind-over-matter theories, Crowley's thelema, and Tesla's strange ability to work in an alternative frame of space-time reference that seemed as real to him as our familiar newspaper stand does to us.

Another significant part of the giant Russian chess game of complex circumstances, cultural influences, social forces, political threats, and counter-threats that were woven through St. Petersburg society around the turn of the century was a widespread fascination with occult and paranormal phenomena — similar to the grip that mediums and their seance rooms had on Victorian Britain.

Russia was full of professional wonder workers, most of whom were making satisfactory livings from the credulity of those willing and able to pay for spells, charms, talismans, Tarot readings, divination, and various other kinds of real or imaginary magical assistance.

The Tsarina, desperate for a son, fell victim to an unwholesome seven-year parade of such miracle-mongers, including a French mesmerist calling himself Dr. Philippe, who induced nothing more useful to the Romanov dynasty than an embarrassing psychosomatic phantom pregnancy. But Rasputin's prayer of faith, and his confident prophecy, preceded the birth of the longed-for Tsarevitch Alexei. Tragically, Alix's Hesse-Darmstadt genes carried congenital haemophilia, and young Alexei's life frequently hung by the slenderest of threads.

Rasputin climbed to unprecedented power and influence on a three-runged ladder: his inexplicable healing powers definitely benefitted young Alexei to a significant extent; the Tsar and Tsarina adored the boy; and so their consequent gratitude to Rasputin knew no bounds. His fame, power, and influence spread through St. Petersburg like fungus invading a damp cellar.

According to the gossip, there was almost nothing he could not do. When one ethnic group dislikes another, it tends to circulate (and to actually believe) wildly exaggerated propaganda concerning the genital anatomy and sexual prowess of the alien group. According to rumour, Rasputin was a one-man stud farm. Had he been alive today, he would have topped the poll for the man least likely to need Viagra. Rumour also credited him with the ability to drink enough vodka to thaw out a Siberian mammoth, and still be able to walk. His physical strength and stamina may also have been exaggerated, but not, perhaps, as much as his drinking and sexual feats. About his enormous bodily strength, there is some dispute: but that is probably due to the relative difference between a hardy Siberian wagon driver and an effete St. Petersburg aristocrat. Some researchers doubt the accuracy of the episode in which Rasputin was said to have killed two attackers by lifting them off the ground simultaneously and smashing their heads together. A competent heavyweight martial artist could undoubtedly do it today, and given Rasputin's natural ambition and aggression, his fiery temper, and mind-over-matter capabilities, the present writers are inclined to think that this particular episode is historically accurate rather than otherwise.

The genuineness of his supernatural powers is much harder to assess. It is claimed that he could make flowers blossom by holding them in his hand and blessing them. It is asserted that he healed a severely physically handicapped man so that he stood up and walked immediately. Rasputin is also credited with having carried out hundreds of equally beneficial but less spectacular cures. The clearest demonstration of his paranormal powers, however, came right at the end of his wild, turbulent life.

He prophesied his own death: "If I die at the hands of the Russian people, the Tsar and his descendants will be safe for centuries. If I die at the hands of the aristocracy, this River Neva will run red with their blood, and the Tsar's family will all be dead within two years."

A young Russian nobleman, Prince Felix Yussopov, had escaped from Kaiser Wilhelm's Germany in 1914. He returned to St. Petersburg, aghast at what was happening to his beloved Russia socially, politically, and militarily. The Tsar's personal command of the outdated and poorly equipped imperial Russian forces was having about as much effect on the highly efficient, mechanized, and modernized German army as a well-intentioned jellyfish would have in a lethal fight with a shark.

Yussopov and a handful of fellow conspirators launched a "Rasputin must go" campaign. On the night of December 29, 1916, Yussopov invited Rasputin to his palace, using his beautiful young wife Irina, the Tsar's niece, as bait for the sexually insatiable Grigory.

The other conspirators included Dr. Lazavert, who also acted as chauffeur to fetch Grigory to Yussopov's palace, Vladimir Purishkevich, leader of a right-wing party in the Russian Parliament (the Duma), and Captain Soukhotin, an old and trusted friend of Yussopov. Duke Dmitri Pavlovich was also a member of this determined group.

Yussopov had acquired a crystallized form of potassium cyanide, which Dr. Lazavert ground up very finely after donning his surgical gloves first. He then sprinkled enough cyanide to kill six people inside each cream cake, and carefully replaced their lids. If it is assumed that as an experienced doctor, Lazavert knew more than a little about toxicology, Rasputin should have died immediately after swallowing the first mouthful.

The victim duly arrived and was fed the poisoned cakes, along with Madeira in a poisoned glass. For several minutes, what had confidently been expected to kill him instantly had no effect at all, then he complained of a slight burning sensation in his throat. When, after some two hours, the poison appeared to be totally ineffective, Yussopov went and fetched a small Browning revolver from his desk drawer. On the pretext of showing Rasputin a crystal crucifix, Yussopov stood up and shot him through the heart. Rasputin collapsed, twitched for a few moments, and lay still. Dr. Lazavert declared him well and truly dead. The conspirators left him lying inert on the basement floor, but Yussopov felt more than a little uneasy. He went back to make sure. To his horror, Rasputin's eyes twitched open and he got to his feet. Yussopov, overwhelmed with terror, looked at Grigory in helpless disbelief. Foaming at the mouth, and shouting Yussopov's name over and over again in furious anger, Rasputin seized the prince by the shoulders and tore away an epaulette. Yussopov, by his own account, was now convinced that Satan had magically resurrected his terrifying servant. Somehow, he broke free of Rasputin's terrible grip and raced upstairs for help.

Purishkevich drew his revolver and came to assist the young prince. To their horror and amazement, Rasputin was already running towards the gate shouting, "I will tell the Tsarina!" The conspirators could not afford to let that happen.

Purishkevich fired several shots at the running figure. One hit him in the back, another struck his head. Rasputin went down, but he was still alive, despite three bullets and enough poison to kill a herd of elephants. Purishkevich was taking no chances. He slammed his heavy boot into Rasputin's head three or four times. Yussopov was still doubtful. He raced indoors for a club, and came back to smash it across Grigory's temples repeatedly.

Dmitri Pavlovich and the other conspirators finally dropped the body through a hole in the ice on the Neva. When it was found, a post-mortem revealed that Rasputin had died from drowning: the poison and bullets alone had not been sufficient.

Various interesting explanations have been advanced. Did a nervous pharmacist supply some harmless substitute to Yussopov instead of deadly cyanide? Did Yussopov invent the story of the poison? How reliable was Dr. Lazavert's original opinion that the first bullet — the one fired from Yussopov's light calibre Browning — had penetrated Rasputin's heart and caused death? Had Purishkevich's two later bullets produced only flesh wounds after all, and what had all the kicking and head battering achieved?

It is one of life's ironies that an incredibly lucky aviator can survive a fall of thousands of feet without a parachute, while another person will trip on an uneven pavement and die as a result.

If the cyanide in the cakes and Madeira was, indeed, cyanide, and if all three bullets had struck vital spots, if the kicking and head pounding had shattered Rasputin's skull and irrevocably damaged the vulnerable brain beneath, how had he survived for long enough to die by drowning?

Whatever the answer, Rasputin was undoubtedly one of the world's most mysterious people.

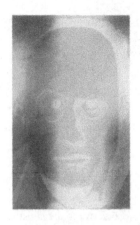

Chapter 9

The Man in the Iron Mask

The identity of the famous masked prisoner remains one of the most intriguing unsolved mysteries of all time. The stumbling block on which so many of the best theories falter is the *reason* for it all. Why would a monarch as powerful, as intelligent, and as ruthless as Louis XIV, the incomparable Sun King of France, feel the need to keep the mysterious prisoner alive for thirty-four years? Why run such a protracted risk, when the prisoner had information so important and dangerous that it was never to be disclosed to anyone on pain of death?

Louis never suffered from scruples. He knew as well as any other scheming politician of his day that the only guaranteed silencer is a coffin. The paradox remains: if what the masked man knew was as dangerous as all that, why did Louis let him live?

Leaving aside all humane motives — for Louis was as free of morality as an autoclaved scalpel is free of bacteria — a prisoner is kept alive only as long as his all-powerful captor believes he has *information* that the captor wants. There are graduated scales of danger versus advantage, on which the shrewd, pragmatic politician weighs everything carefully and objectively. If the danger caused by the prisoner's knowledge getting out is greater than the advantage of acquiring it for the captor's own use, then the logical course is to kill the prisoner as quickly as possible. On the other hand, if the advantages the knowledge could bestow are significantly greater than the dangers of its passing to enemies or rivals, then the logical course is to keep the prisoner alive. But what about torture? There were plenty of diabolical machines and numerous sadistic experts to use them in the prisons Louis XIV had at his disposal. There were experienced torturers galore, who would have been only too willing to gain the king's favour by guaranteeing to extract the important information he wanted. So why didn't Louis use them? Once the vital information had been fully extracted, the masked prisoner could be placed in the safest custody of all — the Central Paris Cemetery.

It is again necessary to evaluate the relative importance of the information Louis wanted against the relative danger of its falling into the wrong hands if the masked prisoner talked other than to the King. If the value Louis, himself, placed on that knowledge was very high indeed, then torture might have been out of the question. The experts who worked with whips, racks, thumbscrews, pincers, and branding irons were not medical experts. A victim who might appear sturdy enough, could have a sudden, fatal heart attack after just one more quarter turn of the rack. Suppose the information was so important to Louis that he wasn't prepared to take that risk.

Does this have the makings of a classical Mexican stand-off? The masked prisoner knows that the King would do anything at all to obtain the secret information. He is as wily, as devious, and as politically experienced as Louis himself. He knows the rules of the power game every bit as well as the

What was the secret identity of the Man in the Iron Mask?

84

Sun King does. If he gives Louis the information, he will be killed. If he does not give Louis the information, he will live in relatively comfortable conditions for the rest of his natural life.

Someone once asked Maurice Chevalier what it felt like to be alive at 80. With a twinkle in his eye, Chevalier replied: "It's wonderful when you consider the alternative!" Asked whether they would rather be dead, or be a masked prisoner, most people would give the same kind of answer as Chevalier did.

The real riddle of the Man in the Iron Mask was not so much who he was, as what great secret he knew. Undoubtedly, the two answers overlap to a considerable extent: as with solving a simultaneous equation in algebra, once you've found x, it's relatively simple to unmask y.

What do historians know already about the Man in the Iron Mask? Alexandre Dumas, in his famous novel, suggested that the masked prisoner was either Louis XIV himself, or his twin brother, and variations of this "royal relative" hypothesis form the first broad category of theories.

Louis XIII and his queen, Anne of Austria, were married for twenty-two years. For the first thirteen years of their union they had no children because, so it was rumoured, the King was impotent. Then, almost miraculously, especially as they had been separated for years, the machiavellian Cardinal Richelieu arranged a rapprochement. There was ostensibly a brief, but biologically effective. reconciliation between Anne and Louis XIII, as a result of which the future Louis XIV was conceived.

Some researchers believe that Richelieu himself was the father. Other suggestions name one of the many illegitimate sons of Henry of Navarre, who was not specially noted for fidelity or chastity. If that was the case, Louis XIV would have had genuine Bourbon genes in his pedigree. Either theory could explain why it was noticed at court, with politely raised eyebrows, that the strong and vigorous young Louis XIV looked nothing at all like his feeble, supposed father.

While searching through the Bibliotheque Nationale in Paris, a painstaking French historian named Maurice Duvivier, who worked conscientiously between World Wars I and II, eventually discovered references to a man named Eustache Dauger. This Dauger was an unsavoury character who had been born in 1637 as the third son of a minor landowner from Picardy, named Francois Auger de Cavoye. Eustache's mother was Marie de Lort de Serignan, a nubile young widow from the ancient and mysterious Languedoc area, from which Bérenger Saunière, the enigmatic priest of Rennes-le-Château, also came.

Francois Auger, Eustache's father, was none other than Cardinal Richelieu's unswervingly loyal and discreet captain of the guard. Had

Francois's additional special duties for the unscrupulous cardinal extended to making Anne of Austria pregnant at the time of her "miraculous reconciliation" with the chronically impotent Louis XIII? No doubt, it would have suited Richelieu's plans to have a young successor to the effete Louis XIII, whom he could manipulate and control as effectively as he had controlled his father.

As Richelieu's captain, Francois enjoyed unrestricted access to the French court, as did Marie of Languedoc and their eleven children. During his boyhood, Eustache, who was just one year older than his royal playmate, was a regular companion of the future Louis XIV.

Eustache's elder brothers died in battle, so that by 1654, while still in his teens, he became the eldest surviving son. From this point on, the shadier side of his character began to develop. He was suspected of involvement in a number of Black Masses, and was also implicated in the death of a young page boy at court. By 1664, he had been disinherited, and was forced to sell his commission to survive financially.

This Dauger hypothesis now supposes that the ne'er-do-well Eustache, desperate for money, made the gargantuan mistake of trying to threaten Louis XIV with disclosing the secret of his true parentage: Eustache's own father, Francois, the former captain of Richelieu's guard.

Perhaps this foolhardy attempt to shake down a character as tough, as resolute, and as powerful as Louis XIV, was not Eustache's only major error. Was he also involved in some sort of espionage adventure on behalf of a foreign power, of which Louis XIV might well have disapproved? Or had he been working as a clandestine courier for Louis and another monarch, before Louis realized that Eustache was not to be trusted with anything as confidential as that?

Considering what had become of his father, Charles II of England had cause to be extremely cautious in matters of state. If, as has been suspected, Charles II was secretly plotting with Louis XIV to restore a Catholic monarchy in England, Eustache could well have been the go-between for the two kings. Charles's sister Minette was also Louis's sister-in-law. In December of 1667 — a significantly early date for researchers into the mystery of the Man in the Iron Mask — Charles wrote to Minette: "much secrecy is necessary for the carrying out of the business ... nobody shall know anything of it but myself and one person more." This "one person more" might well have been Louis XIV, of course, but the phrase could also have referred to the king's messenger.

The man who was destined to become the famous masked prisoner was arrested at Dunkirk (then an English possession) in July of 1669, as he was either entering or leaving France. The Marquis de Louvois, the French minister of war, sent strict instructions about this prisoner to Monsieur de Saint-Mars, governor of the prison-fortress at Pignerol, not far from Turin in northwest Italy. In essence, the prisoner, whose name was actually given as Eustache Dauger in Louvois's letter, was to be held with maximum security, and never allowed to give any information about himself. He had to be placed in a cell with no access of any kind to the outside world, so that no one could communicate with him, and he, in turn, could communicate with no one. There also had to be double doors so that no guards could hear anything the prisoner might say. Saint-Mars himself was to take the prisoner's daily necessities to him, and was on no account to discuss anything with him other than the basic essentials of everyday living. Should Saint-Mars ever suspect that his charge was attempting to say anything else, the prisoner was to be killed instantly.

Saint-Mars wrote back acknowledging safe receipt of both the prisoner and Louvois's orders regarding him, via Monsieur de Vauroy, the military governor of Dunkirk. Saint-Mars promised to obey them punctiliously, and had, with de Vauroy as witness, told the prisoner that if he ever attempted to speak other than about his daily needs, then he, Saint-Mars himself, would run him through with his sword.

There were other, even stranger instructions concerning the treatment the mysterious prisoner was to receive. He was to be spoken to politely; he was to be allowed as many prayer books as he wanted; he was to be allowed to hear Mass on Sundays and Feast Days, and to make his confession three or four times a year. He was also to be given musical instruments to amuse himself if he so wished.

Over the years, Saint-Mars commented favourably on the prisoner's attitude. According to the Governor, the prisoner was a lamb, docile and submissive, accepting his fate without any resentment, as though he had expected something much worse. On one occasion when the man was taken ill with what Saint-Mars described as "a mild fever," both Louis XIV and Louvois demanded to be kept closely informed if the condition became more serious, and Saint-Mars was ordered to do everything possible for the prisoner's comfort, and to aid his recovery.

In 1678, Saint-Mars was promoted from the Pignerol to be governor of the prison-fortress of St. Marguerite, not far from Cannes on the French Riviera. The Man in the Iron Mask went with him.

Twenty years later, in March of 1698, Saint-Mars was promoted to be governor of the Bastille itself, the great prison-fortress of Paris. Once again, he took the masked prisoner with him. Several overnight stops were necessary at inns along the route from St. Marguerite to the capital, and Saint-Mars and his entourage attracted considerable attention.

Contemporary evidence indicates that the prisoner's mask was made of black velvet, rather than iron. Charles Brisot, a landlord at Digoin, said that the masked prisoner was led to a small private room behind the taproom, and guards were posted outside the door. When Brisot entered with the supper tray, the masked man was sitting bolt upright in his chair, with a wine beaker in front of him. Saint-Mars was directly opposite his prisoner, with a pair of pistols lying on the table, cocked and primed ready for instant use. Brisot put the tray down as quickly as he could, bade them "Bon appétit," and left. His assumption was that the prisoner would have opened or removed his velvet mask in order to eat as soon as he and the Governor were alone at the table.

There are two versions of a story that most researchers and historians regard as apocryphal, but that has nevertheless persisted down the years. The first rendering relates that during this journey from St. Marguerite to the Bastille — part of which involved going through the mysterious Languedoc region from which Eustache Dauger's mother came — the prisoner scratched his name and a brief message on a plate, and threw it from the window of an inn. A shepherd found it and brought it to one of the guards, who immediately took him to Saint-Mars. The Governor looked thoughtfully at the plate, then at the shepherd. "Have you read this message?" he asked, his loaded pistols not far from his hand.

"No sir," answered the shepherd, and smiled. "I cannot read, sir."

Saint-Mars smiled back and his hand moved from his guns to his purse. He gave the shepherd a gold piece and said: "You are a very lucky man."

"Because I have been given this gold piece?" asked the grateful shepherd.

"No," said the Governor, "because you cannot read!"

The second version is almost identical, except that it sets the episode in St. Marguerite instead of en route to Paris, and the happily illiterate man who finds the plate bearing the message is a fisherman instead of a shepherd.

The death of the Man in the Iron Mask on November 19, 1703, and the extraordinary precautions which were taken immediately afterwards, only serve to deepen the mystery. Etienne du Jonca was the king's lieutenant in the Bastille when Eustache Dauger (if, indeed, the masked prisoner *was* Eustache Dauger) died quietly and peacefully. These are Etienne's words as recorded in his journal:

> On the same day, November 19, 1703, the unknown prisoner, always masked with a black velvet mask, whom M. de Saint-Mars, the governor, brought with him when he came from the Ile Sainte-Marguerite, and had kept for a long period, this same prisoner being slightly unwell as

he came out of Mass died this evening at about ten
o'clock. The illness did not seem serious. It could scarcely
have been slighter.

Etienne went on to record that the mysterious masked prisoner had been
buried in St. Paul's churchyard. The burial register there revealed that
someone whose name was given as Marchioly, aged around 45, had died in
the Bastille on November 19 and had been buried the following day. This
entry was signed by Major Rosarge of the Bastille and a military surgeon
named Reilhe.

The next category of theories concerns the repayment of treachery.
Further research revealed that no such person as Marchioly seems to have
existed. The nearest name to it belonged to another of Louis's prisoners, a
count named Ercole Mattioli, who had at one time been the state secretary
to the Duke of Mantua. The story was that the Duke was in need of cash,
and Louis XIV made him an offer for the fortress of Casale, which would
have been strategically important to the French. Mattioli was given the price
of the fortress in cash, but failed to pass it on to the Duke. The Duke,
naturally enough, refused to hand over the fortress to Louis. The Sun King
decided that it wasn't worth going to war over it, and bided his time until
something could be done about Mattioli. In due course, a small French
raiding party abducted him and took him to Pignerol, where he was left in
the highly secure care of Saint-Mars.

The strength of this theory lies in a twofold reason for the masked man's
imprisonment. He was a foreign national, and Louis did not want the
embarrassment of an international incident over the affair. It would not
have been diplomatic to have broadcast the news that France was attempting
to buy the fortress of Casale from the Duke of Mantua. Neither would
Louis want to make public his error in allowing himself to become the
victim of Mattioli's confidence trick. No mafia godfather or gang leader
wants the word on the street to invite other would-be confidence tricksters
to take him down. To be regarded as vulnerable is to become vulnerable.
Mattioli's disappearance then sends a distinct message to any of his
confederates who might have been aware of what had happened to the Sun
King's Casale money: don't take liberties with Louis XIV. If Mattioli knew
where Louis's missing money was hidden, then there was a good reason for
keeping him incommunicado. Was Louis also hoping that a promise of
Mattioli's release in return for the missing money would encourage the
masked prisoner to reveal its whereabouts — hence the long imprisonment?
Mattioli would undoubtedly have suspected that the minute he gave Louis
that information, he would be released to heaven, hell, or purgatory rather

than to his old home in Mantua — hence his stubborn refusal to let Louis know where the money was.

Another theory worth airing links the Man in the Iron Mask with Nicholas Fouquet, the former minister of finance to Louis XIV. Fouquet was at one period so rich and powerful that he almost rivalled Louis himself, and Nicholas had a younger brother, who was a secret agent. This younger Fouquet encountered Poussin, the painter, in Rome, and wrote a report of their meeting to Nicholas. In essence, it appeared that Poussin had a secret of immense value, a secret "that kings would give their all to obtain," or so the painter said. In young Fouquet's letter to his elder brother, he maintained that Poussin would be glad to place this great secret into their hands. Fouquet, Senior falls from power and is replaced by Jean-Baptiste Colbert.

Fouquet was Louis's prisoner for a long time, but his imprisonment was known about, and apparently clearly recorded. What if a very clever exchange was made? Fouquet was arrested in 1661, and his trial dragged on for three years. On Louis's personal intervention, Fouquet was incarcerated in Pignerol and supposedly died there in 1680. But could there have been more than one masked prisoner? Once an identity is hidden behind a mask in a cell, which only the Governor himself ever enters, who is to say whether the man who first entered that cell is the same masked prisoner who eventually dies there? What if Eustache Dauger, Louis XIV's half brother, was the original prisoner, but that he died on March 23, 1680 — the date normally recorded for Nicholas Fouquet's death? On secret orders from Louis himself, Dauger is carried off in the carefully sealed coffin labelled Fouquet, and Nicholas becomes the new Man in the Iron Mask. The same stringent security applies until Fouquet eventually dies in the Bastille, well into his 80s.

The official Bastille report estimated the age of the mysterious prisoner who was buried in St. Paul's Churchyard in Paris as between 40 and 50. It seems unlikely that a man of nearly twice that age could produce such an estimate, but what *was* the mysterious secret that Poussin the painter passed over to the Fouquet brothers, the secret that "kings would give their all to possess"? In the case of Louis XIV, it wasn't likely to have been money: admittedly, he was a big spender, but money was never a problem to him. To have everything except your vanished youth must be singularly frustrating for a monarch as powerful as the Sun King.

Poussin and other enigmatic members of the painters guild were apparently involved in the arcane secret of Rennes-le-Château down in the mysterious Languedoc, from where Francois Dauger's wife, Marie, also came.

In the 1880s, Saunière, the parish priest of Rennes, discovered whatever mystery had lain buried there for centuries, and became immensely rich. It has always been hinted by some Rennes researchers that the so-called "Treasure of Rennes" was not gold or jewels, but some strange knowledge, an eldritch secret that could produce wealth if used correctly. One tower of the ruined Château Hautpoul, which gives its name to the village, is called the "Tower of Alchemy." The ancient alchemists such as Paracelsus had two main quests. The first was for the Philosopher's Stone, which would change base metals into gold; the second was for the Elixir of Life, which would restore youth and prolong the user's days almost indefinitely. It was this precious elixir that the legendary Count of Saint-Germain was said to possess. Is it even remotely possible that Poussin's secret concerned this priceless Elixir of Life? Even if it did nothing more than add another ten or twenty vigorous years to a person in middle age, would not kings — as Poussin suggested — give their all to possess it? Had Fouquet had access to a sample of it before being imprisoned in the Pignerol, before being switched with Dauger in March of 1680? Is that why a man of nearly 90 looked nearer to 40 or 50 when he was finally buried in St. Paul's Churchyard? The Fouquet theory totters on the brink of the gulf of incredibility, but there are links between Fouquet, the Languedoc riddles, and the mystery of the masked prisoner. There is also a link between one of Poussin's most enigmatic paintings, *The Shepherds of Arcadia*, Louis XIV, Colbert, and Rennes-le-Château. In *The Shepherds of Arcadia*, Poussin depicted three shepherds and a shepherdess standing beside a mysterious table-tomb in a wild, romantic landscape strongly reminiscent of the area around the hilltop village of Rennes-le-Château. Such a tomb — an exact copy of the one in Poussin's canvas — actually stood at Arques, barely a stone's throw from Rennes. Some researchers into the Saunière mystery have put forward evidence suggesting that Colbert sent an expedition to investigate this curious tomb and its environs almost as soon as he had replaced Fouquet as Louis XIV's minister of finance. There is also evidence that Louis went to great pains to acquire Poussin's *Shepherds of Arcadia* canvas, and that it hung for many years in the Palace of Versailles.

Another far less mysterious and esoteric theory links Fouquet and the Dauger family with a plot to discredit Louis XIV by proving that Eustache was indeed his half brother, and that the Sun King's real father was not Louis XIII at all, but only Francois Dauger, captain of Richelieu's guard. This scenario brings in another strand of the Rennes mystery involving the ancient Merovingian kings. Their dynastic founder was Mérovée the Twice Born, a thaumaturgical monarch, whose mother, according to legend, had been seduced by some sort of intelligent aquatic creature called a Quinotaur. The mystical Merovingians — like Shakespeare's Prospero in *The*

Tempest — had neglected the day-to-day business of government, and had concentrated on their magical books. In consequence, the mayors of the palace had acquired more and more political and administrative power, until they had finally overthrown the Merovingians and started their own dynasty, the Carolingians. The strength of the Merovingians had lain in the Languedoc, and it was rumoured that some had secretly survived the Carolingian usurpation. If this was true, and if Eustache Dauger could be produced to discredit Louis XIV's claim to legitimacy, and hence, to the French throne, then a Merovingian contender from the Languedoc could be put forward. What if Marie Dauger's first husband — from the Languedoc — had been a secret member of that strange and ancient Merovingian line? Had she even been carrying his child when, as a young widow, she married Francois? Could Fouquet, bitterly angry and resentful about the way Louis had treated him, have been a party to such a Merovingian plot?

Yet another line of investigation involves the possibility that the masked prisoner was a certain Surgeon D'Auger, whose name cropped up in connection with the poisonings and Black Masses that rocked the French Court in the 1660s and 1670s. The very astute Nicholas de la Reynie, chief of the Paris police at the time, uncovered a web of poisoners and black magicians operating within the nobility. The motivation behind these sinister and revolting Black Masses, which involved child sacrifice and nauseating ceremonies, was usually to enable a power-hungry lady-in-waiting to become the influential mistress of a highly placed minister, or even the King himself. Madame de Montespan, for example, became Louis's mistress after attending a Black Mass, and her descent into black and blasphemous magic accelerated as she tried additional spells to retain his favours. When de la Reynie arrested the ringleaders, she was lucky to escape with her life. Forty or so of the others were executed, including the excitingly beautiful Catherine Monvoisin, who had the unenviable reputation of being the most notorious of all the magicians and poisoners arrested. Surgeon D'Auger's name was associated with several of these poisoning and witchcraft trials in 1679 and in the following year, but he had vanished mysteriously a decade before. Could it possibly have been Surgeon D'Auger, rather than Eustache Dauger, who was arrested in Dunkirk?

The final strange factor in the mystery of the masked prisoner — whoever he really was, and whatever the true reason for his prolonged incarceration — was the elaborate precautions that were taken to remove all possible traces of him from his cell in the Bastille after he died. The floor tiles were taken up. The plaster was scraped from the walls. All the furniture was chopped up and burned. Nothing on which he might conceivably have left a message for posterity remained.

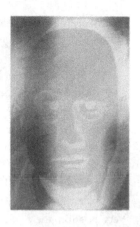

Chapter 10

The Strange Case of Joan Norkot

Sir John Maynard (occasionally rendered "Mainard") was one of the original members of the Long Parliament of King Charles I. He lived on to greet King William III when he acceded to the throne in 1688. During his long life (he died in 1690 at the age of 88) John was generally regarded as a rational and intelligent member of the legal profession. In fact, it was as Father of the Bar that he officially congratulated King William, the former Prince of Orange, on his accession to the English throne.

As a serjeant at arms, Maynard understood the rules of evidence better than many of his seventeenth-century contemporaries. When colleagues referred to Maynard as "the old Sergeant," it was used as an expression of their respect.

After Maynard's death, a manuscript version of the Joan Norkot affair was found among his papers. The story it told was so strange and unusual — even for the superstitious century in which the psychotic and sadistic Matthew Hopkins had made a living out torturing and executing those he denounced as witches — that Maynard's manuscript was copied by a Temple member named Hunt.

He, in turn, gave a copy to Dr. Henry Sampson, who included it in his own records. From there it eventually found its way into *The Gentlemen's Magazine* of July 1851. Valentine Dyall — famous for his "Man in Black" radio series in the 1940s — then put it in his collection of *Unsolved Mysteries* in 1952, along with an interesting theory which he suggested as a possible solution.

According to the Maynard manuscript Hunt copied and gave to Sampson, Joan Norkot had lived in Hertfordshire in the early years of the seventeenth century. There were six in the household: Joan herself, her husband, Arthur Norkot, their infant son, Joan's sister, Agnes, and her husband, John Okeman, together with Joan's mother-in-law, Mary Norkot.

According to the available evidence, Joan seems to have been an attractive, intelligent young mother, who ran her household well enough. Very possibly the other two women resented both her attractiveness and her dominant role as head of their household.

Gossip would have been of major importance in rural Hertfordshire in those days, and part of their resentment might have taken the form of sowing seeds of suspicion about Joan's fidelity. Shakespeare's *Othello* had not long been written, and Iago's cunning destruction of Desdemona might have had its real-life parallel in the Norkot catastrophe.

On the morning of the tragedy, the family claimed that they had discovered Joan dead in bed, still holding her infant son in her arms. She had either been the victim of a violent attack, or she had committed suicide. The family preferred the suicide theory. They claimed that Joan and Arthur had been far from happy, and that Arthur was suspicious that his attractive young wife was having an affair. The family gave further evidence that on the night prior to Joan's death, she had been in a very unhappy and despondent mood. In their opinion, she had cut her own throat.

The coroner and his jury were not inclined to accept the suicide theory, and neither were Joan's friends and neighbours. If she had been having an affair, her lover may well have been one of the foremost protesters against the suicide story. Supposing that he and Joan had planned to leave together, and that she had told Arthur she was going, could that have been the trigger for the final tragedy in the bedroom?

Mary Norkot and the Okemans claimed that on the night of Joan's death, her husband Arthur had been visiting friends and had not returned home. Later investigation revealed that the friends he was supposed to have visited hadn't seen him for years. Close scrutiny of the cottage revealed even more inexplicable circumstances. There had evidently been an unsuccessful attempt to clean a considerable quantity of blood from Joan's bedroom floor. The mark made by the point of the knife with which Joan was supposed to have cut her own throat showed clearly that it had been flung into the floorboards from outside the bedroom. Another

Shakespearean parallel perhaps? Lady Macbeth had taken the fatal daggers back to the chamber in which Duncan had been murdered.

As if the throat-cutting had not been adequate, medical examination showed that Joan's neck was broken as well. When her body was discovered with her child still in her arms, she was lying in the bed, and there was no sign of disturbance or struggle. The utter impossibility of the suicide theory was instantly clear to Joan's friends and neighbours. She could hardly have cut her own throat and then climbed quietly into bed and broken her own neck.

Neither could she have broken her neck first and then climbed peacefully into bed and cut her throat — not to mention getting up again immediately afterwards to throw the tell-tale knife into the bedroom floor, with its handle towards the living room.

The inquest jury made a successful request for an exhumation, which was witnessed by a local clergyman, the jurors themselves, and numerous friends and neighbours. Joan had been dead for a month when this exhumation took place, and it was not a sight for the faint-hearted. Along with many other superstitious seventeenth-century ideas, it was believed that the corpse of a murder victim would bleed if it was touched by the murderer.

Arthur Norkot, his mother, Mary, and the Okemans were lined up as murder suspects and ordered to touch Joan's decomposing body. According to Maynard's carefully written account, her "livid, carrion-coloured" features began to perspire so that drops of water ran down on to her face. Her complexion then changed and became, in Maynard's words, "a lively and fresh colour." One of Joan's eyes opened and closed three times. Her wedding-ring finger was also raised three times and then pulled in again. Drops of blood fell from it onto the grass beside her grave. The body then relapsed into its former lifelessness.

A formal verdict of "murder by person or persons unknown" was brought in, and the four suspects were duly tried at Hertford Assizes. To the great surprise and disquiet of all concerned, they were acquitted. An interesting legal procedure was then invoked, and an appeal was launched in the name of Joan's infant son.

The original murder trial had been conducted under Judge Harvey. The appeal was heard by Chief Justice Nicholas Hyde. He made a point of asking who else had seen the strange phenomena at the exhumation, and was assured by the clergyman who was giving evidence that the whole company had seen it, and that many additional witnesses could easily have been obtained had their supporting evidence been required.

It seemed from the evidence at the appeal that no one apart from the Norkots and Okemans had been in the cottage on the fatal night, that Joan could not have inflicted the injuries on herself, and that one or more of the suspects had killed her.

Okeman seems to have been a relatively simple soul, who was apparently bullied and browbeaten by the others into becoming an accessory after the fact. He was acquitted. The other three were sentenced to death. Agnes was found to be pregnant before the sentence could be carried out, and did not hang. Arthur and Mary did.

If Joan Norkot really had returned fleetingly from the dead to seal the fate of her killers, she must certainly qualify as one of the most mysterious people who ever lived. But are any other explanations available?

Valentine Dyall suggested that there were two exhumations, not one. The medical examiners, he thought, might have been totally convinced that Joan could not have committed suicide, yet doubted whether their scientific evidence would be given sufficient weight in that superstitious age. According to Dyall's theory, the doctors carried out their own secret exhumation prior to the public one, and rigged some thin, barely visible thread on the corpse's eyelid and ring finger. A small fragile container of blood, or some fluid that sufficiently resembled blood to deceive the onlookers, was also attached to the finger. If the threads were fixed to the coffin lid, or surreptitiously operated by one of the doctors or a trusted accomplice, such devices might just have worked.

Pursuing another theory — that Joan had given Arthur genuine cause for concern about acquiring a new partner and leaving him — raises the question of that new partner's involvement in the phenomena reported from the exhumation. Did he, rather than the doctors, rig Joan's body so that the eyelid and finger would move as they did when her coffin was opened? Were he and the medical examiners working together, and was he, perhaps, their secret accomplice?

And what about the motive for the murder? If that elusive factor could be analyzed, would it contribute anything to solving the central paranormal mystery of a corpse that had been decomposing for a month, and that then changed colour, perspired, opened and closed one eye, and literally pointed an accusing finger at the alleged killers?

What if Joan had decided that she didn't want to live a double life any longer? What if she had decided to tell Arthur that he was not the father of her son, and that she was about to leave him and take the boy with her? Would that have triggered a violent emotional response from Norkot? Did his mother loyally try to protect her son from the inevitable consequences of his desperate outburst? Were the Okemans involved simply because they had the misfortune to share the same cottage?

Alternatively, was Joan's hypothetical lover involved in her death? Had he been in the cottage the whole time, secretly admitted by Joan? Did he decide that their affair was getting too complicated? Was Joan's reported dark mood the result of his telling her that they would have to bring their relationship to an end? Did he kill her when she reacted explosively to his decision? Had he found a way to escape from the cottage unobserved before Joan's body was discovered, leaving the Norkots and Okemans to face the consequences of her death?

How significant is Joan's broken neck as an addition to her severed throat? A powerful martial artist could snap a human neck easily enough, but who in the Norkot cottage would have had the necessary knowledge or strength to do it to Joan? Mary and Agnes could possibly be ruled out on the grounds of insufficient physical strength. Okeman and Arthur would probably have had enough muscle, but without the special knowledge of exactly where to apply that strength, they would not have found it easy.

Is there the remotest possibility that Joan's neck had been broken in an accidental fall? Would her panic-stricken family then assume that they would be blamed because of the widely known rift between Joan and Arthur? And what if the fall that broke her neck had not been accidental? Suppose that Arthur's hypothetical violence had not involved using a knife, but that he had hurled Joan against the wall, or to the cottage floor?

The realization then dawns on the family that suicides do not hurl themselves against floors or walls: one of the commonest methods — and one that would have occurred to the Norkots and Okemans — would be throat-cutting. So Joan's throat is cut after her death to make it look as if she had done it herself. When the broken neck is discovered by the medical examiners, the family's attempt at concealment rebounds horrendously and proves that Joan could not possibly have inflicted both fatal injuries on herself.

There are other possible explanations for the exhumation phenomena. Were the witnesses lying? Was Sergeant Maynard lying? Did Hunt make up the story and not copy it from Maynard's manuscript? Did Henry Sampson concoct the whole thing? Or was the editor of *The Gentlemen's Magazine* responsible for the tale in 1851? Very few things are certain. Perhaps nothing at all is absolutely certain. But there are comparable probabilities. That the sun will set tonight and rise again tomorrow is a probability of more than 0.9999.... That you will see a sixty-ton steam locomotive lift itself gracefully into the air and fly across the Rockies is a probability of less than 0.0000 ... 01.

The chance that an honest and intelligent man like Sir John Maynard concocted such a strange tale is very low. The chances of dishonesty among men like Hunt, Sampson, or the editor of *The Gentlemen's Magazine* are probably equally low. However, when a number of remote probabilities are added — as when we buy several lottery tickets — they *may* become more significant.

As far as is known, there is no natural biological explanation for what was reported about Joan Norkot's corpse. If the witnesses were speaking the truth, and if they really observed what they thought they had observed, is there some weird psychic explanation? Did Joan's spirit return briefly to point out her murderers? Did something else, such as the "evil spirits" mentioned in many religious texts, animate the corpse?

It is remotely possible that some form of autosuggestion, or hypnotically induced hallucination, could have led the witnesses to think that they were observing strange phenomena, when they actually had no basis in objective physical reality. But the chances of that are very low indeed. So Joan Norkot must remain one of the world's most mysterious people. Whatever the Hertford jury decided nearly four centuries ago, today's Norkot jury is likely to remain out for some time.

Chapter 11

Spring-heeled Jack: The Terror of Victorian London

One of the strangest terrors of Victorian Britain, and especially of Victorian London, was the amazing character known as Spring-heeled Jack. Although there had been a few odd reports of a strange jumping man as early as 1817, it was not until September of 1837 that Jack made his first recorded appearances. Victoria had been queen for only a few months when Jack leapt over a cemetery wall near Barnes Common and frightened a businessman who was walking home that way after working late. Very soon afterwards, the same sinister leaping creature also attacked a London girl, a youngster named Polly Adams, as she was coming home from Blackheath Fair. He tore the top of her dress away with hands which she described as being more like iron claws. Three other victims of similar attacks all verified Polly's description of him: very tall and thin, but far stronger than such a lightly built man would have been expected to be. She also gave an account of a separate episode that had taken place a little earlier in which a man with bulging eyes had accosted her. Apart from commenting on those prominent eyes, the other witnesses also said that Jack had pointed ears — and this was a century and a half before anyone saw Mr. Spock on board the starship *Enterprise*. Spring-heeled Jack's bulging, glowing eyes terrified the girls, who had probably filled their minds with images of medieval demons by this time. They all reported that he spat blue and white flames. Victims of some later attacks were reportedly blinded by them.

Another young female victim was Mary Stevens, a servant girl who had been visiting her parents in Battersea and was walking back to her employer's home in Lavender Hill. At the entrance to the aptly named Cut Throat Lane, Mary was seized by a tall, thin attacker who threw his long arms around her and held her helpless in a vice-like grip. Her screams and struggles attracted help. The mysterious attacker laughed demonically as he, she, or it bounded away. A similar sudden, wild appearance by this grotesque jumping oddity a few days later terrified a pair of coach horses that bolted, causing an accident in which the coachman was severely injured.

Some of the most useful pieces of evidence Jack ever left were strangely deep footprints in soft, damp soil, when he attacked a woman near Clapham Churchyard. It was suggested by a number of those who examined the marks that Jack had possibly fixed mechanical jumping devices to his shoes.

There was undoubtedly an imaginative streak in the Victorian public, to which the character of Spring-heeled Jack made a strong appeal. Several stories about him were featured in the popular Victorian "Penny Dreadfuls," and these no doubt added fuel to the speculative flames. Rumours, myths,

Spring-heeled Jack — the terror of Victorian London. Who was he, and what secret powers did he possess?

and urban legends about Jack varied widely. He had been described as a white bull in one area, a huge polar bear in another, and a gigantic baboon in the third. He was also said to have worn brightly polished brazen armour during one attack, and burnished steel armour during a different episode. One of his homelier pranks was to disguise himself as a London lamplighter and walk through the darkening streets on his hands, carrying his ladder on his long, wiry legs.

On one occasion, a victim who escaped from Jack's clutches without anything much worse than a fright, said that she had seen the letter "W" emblazoned on the costume below his cloak. An elaborate crest and coat of arms were embroidered above it.

Henry de la Poer Beresford, the Marquis of Waterford, had been an outstanding oarsman and boxer at Eton and Oxford. He had the kind of physique and co-ordination that would have enabled him to carry out at least some of Spring-heeled Jack's minor feats. It is also possible that his boxing career left him slightly brain-damaged, which could, perhaps, have accounted for some of his more eccentric behaviour. Beresford and some of his equally wild friends were notorious for throwing eggs at people as their coach galloped past, and in 1837, he literally painted not only a town, but one of its night watchmen red as well. On another occasion, he once suggested to a railway company that they could arrange for two trains to crash head-on at his expense so that he could witness it. He was callous enough to evict thirty of his tenants on one occasion without providing either a valid reason or fair notice. Physically and mentally, Waterford's character seems to fit in with Spring-heeled Jack's performances as they were generally reported. Did the "W" on the tunic stand for Waterford? The problem with this theory, however, is that Waterford died following a riding accident in 1859, and Spring-heeled Jack was still creating havoc until at least 1904.

Some of the wilder theories far surpassed pointing the finger of suspicion at young Waterford. Jack was said, among other things, to be a mentally ill circus acrobat, a fire-eater from a sideshow, even a kangaroo that had been trained and dressed up by a zoo-keeper with a bizarre sense of humour. To speculative thinkers of our own day, rather than those of the Victorian epoch, Jack seems more like an extra-terrestrial than a kangaroo in fancy dress.

Is there any possible connection between the Victorian sightings of the Spring-heeled Jack phenomena and the reports of Owlmen and Mothmen that come mainly from the Canadian and American side of the Atlantic? Reported sightings of such beings abound. A motorist travelling from Point Pleasant towards the Chief Cornstalk Hunting Grounds in West Virginia along Highway 2 suddenly spotted a very large humanoid figure blocking the road ahead of her. Its wings were so vast that the whole thing resembled a small aircraft, and it took off vertically just ahead of the car. In November 1966, it was seen again in the Point Pleasant area, this time by two couples, Mary and Steve Mallette and Linda and Roger Scarberry. Two strange red eyes, like those attributed to Spring-heeled Jack in London over a century earlier, were peering out at them from a derelict industrial area. The Mallettes and Scarberrys saw a grey, apparently slow-moving creature over seven feet tall, with large wings folded behind its back. They accelerated hard to get away from the thing, but it seemed able to fly alongside them without flapping its wings, even when they were going at a hundred miles per hour.

In 1976, two teenage girls saw something remarkably similar in the woods near Mawnan Old Church, in Cornwall, England, a creature that was later researched by leading cryptozoologist Jonathan Downes and recorded in detail in his excellent book, *The Owlman and Others*.

Returning to the earlier British Spring-heeled Jack exploits, by 1838, things had become sufficiently serious for the Sir John Cowan, Lord Mayor of London at the time, to declare Jack an official public menace. Vigilance committees were established to try to catch him, but none of them were successful.

On February 20, 1838, eighteen-year-old Jane Alsop was at home in her father's house in Bearhind Lane in Bow. Fortunately for Jane, her two sisters were there with her. She answered the door in response to loud, urgent knocking. A voice from the wintry darkness outside shouted excitedly: "Bring a light quickly. We've caught Spring-heeled Jack."

Jane ran to fetch a candle. As she stepped outside unsuspectingly with it cupped in her hands, the mysterious visitor grabbed her: it *was* Jack. The tough little East End teenager put up a superb fight and broke away from her mysterious attacker. Her desperate screams brought one of her sisters racing to help. She got Jane away from the strange creature, pulled her inside, and slammed the door against their attacker. From the relative safety of an upstairs window, the Alsop girls shouted for the police, founded by Sir Robert Peel's Metropolitan Police Act only nine years earlier. Spring-heeled Jack was glimpsed by his pursuers as he bounded away through the February gloom of what were then open fields at the back of Bearhind Lane. He dropped his cloak as he ran, but someone retrieved it and escaped with it before the police could examine it. Was it possible that Jack had had an accomplice? Was there, perhaps, a Spring-heeled Jill?

Press reports on February 22 contained detailed descriptions given by the Alsop girls and other witnesses. Jack had been wearing a helmet together with a long cloak over a costume that resembled shiny white oilskin.

Another possibility was that Jack was not human at all, but an extra-terrestrial, or an unknown animal possessing shiny white skin like that of an amphibian or a reptile. The press descriptions also referred to his blazing red eyes, and his ability to spit dangerous blue and white flames.

Taking all the persistent reports together, there can be little doubt that Spring-heeled Jack really existed, and that there was something abnormal and dangerous about him. His exceptional strength and speed and his ability to bound away effortlessly over high walls made him very difficult to capture.

In most of the early attacks reported between 1837 and the 1850s, Spring-heeled Jack seems to have been satisfied with terrifying his victims, tearing off their clothes, and inflicting painful scratches with his cold, claw-like, metallic hands — if, indeed, they were hands. No researcher has ever been able to decide exactly what sort of man, machine, alien, or phenomenalist entity Spring-heeled Jack really was.

As the years passed, however, the attacks grew more vicious, the injuries Jack inflicted more severe, and, in some cases, permanent. Lucy Scales was a victim of one of these disabling later attacks. Her father was a butcher in Limehouse. Lucy had been out to visit her brother, and was returning home through Green Dragon Alley, when Spring-heeled Jack appeared. He wore the same long cloak and tight-fitting, shiny white oilskin outfit that earlier witnesses had described. The blue and white fire he spat into Lucy's face blinded the girl.

That was serious enough, but his next recorded attack, which took place in 1845, proved fatal for the victim. It happened in broad daylight in the Jacob's Island district of Bermondsey. Young Maria Davis was one of the sad little teenage prostitutes who plied their trade there. Eyewitnesses described how Spring-heeled Jack bounded at the girl as she was crossing a narrow wooden bridge. He seized her by the shoulders, breathed his vicious blue and white fire into her terrified face, then flung her down into Folly Ditch — a deep, open sewer that oozed foully below the bridge. Maria drowned in it before passers-by could get her out.

During the middle of the nineteenth century, Jack was reported to have been seen all over the place, but chiefly in the Midlands. In the 1870s, he even attacked some military establishments, where tough, veteran sentries were as startled by him as the girls he'd attacked in the London area. Some soldiers reported being slapped in the face by "a man with an icy hand — like the hand of a corpse." That compares interestingly with the descriptions of earlier victims, whose clothes were torn off by "hands that felt like iron claws."

At North Camp, part of the famous old military installation at Aldershot, Jack approached a sentry, ignored the formal challenge and leapt clean over the sentry box. The soldier did his duty and fired, reporting later that he was certain Jack had been hit. Hit or not, the strange creature bounded on its way as if nothing had happened. Jack had also been fired at by angry citizens in Lincoln, but their bullets and buckshot had had no apparent effect on him, either; he merely leapt on his eccentric way through their historic city streets.

In Caistor on the Norfolk coast during the late 1870s, almost everyone in the village came out to watch Jack leaping from one cottage roof to another. This time, the eyewitnesses commented on his large ears, and said that his costume was more like sheepskin than his normal shiny white oilskin.

Ten years later, he was observed in Cheshire, over three hundred miles away on the west of England. On this occasion, Spring-heeled Jack leapt into a room where a girl sat playing the piano. He didn't touch her, but contented himself with sweeping all the ornaments from a shelf, and bounded away before anyone in the house had fully realized what was happening.

His last recorded British appearance was in Everton, on William Henry Street, in September of 1904. On September 25, *The News of the World* printed a story about this Everton appearance, reporting that Jack had amazed witnesses by jumping as much as twenty-five feet into the air. On this occasion, as with the pianist in Cheshire, Jack harmed no one, but seemed content to entertain the crowd with his phenomenal athletic powers. He ended the show by bounding clean over a house and disappearing. Although that was his last recorded UK sighting, something very much like him was reported from the USA.

One blisteringly hot June night in Texas during the summer of 1953, three Houston friends were sitting outside their apartment building in a vain attempt to get some relief from the intense heat. They reported seeing a huge shadow passing across the lawn in front them, and then, in their words it "seemed to bounce up into a pecan tree." By the dim, greyish light that revealed the strange shape in the tree, it seemed to them to be a very tall, thin man, wearing tight-fitting clothes under a large cape. The witnesses also noticed his boots. Rather than bounding away as Spring-heeled Jack had done when he had made most of his previous dramatic exits, this mysterious figure in the pecan tree gradually seemed to fade. From the other side of the street, the Houston witnesses heard a weird swooshing sound and thought that they could see a rocket taking off from that vicinity. The investigating police officers to whom the witnesses reported this strange episode were of the opinion that their evidence had been given in good faith and that the witnesses were honest, well-intentioned, and genuinely frightened by whatever they thought they had seen in the pecan tree.

As with most reported sightings of unexplained phenomena, there are numerous rational and logical alternatives that could be thought to provide common-sense, everyday explanations for Spring-heeled Jack. In the Aldershot sentry episode, there is always the possibility that the sentry in question had been engaged previously in military training manoeuvres that had necessitated using blank rounds during the exercises. If his rifle still contained blanks when Spring-heeled Jack leapt over his sentry box, that would account for the ineffectiveness of the shots he reportedly fired at Jack at close range.

The episode on William Henry Street in 1904 was reported in the *Liverpool Echo*, which also mentioned a man in the area who suffered from some form of religious mania. He had accused his wife of being demon-possessed, and was said to have leapt from rooftop to rooftop to escape from the police and fire brigade. Were the two stories compounded in some way, or did some of the superstitious residents of William Henry Street think they were watching the infamous Spring-heeled Jack, when they were, in fact, only watching the antics of a mentally ill neighbour?

There is compelling evidence on both sides of the argument: Jack could have been a series of errors of observation made in good faith, a cruel hoax begun by Waterford that was improbably prolonged by a string of impersonators, an extra-terrestrial cyborg, or, just possibly, a very remarkable freak of nature — the springiest branch on Darwin's evolutionary tree.

Chapter 12

Coinneach Odhar: The Brahan Seer

To the names of Nostradamus and Mother Shipton must be added that of Coinneach (the Gaelic form of the Anglicised "Kenneth") Odhar, known as the Brahan Seer.

The Outer Hebrides, where he was born on the Isle of Lewis in 1600, are strange and lonely places with many mysterious myths and legends attached to them: but none stranger than the unknown fate that befell the three missing lighthouse keepers of Eilean Mor. This egg-shaped protrusion of Gneiss granite rises over two hundred feet out of the northern Atlantic, and is the largest of the Flannan Isles, also known as the Seven Hunters, which are situated fifty-eight degrees twenty minutes north, by seven degrees forty minutes west — roughly fifteen miles out into the Atlantic on the Canadian side of the Outer Hebrides.

Had Coinneach still been around on December 15, 1900, his strange psychic powers might have untangled the mystery of what really happened to James Ducat, Donald McArthur, and Thomas Marshall. The duty roster shared by the four keepers of the Flannans Lighthouse meant that one man took a month's shore leave on Lewis or one of the other Outer Hebridean islands, while the remaining three were on duty maintaining the lighthouse.

Joseph Moore was on leave when the Flannan light failed to appear on the night of December 15. The weather was so appalling that the Northern

Lighthouse Board's stout little *Hesperus* was unable to cross the fifteen miles or so of raging northern Atlantic until Boxing Day.

The kind of grim eeriness that had accompanied so many of Coinneach's dark prophecies centuries earlier now hung over the sea-lashed Flannans as the relief party landed. That day, Joseph ran to the lighthouse, calling his friends' names as he ran. The unsecured door swung ominously on its hinges. Their pet parrot — by then almost starved to death on its perch — managed to squawk a feeble greeting. Breakfast was set for three. One overturned chair lay on the floor beside the unused breakfast table. Everything else was perfectly neat and tidy. The log had been made up for Saturday, December 15, and everything was then perfectly in order.

Moore and his two shipmates from the *Hesperus* searched every inch of the island — scarcely five hundred by two hundred metres. They noted that two sets of oilskins were missing; the third hung in its accustomed place. They also found that a tool chest, which should have held ropes for working on the jetty, and which was normally kept on a ledge a hundred feet *above sea level*, had been swept away. A crane situated seventy feet above the sea was also found covered, with the tangled ropes from that same chest. Their conclusion was that massive waves over a hundred feet high had torn the chest from its ledge.

Coinneach Odhar would have been familiar enough with the morbid legends attached to those seven gaunt granite islands, and none of the Hebrideans of his day would have gone there voluntarily, except in the

The amazing Brahan Seer, whose prophecies equalled those of Mother Shipton and Nostradamus.

most pressing emergency. Certainly, none would have stayed there overnight. Among the weird legends attached to the Flannans was the story that dark, magical forces on the islands were able to transform men into birds, and even as recently as 1900, there were those who believed that that was what had happened to Ducat, McArthur, and Marshall. The sinister Flannans were certainly fitting neighbours for the Brahan Seer. Like Robert Nixon, who lived two centuries before Odhar and was generally known as the "Cheshire Prophet," Coinneach came from a basic farm-working background.

Accounts of Coinneach's strange prophetic powers reached Lord Mackenzie of Kintail, who was Coinneach's feudal chief. Mackenzie promptly sent for him and installed him as a tenant on land near Brahan Castle, close to the Cromarty Firth. Not long afterwards, Mackenzie died, and his estates passed to the Earl of Seaforth. Coinneach continued to live and prophesy at Brahan.

One early tradition associated with his occult powers accounts for them by suggesting that he had found a magic stone at Baile-na-Cille in Uig, possibly while he was ploughing there, and that it had been deliberately left by the fairies for him to find. This tradition records that the stone was white and had a hole through it. Another version of the legend of its acquisition describes it as blue and transparent, and adds that his mother was given it by the ghost of a Norwegian princess who lay buried in the graveyard at Baile-na-Cille.

Such strange and powerful gifts of supernatural origin traditionally exacted a heavy price from the man or woman to whom they were given. Whatever his clairvoyant powers might have been with the aid of the stone, Coinneach either went blind in one eye or developed a bad squint as a result of using his miraculous gift. He was afterwards known as "Cam" (a word meaning "squinting" or "one-eyed" in Gaelic) for that reason.

In the Middle Ages, and for several centuries afterwards, ploughmen, in particular, were likely to unearth ancient British, Roman, or Saxon gold, which had been hidden in the ground for safety during the frequent periods of war, invasion, and unrest. These discoveries were sometimes referred to as fairy gold. In the same way, when flint tools and arrowheads were unearthed by the plough, the finders thought they had been made by the fairies and probably possessed magical powers as a result. Neolithic stone tools with holes through them would also be highly prized by superstitious medieval finders, who would then look through the hole in the expectation of seeing visions of the future, or of finding one of the hidden gateways to the fairies' enchanted lands. There were also fond expectations that peering through the hole might reveal the whereabouts of fairy gold.

One of the many legends associated with Coinneach's alleged possession of such a magical Seer's Stone was that its first function had been to save his life by revealing that a meal he was about to eat had been liberally laced with poison by his enemies.

Andrew Lang (1844–1912) was a painstaking and thorough member of the Society for Psychical Research, who devoted a great deal of time and careful objective thought to investigating the phenomena of second sight, which so many of the old Scots "taibhsear" like Coinneach were said to possess. His prolonged studies led him to the conclusion that the phenomena were genuine.

Not everyone shared Lang's opinion, however, especially some of Coinneach's contemporaries. One elderly neighbour, Duncan Macrae of Glenshiel, asked Coinneach to foretell the circumstances of his death. "By the sword, aye, by the sword," replied the Brahan Seer positively. Macrae and several of his friends and neighbours found it highly amusing. Men of Duncan's age rarely, if ever, died in battle — even in seventeenth-century Scotland. In 1654, however, the grim prediction came to pass. General Monck and his Parliamentarian soldiers were on their way to Kintail, when they met the elderly Duncan strolling innocently in the hills. When the Parliamentarians spoke to him in a language he couldn't understand, the old man reached for his broadsword. Monck's men promptly killed him.

Unlike the wealthy customers of the highly commercialized Greek oracle at Delphi, very few people seem to have gone as clients to ask Coinneach direct questions. What happened much more frequently was that the Brahan Seer would suddenly feel compelled to utter a prophecy — rather like Coleridge's Ancient Mariner, who was apparently constrained by some psychic urge to tell his story of the albatross to certain people who were invariably pointed out to him by his supernatural controller. Such was the case with Coinneach's strange pronouncement that a woman would weep over a Frenchman's grave in the burial place at Lochalsh. Sure enough, a Lochalsh girl married a Frenchman whom she greatly loved, but he died young, and her neighbours watched the heartbroken young widow crying beside his grave every day. A similar personalized prophecy concerned the death from measles of a woman named Baraball n'ic Coinnich — or Annabella Mackenzie, in its Anglicised form. She lived in the village in the latter part of the nineteenth century, two hundred years after Coinneach's time. As she lived to be well over 90, it seemed highly improbable that she would ultimately succumb to measles: but she did. Again, unlike the commercialized prophecies of classical Delphi, Coinneach's forecasts often went far into the future: so far, in fact, that there could be no financial advantage in them for the seer, or for those of his contemporaries who heard them. They were set so far into the future, on several occasions, that they would not even have served the purpose of enhancing Coinneach's reputation — a consideration that was undoubtedly a significant motive, however, in the minds of some other so-called seers. The value of these long-range predictions is their evidential value to researchers of the paranormal.

Crossing Drummossie one day, Coinneach paused and uttered a dark prophecy foretelling the tragic fate of the Scots army that was destroyed while fighting for Charles at Culloden over a century after the Brahan Seer's prophecy was made on the precise spot where the grim battle would be fought.

Just as Merlin was once credited with the uncanny power of being able to teleport the huge blocks of Stonehenge, so Coinneach prophesied that a great stone weighing nearly ten tons would be taken from its place on the land where it marked the boundaries between Culloden and Moray, and erected again in the ocean at Petty Bay. During the great storm of 1799 — similar in fury to the one that swept away the first Eddystone Lighthouse and its designer in 1703 — the Culloden-Moray stone was torn from the ground and deposited in the sea some 250 yards from the shore, just as Coinneach had prophesied.

He also predicted that the sulphurous waters of Strathpeffer — normally shunned by the locals who regarded them as toxic — would one day become a famous health spa like Bath, Cheltenham, Epsom, or Matlock Baths. That, too, came to pass in 1818, when the Strathpeffer Spa was opened.

Another of the Brahan Seer's prophecies concerning bodies of water also came true almost three hundred years after it was uttered. Coinneach said that a loch somewhere above Beauly would be responsible for a flood that would destroy a nearby village. It seemed geographically, topologically, and hydrologically very unlikely. Then a twentieth-century hydro-electric dam across the River Conon failed at Torrachilty in 1966, and flooded the village of Conon Bridge, just as Coinneach had predicted.

One of Mother Shipton's most interesting Yorkshire prophecies concerned the coming of the railways, centuries after the Knaresborough Wise Woman's death, and Coinneach had a glimpse of something similar. The Brahan Seer said that strings of black carriages, without horses or bridles, would be drawn through the Scottish Highlands by a fiery chariot; not a bad description of a steam train coming from a man who never saw one.

Coinneach also foresaw the coming of the Caledonian Canal. He prophesied that one day, ships would sail behind the enchanted hill of Tomnahurich not far from Inverness, and once the canal was completed and opened in the 1820s, they did. Another of Coinneach's prophecies concerned the allegedly enchanted, fairy-inhabited land of Tomnahurich itself. Common land in Coinneach's day, he said it would eventually be placed under lock and key so that the fairies who dwelt there would be trapped within it. It was actually turned into a cemetery during the nineteenth century, fenced off, and provided with a locked gate. It is open to conjecture whether the so-called fairies — especially if they were some type of half-remembered, pre-Christian, pagan nature-spirits — were trapped by the iron fencing, with its locked iron gate, or by the Christian ceremony consecrating the ancient ground itself. Iron — such as that used in railings — was always regarded as a reliable psychic defence against witches, wizards, demons, and supernatural beings of all types.

But Odhar's grimmest and best-remembered prophecy was uttered just before he died, the victim of the spiteful, misdirected anger and jealousy of the Countess Isabella, his master's wife.

The Seaforths had been loyal monarchists during the Civil War, and at the Restoration, Charles II had rewarded them generously with extra lands. A little later, the King sent the Earl to France on royal business, and he failed to write to the countess for several months. Isabella called in the Brahan Seer to see if he could provide any information about the Earl.

"I see him in a luxurious room. He is well and happy, but he is not yet ready to return home," said Coinneach. The suspicious Isabella demanded to know more. True to his seer's calling, Odhar said that her husband was apparently enjoying the company of a beautiful Parisian lady.

Isabella went berserk and ordered Coinneach to be burnt to death in a barrel of tar. Before the sentence was carried out at Chanonry Point on the Moray Firth, the Brahan Seer gave his last terrible prophecy concerning the downfall of the House of Seaforth.

The last of the line would be deaf and dumb, and he would live to see his four sons die before him. One of his daughters would come white-hooded from a strange land to the east, and kill her sister. They would know when the dreaded prophecy was about to be fulfilled because four great lairds — Raasay, Gairloch, Grant, and Chisholm — contemporaries of this last Seaforth, would have buck teeth, a harelip, low intelligence, and a stammer. The doomed Coinneach also foretold that there would be a prolific stag-laird of Tulloch who would kill four of his wives, but predecease the fifth.

The Brahan Seer's last fatal prophecy came true in horrendous depth and detail. The last Seaforth was Francis Humberstone Mackenzie, who was born in 1754. As a reward for his services, and those of his valiant Seaforth Highlanders during the Revolutionary Wars against France, he was named Baron Seaforth of Kintail, and later became the governor of Barbados in 1800 — shortly before the governorship of the famous Lord Combermere, who was in charge of the island at the time of the moving coffins mystery in the sealed Chase Vault at Oistins, near Christchurch.

Seaforth was deafened by scarlet fever when he was a boy, and gradually lost his power of speech as well. All four of his sons died before he did. At the time when Francis Humberstone Mackenzie died, Sir Hector Mackenzie of Gairloch was noted for his very prominent front teeth. The harelip belonged to Chisholm of Chisholm. Laird Grant had severe learning difficulties, and Macleod of Raasay stammered badly.

Another element of the prophecy, the stag-laird of Tulloch, was Duncan Davidson. Four of his wives died in childbirth, but the fifth outlived him. His nickname "the Stag" arose because he fathered at least thirty illegitimate children in the area.

Seaforth's daughter Mary had married Admiral Hood, and when he died, she returned home from India as a widow, wearing a mourning costume that included the traditional white hood. One day, while Mary was out driving in the woods with her sister Caroline, the horses bolted, their trap overturned, and Caroline was killed. Every terrible event that the Brahan Seer had prophesied for the last of the Seaforths had come to pass.

The historical evidence for the man and for the genuineness of his prophecies is persuasively strong. But what does prophecy itself mean, and what are its implications for human life, for morality, theology, and philosophy?

If gifted seers like Nostradamus, Mother Shipton, Robert Nixon, and Coinneach Odhar are really able to see and predict a future that *inevitably* comes to pass, what happens to human moral choice, and that most precious of all commodities: free will? For that matter, what happens to justice? If Jack the Ripper was destined to be a serial killer, and Saint Francis was destined to be a holy man, does either deserve praise or blame for his actions? Are we morally justified in executing a mass murderer, or in praying at the feet of some great and good religious leader, if neither of them had one iota of choice about what they did with their lives?

But if seers can see the future, doesn't it have to be *there* in some sense in order to be observed? If everything is preordained and laid out ready for us, so that we merely trundle along our tracks with no power to steer away from future certainties, everything is an illusion. We cannot choose to rescue a drowning man from a raging ocean at risk of our own lives. We cannot volunteer to nurse lepers knowing the grave risk of infection. We cannot say yes or no, of our own free will, when a potentially loving partner asks us to marry him or her. We cannot decide whether to make a deathbed confession, or to take our darkest secrets to the tomb with us. If the whole future is already written in some vast book of destiny ready for the seers to read, then life loses all point and all purpose; we might just as well lie back and let things happen.

That scenario is too negative to be true. It contradicts all the life experiences of the indomitably courageous woman and the aggressively tough and determined man. Whatever the seers can see cannot be inevitable. The future has to be an infinite series of probability tracks. We are the captains of our fate, the masters of our destiny. Shakespeare was right when he wrote in *Julius Caesar*: "The fault's not in our stars but in ourselves."

But accurately fulfilled prophecies like Coinneach's won't just bow quietly and leave the ring. They are stubborn facts, and they demand their right to be heard during this debate.

We believe that Dickens was on the right track in *A Christmas Carol*. Grumpy, selfish, antisocial old Ebenezer Scrooge sees the hazy outline of a Christmas yet to come, in which both he and Tiny Tim are dead. When he asks his spirit guide if these things are inevitable, it replies that they are *if nothing changes in the present*. In other words, the assassin's bullet will hit the president *unless* one of the president's bodyguards shoots the assassin first, or flings himself altruistically in the path of the bullet meant for his leader. The key word always has to be "unless."

There are certain grim possibilities facing our planet: overpopulation, nuclear, biochemical, and bacteriological Armageddons, global warming, and even worse ecological nightmares. The prophets may see them, but they can still be averted if we all try hard enough. So it was in Dickens' happy ending that Tiny Tim did not die, and Scrooge himself, with a new lease on life, became a second father to the boy.

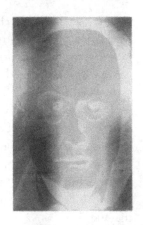

Chapter 13
Saunière, Boudet, and Gélis

The mystery surrounding the "Priest's Treasure" at Rennes-le-Château is now so well known that a brief preliminary outline is enough to introduce three of the most mysterious people — all priests — who featured prominently in that affair.

During the 1880s, it seems that something of great value was discovered at Rennes, and from then until his death in 1917, Bérenger Saunière, the parish priest, spent lavishly on redecorating and refurbishing the church, on various extravagant building projects, and on having a good time in general. Argument has raged about the source of his mysterious wealth ever since. The weirdest, wildest theories have suggested that he was in league with demons such as Asmodeus, whose grotesque statue still stands just inside the little village church of St. Mary Magdalene, or with alchemists and black magicians. Some researchers think that Saunière found Visigothic treasure hidden in a royal tomb in a labyrinth below the church. Other theories involve mysterious secrets older than the sphinx, secrets known to Hermes Trismegistus or Melchizedek — secrets that left Egypt with Moses and the Israelites, and eventually made their way to Rennes via the Albigensian heretics or the Knights Templar. Some researchers think Saunière was a blackmailer, or that he charged exorbitant fees to say chantry Masses for the wealthy dead. There are also several popular versions of a quaint genealogical theory involving Jesus being married to Mary Magdalene, and suggesting that she and Christ had children who eventually married into the ancient royal Merovingian dynasty of France. Most serious Rennes researchers tend to regard this idea with mild amusement: it doesn't account for the money Saunière spent.

Poussin the painter may have been involved in the Rennes treasure conspiracy, along with Fouquet, the one-time finance minister to Louis XIV, and Victor Hugo, the writer.

The central figure in the Rennes mystery seems to be the enigmatic parish priest, Bérenger Saunière. He was born nearby on April 11, 1852, in the tiny hilltop village of Montazels, next to Couiza in the high valley of the Aude.

The Saunière family were dedicated monarchists, and Bérenger's father worked for the Marquis of Cazemayou. Bérenger was the eldest of the seven Saunière children and his brother Alfred also went into the Church.

The family's attractive terraced house stood close to a curiously carved fountainpool in the centre of Montazels. This curious old pool was decorated with three weird, semi-human, semi-aquatic figures often referred to as Tritons, but sometimes called "griffouls" by the local people. They are possibly connected to the ancient legend that Mérovée, founder of the dynasty, carried mysterious non-human genes as a result of his mother's aquatic sexual encounter with a strange, intelligent marine being known as a Quinotaur. This, in turn, links with the Merlin and Arthur sea-babe legend, as well as with the mysterious ancient traditions preserved by the Dogon tribe, relating how intelligent amphibian aliens known as the "Nommos"passed on their wisdom to the Dogon.

One of the earliest mysteries connected with Bérenger is whether his ultra-royalist parents hinted to him that the Saunières — a very old Languedoc family — had Merovingian blood themselves. After the Carolingians usurped the Merovingian throne, it was assumed that all the old, legitimate dynasty had been wiped out for political reasons. But what if it hadn't?

When Saunière became immensely rich, possibly as a result of unearthing Visigothic or Merovingian treasure, none of the villagers ever disputed his right to combine his role as parish priest with that of grand seigneur of the district. It was as if those who knew the history and traditions of the Languedoc and the secret family history of the Saunières accepted it as right and proper for them to "inherit" whatever it was that Bérenger had discovered there.

If Saunière knew himself to be descended from one of the most ancient royal lines in Europe, it would explain his ability to negotiate with the

Austrian Habsburgs on equal terms — as he was thought to have done — and to treat the singularly unpleasant, querulous, inquisitive, and bureaucratic Bishop de Beauséjour with the contempt he deserved.

In 1874, Bérenger passed the entrance examinations for the Grand Diocesan Seminary, where he endured five years of what must have been, for a man like himself, tedious and irksome religious study. One of the theories about Saunière is that he was, at heart, simply a vigorous, worldly, hedonistic character with no real religious conviction. He believed passionately in his secret Merovingian or Visigothic lineage, and in the existence of some great ancient treasure concealed in or near the ancient church at Rennes, which were said to stand on Visigothic foundations. He forced himself to endure five years of austere misery in the Diocesan Seminary simply in order to get ordained and to obtain the living of Rennes-le-Château. The village priest there, he could well have argued to himself, would have the best possible vantage point from which to search for the fabled treasure of Rennes.

He was duly ordained in June 1879 and appointed first as assistant priest in the Parish of Alet. Three years later, he became the Curé of Clat, and worked there for another three years. His dreams came true, and all the long years of struggle came to fruition on June 1, 1885, when he was given the living of Rennes-le-Château.

As a fanatical Royalist, Bérenger preached two unequivocal anti-Republican sermons on October 4 and October 18 of that same year. This did not endear him to the victorious anticlerical Republican politicians who won the elections in Aude shortly afterwards. He was sent off to be a lecturer in the Narbonne Seminary for a few months while the political dust settled, but he was reappointed to Rennes-le-Château in July of 1886.

According to one account of the discovery of the controversial coded manuscripts leading Saunière to the treasure, they were found inside a Visigothic altar pillar while repairs were being carried out in 1887. A more reliable version of the story relates how Saunière's verger, Monsieur Captier, found a parchment inside a secret compartment in an old wooden pulpit support, and took it to the priest shortly before Saunière became wealthy. One decoding of these strange documents alleged that Poussin "guarded the key" to the treasure.

There was certainly something very odd about Poussin's paintings. Our great friend, George Young, the Nova Scotian author and researcher, is an expert in the ancient Ogham script, and he has demonstrated that the fingers and hands of many characters in Poussin's canvases could well be intended to represent Ogham letters. If George is right — and his research deserves considerable respect — then Poussin has cunningly encoded secret messages into his paintings.

Roundabout 1888, Saunière and Abbé Boudet of Rennes-les-Bains became acquainted. Henri Boudet was fifteen years older than Bérenger, and a man of much deeper scholarship than his young colleague. His parish of Rennes-les-Bains had been a Roman settlement at one time, but ancient cromlechs in the area provided evidence of occupation that went back far beyond the Roman Empire. Boudet was a linguist and a historian, albeit a rather eccentric one, and his life's work was a tantalizing and enigmatic book, *La Vraie Langue Celtique et le Cromleck de Rennes-les-Bains*. Many of the best authorities on the Rennes-le-Château mystery believe that the intellectual Boudet was the real power behind Saunière. Boudet was the brain; Saunière was the muscular, energetic young body.

In 1891, Saunière erected a statue of Our Lady of Lourdes near his presbytery with the words "Penitence! Penitence!" carved prominently below it. What was it that Saunière felt he had to be so penitent about at that time?

Maurice Guinguand is said to have given an account of a local lawyer who visited Saunière with a request to translate some Latin documents in connection with a land transfer involving Paul Urbain de Fleury. Does this give a different slant to the *Terrain Fleury* that Saunière himself painted in the church at Rennes-le-Château? By a very curious coincidence, this same lawyer died in a shooting accident while in Saunière's company. Could that have been the reason for the penitence?

In that same year, Bérenger also unearthed an ancient flat stone, like a grave marker, carved in very primitive bas-relief. The stone is still on display in the little museum at Rennes. It shows a figure on horseback carrying a child. Thought by some to represent the Holy Family's flight to Egypt, it might equally well represent the seventh-century King Dagobert II, whose name also appears on one of the controversial coded documents.

The *Terrain Fleury* mural is one of the most interesting and intriguing features in Saunière's richly decorated church. It shows Christ preaching on a hill of flowers, but there are curious details in the painting, which Saunière is said to have executed himself. At the foot of the hill is an old-fashioned drawstring moneybag — with a hole in it. Is Saunière trying to say that he has discovered and spent a little of the legendary Rennes treasure, but that the major part of it still remains untouched?

In 1899, Bérenger purchased various plots of land around the church and presbytery, all in the name of his attractive young housekeeper, Marie Dénarnaud, who had come to work for him as an eighteen-year-old, and who eventually died as a very old lady in 1953. Having admitted that she had shared the secret of the treasure with Saunière, she was unable to reveal it on her deathbed, as she had promised to do, because at the end, a severe stroke robbed her of speech and movement.

On this land he had acquired in Marie's name, Saunière built orangeries, the luxurious Villa Bethania, the Magdalen Tower and several promenades. Substantial amounts of money to pay for all this work must have been coming in from *somewhere*.

Unfortunately, in 1908, lovable old Bishop Billard, who had always treated Saunière with kindly tolerance and understanding, was replaced by the obnoxious Beauséjour, a cantankerous busybody, who would have destroyed a lesser man than Saunière in a matter of weeks. Bérenger proved too tough for Beauséjour, but there was a long, bitter war of attrition, and even Saunière's robust health began to decline towards the end of it. By 1915, Beauséjour's petty spite had deprived Saunière of his parish, but in 1916, Bérenger came back from a pilgrimage to Lourdes, fighting fit and full of new building plans. He was going to erect a tower fifty metres high; he was going to put a rampart all around Rennes; he was going to arrange for a piped water supply to every house in the village. These plans, however, were never realized.

Émile Saunière wrote an account of his famous relative's life, in which he recorded that Bérenger had a heart attack on January 20, 1917, and his condition worsened and he died two days later. But widespread rumour and gossip in the village told a different story. Mysterious visitors had called on Saunière shortly before his "heart attack." Father Rivière, who came to take Bérenger's dying confession, was so shocked and traumatized by what Saunière told him that he had a nervous breakdown and was unable to work for months afterwards. The mysterious priest's body sat in state, covered by a red cloth with pompoms on it. All the villagers filed past to pay their last respects and each plucked a pompom as a memento.

If any man knew the truth behind Saunière, it was his equally mysterious friend and colleague, Abbé Henri Jean-Jacques Boudet, up at the neighbouring parish of Rennes-les-Bains. Some Rennes researchers believe that Boudet was the puppet-master concealed in the shadows behind the stage, while Saunière, his puppet, danced in the limelight.

Boudet was born on November 16, 1837, at Quillan. A local priest noticed the lad's high intelligence and paid for his education. Boudet was ordained on Christmas Day, 1861, at the age of twenty-four, and he was appointed to the living of Rennes-les-Bains by the amiable Bishop Billard in 1872.

Another interest that Boudet and Saunière shared was walking. Each of them would tramp for miles over the Languedoc, looking especially at the ancient stones. Boudet once wrote to his friend Gassaud, another local priest, "I like the winter when the greenery no longer hides the stones ... "

Boudet's strange book about the Celtic language and the local cromlechs was completed in manuscript form in 1880, but it took six more years of careful revising and typesetting before it was eventually printed. The original run of five hundred books cost Boudet 5,382 old francs in gold, an enormous sum of money in those days. Between 1886 and 1914, he sold only ninety-eight copies. He gave a hundred copies to local VIPs, libraries, and charities. Two hundred more were given to distinguished visitors to Rennes-les-Bains, which was a fashionable health spa in those days, similar to Strathpeffer, as forecast by the Brahan Seer.

The remaining 102 copies were destroyed in 1914. Some reports say that this was yet again the vindictive work of the odious Bishop Beauséjour, when he apparently deprived the sick old priest of his living; other evidence suggests that the books were destroyed at Boudet's own request.

The circumstances surrounding the death and burial of the old priest of Rennes-les-Bains were almost as strange as those of his life and his book. He retired to Axat, where his brother had been a lawyer. It is said that Boudet was visited there by sinister strangers just before his death — as was Saunière — and that he died in agony shortly afterwards. Boudet was buried beside his brother Edmond, and the stone covering them both has a carved replica of a book on it.

This may be no more than a symbol that both men were scholars, and the book could merely symbolize legal and theological learning. There is an inscription on this carved book. It could be the numbers 310 and 311, suggesting that the main clue to the Rennes treasure mystery is hidden in Boudet's book somewhere on those two pages. Alternatively, it may be only the Greek word for "fish," the symbol for Christianity in the early Church. The original inscription on the stone book on Boudet's Axat tombstone showed some signs of recent alteration when we visited the cemetery to examine it.

The fact that Boudet had over five thousand gold francs to spend on his remarkable book, rather suggests that he had access to whatever treasure Saunière uncovered at Rennes-le-Château.

The third mysterious priest in the area was Jean-Antoine-Maurice Gélis of Coustaussa. Born on April 1, 1827, at Villesquelande in the Aude district of Languedoc, he was appointed as parish priest of Coustaussa, within sight of Rennes-le-Château, in 1857. By 1897, when Gélis was in his seventy-first year, he had become a very cautious old recluse. He opened the presbytery door to no one except his niece when she brought him food and clean laundry. It was part of his arrangements that the girl had to wait on the step until he had rebolted the heavy presbytery door. Despite all his caution, however, Gélis was brutally murdered, struck down first with heavy Victorian fireirons, then finished off with an axe.

Whoever did the job laid the body out reverently afterwards and left absolutely no trace, although the presbytery floor and walls around the corpse were liberally splashed with Gélis's blood. There was no sign of a break-in, which suggests that the old priest had known the murderous visitor well enough to admit him. *Could that fatal visitor have been Saunière?* Imagine a scenario in which Bérenger had asked scholarly old Gélis to translate something for him from one of the secret parchments Saunière had allegedly found in his church. If that translation had given the shrewd old priest of Coustaussa a clue to what Saunière was up to, he might perhaps have demanded a share of the treasure. Bérenger was powerful and quick-tempered: not the kind of man to play the fool with. In a surge of sudden anger, he strikes Gélis down. The old man staggers up, heading for the window to try to summon help. Saunière seizes an axe and completes his grisly work. Then, overwhelmed with remorse, he lays the body out reverently, perhaps even reciting an appropriate prayer or two over it before letting himself out quietly.

Does this tie in with the Rennes rumours and gossip in 1917, when Father Rivière was said to have had a nervous breakdown after taking Saunière's dying confession?

" ... I shot a lawyer ... and butchered helpless old Father Gélis in his presbytery ... "

Three decaying bodies were exhumed from the lawn of Saunière's home after the Second World War. All three had been shot. They might have been victims of that war, but they might equally well have been would-be assassins who made the mistake of trying to liquidate Saunière — a hard target, and a man very capable of looking after himself.

He was suspected of having had dealings with the Austro-Hungarian Habsburgs, who were believed to have employed unscrupulous secret agents headed by the ruthless Count Taafe. It is easy to imagine the three would-be assassins' shock and disbelief when, instead of an ingenuous and vulnerable village priest, they encountered an ecclesiastical gunman considerably more ruthless and efficient than they were.

Was the mysterious Bérenger Saunière really a remote descendant of Mérovée the Twice Born? Did he uncover an ancient treasure at Rennes as well as a timeless secret? Was shrewd old Boudet masterminding the deal? And who were the mysterious strangers who finally dealt with them both? Perhaps they, rather than Saunière, had also killed Gélis at Coustaussa?

There are also persistent rumours and legends in the Rennes area concerning a mysterious secret society known as "The Priory of Sion." Some researchers believe that they may be far older than the Christian era, and have originally been the guardians of whatever ancient and terrible secret Moses and his people took out of Egypt with them. Other theories regard the so-called "Priory" as little more than a relatively recent hoax perpetrated by a small but politically ambitious right-wing French organization.

If the "Priory" does exist, and if it is genuinely ancient and knowledgeable, it is possible that both Saunière and Boudet were members of it, and that their unexplained wealth came from there.

Chapter 14

George Ivanovitch Gurdjieff

Gurdjieff's original name was George S. Georgiades. The date of his birth is uncertain — somewhere between 1860 and 1880, with 1866 and 1872 being favourite years with disciples and researchers. Irrespective of the precise year, Gurdjieff was born in Alexandropol in Armenia, which was then part of the old Tsarist Russian Empire. He was an Armenian-Greek, who travelled extensively in search of esoteric information and mystical knowledge. He visited North Africa, Central Asia, the Middle East, India, and many other fascinating and exotic places. In 1912 he left Tashkent and travelled to Moscow, where he began to attract a group of disciples that included Peter Ouspensky. He began to teach them what he himself had learnt during his travels and his years of deep spiritual meditation.

Above all, Gurdjieff was a man of intense, exquisite energy. He was a human dynamo. He was more vibrantly alive the whole time than most people can hope to be even when they are at their most excited and most alert. Gurdjieff was a living volcano. He effervesced continuously. He was also a fearlessly combative and buoyant character who coped resiliently with poverty, revolution, civil war, exile, media hostility, and derision. In 1922, he situated his Institute for the Harmonious Development of Man at the Prieuré in Fontainebleau. It closed in 1933, but Gurdjieff himself continued to teach his disciples in Paris until his death at Neuilly on October 29, 1949.

The outline of Gurdjieff's teaching was that we spend most of our lives half asleep — perhaps more than half. Laziness and habit are humanity's worst enemies. We have to be constantly on our guard against the automatic and the robotic. We need to seek the new, the different, the difficult, and the challenging at all times.

Why does time seem so slow and protracted for most of us in childhood, yet seems to accelerate as we grow older? Gurdjieff's answer to that would be that in childhood everything is new. We observe with interested eyes and listen with interested ears. We have not as yet formed many habits. Nothing is automatic for a young child. Holding a pencil requires deliberate and careful thought. Drawing a picture or a pattern requires our full attention and concentration. As we grow older, handwriting or typing skills become automatic. Holding a pencil in the correct position for sketching becomes automatic. After a time, even the skillful, artistic action of drawing the animal, landscape, or flower becomes automatic. Think of riding a bicycle, driving a car, flying an aeroplane, acting on the professional stage, or making a parachute jump for the first time. We are really alive on that first occasion. We are thinking hard about every detail of

George Ivanovitch Gurdjieff: his dynamic energy seemed almost supernatural.

what we are doing. We are fully *aware* of ourselves and of our surroundings, concentrating with maximum intensity. In essence, Gurdjieff's secret lies in finding ways of recapturing that first bottomless reservoir of concentration, the vivid awareness, the excitement — the true joy of living.

The Gurdjieff system of becoming fully "awake" as a sentient being — and staying that way — consists of training ourselves to go beyond our limits physically, mentally, and spiritually. The target that has to be beaten is the target that we achieved yesterday. It may be a matter of running a little farther in the same time, lifting a fraction more weight, serving one extra customer, making one more phone call, writing one more chapter ... solving one more problem. Gurdjieff's answer to life is always "more not less." His mental, physical, and spiritual teaching directives can be summed up as: learn another new skill as soon as you've mastered the one you're studying now; think deeper thoughts; travel to wider horizons; explore ever stranger, wilder, and more challenging concepts; go beyond the boundaries; push your frontiers forward; seek exciting new dimensions; expand your consciousness. Every part of your being must seek to change and grow continuously.

Gurdjieff has been described as a destiny-changer, a man whose amazing teachings can help to steer a disciple's fate in a desired direction; a catalyst enabling others to find themselves and then to alter their lives so that they can become what they really want to be. A sociologist has been described as the kind of man or woman who meets every situation by asking: "Who says so?" It's a healthy, sensible, and independent attitude. Gurdjieff's philosophy appeals in much the same way. His ideas, like the concepts of sociology, challenge the world-taken-for-granted syndrome. The Gurdjieff system vigorously attacks what some of his disciples refer to as "society's consensual lies."

Gurdjieff was like the only person at the party who had had the good sense not to take the tranquillizing narcotics which had sent everyone else into a living-dead trance. He became the vitally important man with the black coffee and icy flannel who saw the urgent need to wake everyone else up before it was too late. Gurdjieff realized that the human sleepers' greatest danger lay in not knowing that they were asleep. The joys of being fully conscious, fully aware, fully awake, fully alive in the Gurdjieffian sense could not come into play as a major motivator until the human sleepers knew that the goal existed. There lay the challenging paradox for Gurdjieff to resolve: if only people knew what they were capable of achieving, they would undoubtedly strive to achieve it — until they know it's there they won't aim for it, and unless they aim for it and reach it, they will have no proof that it's there.

Gurdjieff taught his disciples to mobilize their attention and to concentrate on stimulating their self-awareness. He was a great believer in developing the whole person: head, heart, and hand worked and grew together in the Gurdjieffian realm. There was, for him, an essential reciprocity, a harmonious mutuality about coming fully to life. The craftswoman's hand, mind, and emotional interest in the beautiful object she is carving all work together, and all help to awaken her to higher and more exciting levels of consciousness in the process. Imagine designing and building something like a windmill which is useful, aesthetically pleasing, and environmentally desirable all at the same time. The skillful hand shapes the fabric of the mill. The mind has planned, designed, and worked out the critical path analysis for it: the logical order in which foundations, walls, and roof will be joined together. The cleanliness and positive ecological advantages of the completed mill produce strong emotional satisfaction: hand, head, and heart have been harmonious allies throughout the entire windmill project. If Gurdjieff was alive now he would be a leading protagonist of the Green movement.

Gurdjieff has to be approached as a writer as well as a charismatic teacher. His greatest book is arguably *Beelzebub's Tales to his Grandson*. In this vast work (three large volumes) Beelzebub, a fallen angel, is on a long spaceship journey with his grandson, Hassein, during which he tells him all kinds of things about the human race, its problems, and its potential. Gurdjieff's most enthusiastic supporters would never pretend that it was easy to read. His style makes it almost impenetrable in places, but it is well worth persevering. Another of his works, *Meetings with Remarkable Men*, is a series of autobiographical pieces dealing mainly with Gurdjieff's travels in Asia when he was young. He presents the characters he met there almost as role models, but there is also a subtext and is rich in metaphor and spiritual allegory, which is reminiscent of Bunyan's *Pilgrim's Progress*. One of the best books about Gurdjieff and his work, entitled *Asking for the Earth*, is from the able and informative pen of James George, a former Canadian Ambassador.

If the books written by Gurdjieff himself — and by writers like James George who understood him and his system very well indeed — are an important window into the man and his methods, then his remarkable music is even more revealing. Gurdjieff's music was almost invariably written down and brilliantly arranged for him by the great Russian musician Thomas Alexandrovitch de Hartmann, who lived from 1866 to 1956 — surviving his revered leader by only seven years of his long and productive life. Although Gurdjieff owed so much to Hartmann and his rigorous classical musical training, Hartmann himself said: "It is not *my* music. It is *his*. I merely picked up the master's handkerchief for him."

George Ivanovitch Gurdjieff

The brilliant and generous Russian maestro arranged, scored, and played Gurdjieff's compositions for him. Although not really in the first rank as an instrumentalist, Gurdjieff played keyboard, mouth-organ, and guitar. His musical experience began as a chorister in the cathedral at Kars, and on his many travels he studied the musical styles and forms of Asia and the Middle East. He was also into mantric chanting, and the less orthodox kinds of Western music.

He wrote about three hundred pieces altogether, many of them with Hartmann's help. Some of his later pieces seem to have been specifically intended to accompany his teaching and ideology. His music is very rhythmic and strong, reflecting the man himself. He went in for a great many grace-notes, which glide across into the tone next to them, and give the impression of quarter tones which a piano is unable to play. Gurdjieff was particularly fond of using the elision from a semi-tone to a minor third to achieve the effect he wanted.

Moving from music to dancing was an obvious step for Gurdjieff, and it was as a teacher of religious dancing that he felt most at home and most fulfilled. He referred to the style as Temple Dancing, and thought that it had two major functions. The first was to encourage the development of the dancers themselves: for Gurdjieff a dance, exercise, or movement was like a piece of craftwork, a painting, or a musical composition — it had to do something for the craftsman or woman who performed it, as well as for the audience for whom it was intended. The second great value of Gurdjieff's movements was as a vehicle which would convey his ideology to distant posterity. In some communities, it seemed to Gurdjieff that ritual dances had been performed for centuries, for millennia even, and he valued dancing because it could serve as a cultural transmission medium in this enduring way.

"Nothing is new under the sun," runs the old maxim, which can be profitably coupled with, "The more things change, the more they remain the same." This is particularly true of what Gurdjieff did with the many Eastern Temple Dances he studied, adapted, modified, formalized, and in so doing made uniquely his own. It is worth noting that Kirstein, founder and director of the School of American Ballet in 1934, had been a very attentive pupil of Gurdjieff in 1927. Like Hartmann, Kirstein was generous with his praise for Gurdjieff: "whatever is valid ... springs from Gurdjieff," he wrote. A final interesting point about Gurdjieff's dances is that they were strictly mathematically predetermined, like the Japanese *kata* in martial arts training.

A bright central jewel in Gurdjieff's rich legacy to the posterity that mattered so much to him was his enneagram, a nine-sided figure that can be constructed by drawing a circle and then marking off its circumference into nine equal parts. With 9 at the top of the circle, join 9, 3, and 6 so that they form an equilateral triangle with 9 at its apex. Now join the remaining points in this order: 1, 4, 2, 8, 5, 7. These lines create the rest of the enneagram as shown in the diagram. The vertical height of *any* equilateral triangle — including Gurdjieff's enneagram's special equilateral triangle which touches 9, 3, 6 on the circumference — can be calculated by using *Fanthorpe's Second Constant*, which is the square root of 0.75 and $^3/_4$. This works out to 0.866025. Simply multiply that number by the length of one of the three equal sides to find the vertical height of the enneagram's equilateral triangle.

Not surprisingly, Gurdjieff incorporated his enneagram into a dance which he choreographed at Fontainebleau in 1922, so that the rigorous movements of the dancers turned it into a living, moving symbol incorporating his metaphysical-mathematical principles, the Rule of 3 and the Rule of 7.

Numbers and their meanings were always important to Gurdjieff. He regarded his enneagram as a symbol of perpetual motion, and he saw this as the vital, energizing antidote to the mentally sleeping state from which he sought to rescue his disciples. Through them, he hoped ultimately to rescue the rest of humanity.

Gurdjieff was undeniably a man of mystery — but equally undeniably he was a man of great energy and even greater goodness.

Gurdjieff's amazing enneagram: symbol of abundant life and boundless energy.

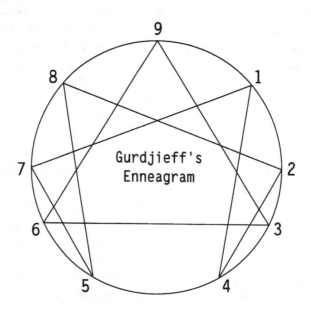

Chapter 15
Helena Petrovna Blavatsky

Helena Petrovna Blavatsky was born on August 12, 1831, the daughter of a Russian army officer named Peter von Hahn, whose ancestors were German. Her mother was a successful novelist, Helena de Fadeef, the daughter of Princess Elena Dolgorukov. When Helena was born, the von Hahn family home was in Yekaterinoslav in the Ukraine.

Helena's strange psychic gifts and apparent powers of mediumship surfaced early. As a child she told her father that she was being visited at night by a spirit claiming to be a woman named Tekla Lebendorff. Not surprisingly, Colonel Hahn thought his imaginative young daughter was making the whole thing up, and used his influence to check the government archives. Not only had Tekla once existed, the data she had supplied about herself to Helena was accurate, as far as Hahn could discover.

In addition to being psychic, Helena was bold and adventurous, which led her governess to remark severely that unless she changed her ways she would never marry anyone — not even an unprepossessing general like Nicephore Blavatsky, who was old enough to be her father. Human nature being what it is, and the teenaged Helena having a fiercely obdurate spirit that thoroughly enjoyed proving opponents wrong, she regarded the governess's remark as something of a challenge. Consequently, she launched her youthful charms at the forty-year-old Russian General so effectively that he proposed to her within a few days. She was seventeen when they married. Their relationship was not a success, and the incendiary Helena — now Madame Blavatsky — solved her matrimonial problems by running away.

Her cousin, Count Witte, maintained that she obtained work as a bareback rider in a travelling circus when she first left General Blavatsky, who was then the vice-governor of Erivan in addition to his high military rank.

Helena's next matrimonial adventure was a bigamous marriage with a romantic opera singer named Metrovitch. Some speculative accounts of her life go so far as to suggest that she probably had a child by him. Their partnership was turbulent, punctuated by numerous sharp quarrels, temporary separations and fragile reconciliations.

The marriage ended dramatically in 1871, when Helena was 40. They were travelling together on the steamship *Eumonia* when its boiler exploded and sank it. Metrovitch drowned, but Helena was rescued by a passing merchantman and taken to Egypt.

Blavatsky went through several difficult years of abject poverty and constant struggle after Metrovitch was killed in the *Eumonia* accident. Most of that time she seems to have worked liked a Romany girl as an itinerant fortune-teller, clairvoyant, and medium.

According to her own account, Helena studied occultism and mysticism

Helena Petrovna Blavatsky

130

under the guidance of various Hindu Mahatmas in India and Tibet during her impoverished travels. Mysterious masters were allegedly training her for the great objective of conveying their spiritual teachings to the materialistic West. She also met and worked for a time with the levitating medium Daniel Dunglas Home.

It was also alleged that she obtained a copy of the *The Book of Dyzan* from a hermitage in the Himalayas, in which a version of the ancient Flood Narrative was recorded. According to *The Book of Dyzan* the first great waters came and inundated seven large islands. The holy people who lived there were saved; the unholy perished. Did reading this grim disaster narrative remind Blavatsky of her own miraculous rescue on the traumatic day when the *Eumonia* went down, and reinforce her conviction that she had been saved for some special purpose?

In 1873 she reached New York. She was a penniless Bohemian figure, wearing a grimy, weather-beaten red shirt, and smoking large numbers of hand-rolled cigarettes in quick succession.

Her life changed dramatically for the better when she met Colonel Henry Steel Olcott, a successful lawyer. She founded the Theosophical Society with him in 1875. The two shared a profound interest in the occult, and the great arguments about Madame Blavatsky's psychic talents — and her integrity — really begin in this period.

To those who believe that she was genuinely gifted with remarkable paranormal powers, she remains a unique woman who wrote amazing books — a miniature library of vitally important, inspired, occult revelations. Her disciples are convinced that she was in constant touch with two great super-beings, Immortal Masters known as Mahatma Koot Hoomi and Mahatma Morya. She was also said to have been in contact with the Count of Saint-Germain, whom some theosophists regarded as another of their secret invisible leaders. A group of them actually went to Paris after its liberation in 1944 in the hope of meeting him, but there was no positive outcome. In 1972, however, Richard Chanfray, claiming to be the Count, appeared on a French television program and allegedly turned lead into gold using nothing more sophisticated than a portable gas heater of the kind favoured by campers.

According to those who believed in her, Helena Petrovna Blavatsky was able to perform many types of psychic miracle. She could produce apports, talk in Russian to the seemingly solid spirit of her dead father, and receive at his hand a medal that had allegedly been placed in his coffin years before. She was also able to relay messages to and from Koot Hoomi and Morya, who were responsible, she said, for giving her the teachings which she recounted in her book *Isis Unveiled*.

To those who did not believe — including Richard Hodgson, the young Australian author of the Hodgson Report, which was commissioned by the Society for Psychical Research — all her supposed paranormal phenomena were faked. She was described as "one of the most accomplished, ingenious and interesting impostors of modern history." Yet that devastatingly critical report was itself severely criticized by Christmas Humphreys and by an American writer named Adlai Waterman in his book *Obituary: The Hodgson Report on Madame Blavatsky: 1885-1960*.

A third possibility lies somewhere between those two extreme positions. Blavatsky could well have had some unusual, paranormal abilities, which she was able to demonstrate on certain occasions — but not all the time.

It is rather more than a flimsy-but-convenient excuse when a medium says that he, or she, is unable to produce psychic manifestations when sceptics are present. Observers *can* sometimes affect an event. A bored or hostile audience can inhibit the finest actress, or the most stirring orator. If psychic phenomena and mind-over-matter experiments do depend to some extent upon a conducive atmosphere and a supportive, encouraging audience, then the presence of scornful, contemptuous cynics can inhibit the very phenomena that they secretly hope to see incontrovertibly demonstrated. Think of the effect a huge crowd of loyal supporters can have on the morale of their team. Fighters are sometimes able to beat stronger, technically superior opponents because the crowd are cheering for the underdog. Experienced doctors and nurses are well aware of cases where the potent but invisible medicine known as TLC (tender, loving care) administered by families and friends has saved the lives of critically ill or severely injured patients.

In 1877, when Blavatsky published *Isis Unveiled*, Olcott testified that it was inspired by her astral visions. Observing her at work, the Colonel described how her pen would be flying at one moment and then she would stop and stare into space as though seeing psychic phenomena. A moment later her pen would dash over the pages again as she wrote down what she had apparently just seen and heard.

Opinions on *Isis Unveiled* are as polarized as opinions about Blavatsky herself. To her faithful devotees and admirers, the book is monumentally impressive. For Blavatsky's ardent supporters, *Isis Unveiled* is evidently the work of someone with vast arcane knowledge who had privileged access to ancient secrets. For critics like Coleman, the book is merely a collection of plagiarized extracts from other works, compiled by an author with very little real knowledge of the subject. Coleman's criticisms might be refuted by the argument that the same external psychic super-beings who inspired Helena could also have inspired the other occult writers, whom she was consequently accused of plagiarism. A parallel problem arises for students of the ancient Greek texts of the synoptic Gospels in the New Testament. Almost all of St. Mark's work appears in both Luke and Matthew. It could be argued that if three writers were genuinely inspired by some Great External Source there would be close similarities when they recorded the same truth.

The basic ideas expressed in *Isis Unveiled* are that the seance room phenomena of the late nineteenth century were all familiar to the great writers, thinkers, and religious leaders of antiquity, and that those same prominent personalities of olden times had themselves been in touch with more advanced spirits than the ones contacted by Victorian mediums. Blavatsky's advice to contemporary spiritualists was to learn from the ancient masters. The old writings on magic and alchemy, she asserted, were not sufficiently understood nor appreciated by readers in the materialistic nineteenth century. In her opinion, given the essential keys by which their coded symbolism could be properly understood, these cryptic old writings held a great many spiritual and scientific truths, which would be of enormous benefit to contemporary humanity, blinded as it was by its obsession with materialism. Blavatsky hinted all through *Isis Unveiled* that she held these necessary keys and that, furthermore, she was working for a mysterious, secret organization of super-beings, who had commissioned her to save nineteenth-century humanity from its suffocating materialism.

She dealt more fully in her later works with the other "six root races" as well as our type of humanity, which, according to her, is the fifth. The first root race was invisible and made of "fire-mist." The second was a fraction more substantial and occupied the remoter regions of northern Asia. The third — whose members sound suspiciously like the remote ancestors of the Yeti and Sasquatch — was similar to gigantic apes. Blavatsky said that they lived in Lemuria, or Mu, another lost continent like Atlantis, but situated in the Indian Ocean. Members of this third root-race were telepathic, but lacked powers of logical reasoning or deduction. The fourth root race was that of the highly civilized and advanced Atlanteans. We, ourselves, are the fifth, and the most solid so far. The pendulum will swing away from our material form again. When the sixth and seventh root races appear, they will be much less solid than we are.

Blavatsky maintained that this arcane knowledge reached her through the aether (or ether), also known as the *"akasa"* (or "empty space") in Hindu writings. Waves in this psychic aether make telepathy and clairvoyance possible.

One interesting anecdote in *Isis Unveiled* concerns Blavatsky's visit to a Greek monastery where she claimed to have seen a monk reading a copy of a rare manuscript written by Theodas, who was said to have been a scribe at the old library in Alexandria.

Egyptian and Babylonian priests claimed that their oldest manuscripts dated back for hundreds of centuries. While this kind of dating is hard to accept, it has to be admitted that almost nothing is known today of what the innermost store rooms of the Serapeum and Brucheum in Alexandria contained. There were at least half a million documents there, and some of those may have been of awesome antiquity. It is also possible that Cleopatra may have ordered some of the most interesting and important documents to be stored safely — as happened to the Dead Sea Scrolls at Qumran a few years later.

Some ancient traditions state that the most precious of the sacred Egyptian writings from Alexandria were hidden in a secret vault shortly before a disastrous fire destroyed the rest. The location of this vault was said to have been guarded by a secret fraternity, who passed it on down the generations. Could this location have been known to the Priory of Sion, who were said to understand and protect the ancient secrets buried at Rennes-le-Château?

When the great Cathar (or Albigensian) stronghold at Montségur, not far from Rennes, was undergoing its last terrible siege in 1244, the bravest of the Cathar warrior-mountaineers who were defending it, slipped away under cover of darkness, carrying with them some great and mysterious treasure, which was later described as *pecuniam infinitam* — infinite money.

A few years ago when we interviewed Dr. Arthur Guirdham, the acknowledged world authority on the Cathars and their strange history, he told us that in his opinion those Albigensian heroes were carrying books. Is it possible that those priceless, ancient books had come into Cathar hands after being saved from the Library at Alexandria?

Among her other prolific occult writings, Blavatsky dwelt in some detail upon the mysteries of Atlantis. Rudolph Steiner agreed that her Atlantean theories seemed to be soundly supported by references in the Akashic Records, the conjectural "astral library" preserved in the aether, whose waves supposedly recorded every event in the history of the world.

Blavatsky also wrote a lengthy and spirited defence of Guiseppe Balsamo, alias the enigmatic Count Cagliostro, allegedly an associate of the even more mysterious Count Saint-Germain. What is especially interesting about Blavatsky's defence of Cagliostro is her insistence that Giuseppe Balsamo was not his real name at all, but a cabalistic code given to the boy by Althotas, the legendary Hermetic sage who was said to have educated him much as Merlin was said to have educated the youthful King Arthur. According to Blavatsky, Giuseppe Balsamo meant: "He who was sent ... the Given One ... Lord of the Sun."

In addition to her shorter, specifically directed writings like the defence of Cagliostro, Blavatsky wrote lengthy articles on the cosmos and the parts played in it by paranormal beings such as elementals. The following sample of her work gives an idea of both her style and her preferred subject matter:

> The Universal Aether was not, in the eyes of the ancients, simply a tenantless something, stretching throughout the expanse of heaven; it was for them a boundless ocean, peopled like our familiar earthly seas with Gods, Planetary Spirits, monstrous and minor creatures, and having in its every molecule the germs of life from the potential up to the most developed.... According to the ancient doctrines, every member of this varied ethereal population, from the highest "Gods" down to the soulless Elementals, was evolved by the ceaseless motion inherent in the astral light. Light is force, and the latter is produced by the **will**.

One of Blavatsky's most enduring and influential converts was a professional journalist named Sinnett. The astonishing Blavatsky phenomena he witnessed included a cup that "apported" at a picnic — supposedly by the intervention of the invisible Mahatmas. Another Blavatsky spectacular was the miraculous "repair" of a broken cup, although some sceptics felt that this was more in the nature of a sleight of hand conjuring trick than anything paranormal.

Sinnett undertook what he believed to be a lengthy correspondence with Koot Hoomi and Morya — with Madame Blavatsky transmitting letters in both directions, and generally acting as the go-between. Sinnett's questions ranged over a wide gamut of arcane and eldritch topics: Atlantis, Lemuria, who and what the so-called Masters really were, the nature of physical and spiritual evolution, the Moon's occult significance, secret world government, and the riddle of reincarnation.

On the basis of what he believed was coming back to him from the invisible Mahatmas via Blavatsky, Sinnett wrote two theosophical texts: *Esoteric Buddhism* and *The Occult World*, which are still widely read. He and many other energetic and intelligent theosophist speakers and writers continue to perpetuate Blavatsky's teachings.

After struggling with failing health for nearly a decade, the mysterious, intriguing, and controversial Madame Blavatsky finally died of Bright's disease in England on May 8, 1891. She took the secret of whether she was a genuine magician and an inspired psychic teacher or just a clever charlatan to the Woking crematorium with her.

Chapter 16

Sir Francis Dashwood

Ishmael Reed, quoted by Wilson and Shea in *Illuminatus*, declared that the history of the world is the history of secret societies; and Socrates, in an uncharacteristic moment of cynicism, is alleged to have suspected that the gods inflict humanity with paranoia so that we may occasionally glimpse a fragment of the truth.

If Reed and Socrates are on the right track, Sir Francis Dashwood can best be understood within the general setting of the notorious Hell-Fire Clubs: the strange, flamboyantly libidinous secret societies which flourished in Britain during the eighteenth century.

It is characteristic of most secret societies — and Dashwood's group was no exception — to be hierarchical in structure. Unlike Arthur's egalitarian knights at their status-free round table, secret societies tend to revel in elites within elites, and degrees above degrees. The famous OTO (*Ordo Templi Orientis*) for example, is credited with eleven degrees headed by the OHO, the Outer Head of the Order. The Illuminates of Thanateros have only four degrees, and are led by a Supreme Magus with the rank of zero, while newcomers are admitted to the Fourth Degree.

The late Stephen Knight wrote in detail in *The Brotherhood* about a Supreme Masonic Council of the 33rd Degree, and it's significant that some degrees and titles seem to be common to more than one secret society. "Knight" referred to a sixteenth Degree in Masonry, known as "Prince of Jerusalem." An identical title exists in OTO but is only fourth Degree with them.

The priesthoods of the old-world cultures ringing the Mediterranean in ancient times were notoriously secretive: none more so than the Egyptian priests and the mathematically inclined Pythagoreans. Heaven alone knows where their arcane information came from originally. If a highly advanced civilization flourished millennia ago below what is now the vast Antarctic ice-field, a few deep-frozen answers may still lie there. Although the Alexandrian Library was destroyed, and the Roman Emperor Diocletian did his best to annihilate all the quasi-scientific and alchemical textbooks his men could find, residual traces of ancient arcane knowledge almost certainly survived under the protection of the old established secret societies of the Mediterranean ring.

When the Fatimid Caliphs opened their study centre in Cairo, which was equivalent to the best of the medieval western universities, they called it

Sir Francis Dashwood, leader of the Hellfire Club at West Wycombe: what strange arcane knowledge did he and his disciples really possess?

the Abode of Learning. Like the western universities, it also awarded degrees, but these Cairo awards were said to have been accompanied by mystical religious ceremonies: they served as a form of initiation as well as an academic or professional qualification.

The original Grand Lodge of Cairo was understood to have been founded by the Ismaili Sect of Islam during the ninth century, and to have adapted and modified the degree system used in the Abode of Learning. Various splinter groups made further modifications until 1090, when Hasan-e Sabah (better known as "The Old Man of the Mountains") took control of the massive fortress of Alamut in Daylam with his Assassins (or Hashishim). His organization was believed to have seven degrees with Hasan-e Sabah at its head as Grand Master. Following him in descending order were the Grand Prior, the Dais, the Rafiqs, the Fadais (who did the actual killing when ordered to), the Lasiqs and, finally, the ordinary people, who constituted the lowest stratum, or Seventh Degree.

It was said that Hasan-e's recruiting technique was to dose the prospective recruit with hashish and have him carried to a beautiful garden filled with flowers, fountains, trees, and bushes bearing delicious fruit. There were also many beautiful girls, or *houris*, who attended to the recruit's every need. After a second dose of hashish, the potential Fadai was carried back to Hasan-e's palace. When he regained consciousness he was told that he had never left the Grand Master's presence, but had had a brief foretaste of Paradise. He was also assured that he would dwell there in eternal happiness after death, provided he faithfully and unquestioningly carried out his orders on earth now. As a recruiting campaign it was highly successful.

Many secret societies — including the Knights Templar, if some rather questionable accounts of their practices are to be taken seriously — had a tradition of a magical head which, although severed, continued to live and speak. Abdel-Rahman of Damascus was credited with being the editor of an ancient treatise called *The Art of Deception*, which purported to reveal where the severed head trick originated and how it was done. Abdel-Rahman's work is quoted in Daraul's book, *Secret Societies Yesterday and Today*. Rahman's explanation was that one of Hasan-e's disciples stood in a deep, narrow hole in the floor of Sabah's palace, with just his head above ground level. Two tightly fitting, flat, semi-circular metal collars, shaped like two halves of a plate but with a wide hole in the centre for the man's neck, were fastened below his chin to give the impression of a severed head lying on a dish on the floor at Hasan-e's feet. The biblical Salome had asked King Herod for the head of John the Baptist on just such a platter.

To make the deception even more convincing, fresh red blood was poured liberally on the dish. The prospective Fadai was then shown this ostensibly severed head, told that it was a man he knew who had died and visited Paradise, but who had now come back to earth by virtue of Hasan-e's magic in order to describe the joys of Paradise to the would-be recruit. According to Abdel-Rahman's account, this severed head deception was an even more effective recruiting aid than the visit-to-Paradise-via-a-quick-dose-of-hashish technique. To make certain that none of the actors playing the part of the severed head was ever tempted to explain the trick — even assuming that they themselves realized what was going on — Hasan-e followed up his hole-in-the floor illusion with a swift, genuine decapitation. The former "talking head" — now permanently silent — was then displayed on a pole. The purpose was to dispel any lingering doubts that it had been a real severed head with whom the potential Fadai recruit had recently been discussing: the uninhibited sexual delights of the *houris*; the luscious taste of the fruit; and the exquisite colours and fragrances of the everlasting flowers of Paradise.

Unlikely as it may seem, there is just a very faint possibility — but no more than that — that at the highest and most secretive levels of both societies, the valiant and utterly fearless Knights Templar might just have had some highly confidential contact with the equally bold and ruthless Assassins. Even King Baldwin II himself could have made some kind of deal with the Assassins to obtain their assistance against Baghdad. It was hinted that in 1149, the Templars actually aided the Saracens in Damascus against the crusading Emperor Conrad.

It cannot be emphasized strongly enough that almost all the spitefully negative propaganda attacking the Templars was a total fabrication compiled at the instigation of the odious Philip IV. His noxious lies were part of the preparation for his cowardly and treacherous betrayal of their altruistic and heroic order on Friday, October 13, 1307. Not until Goebbels' poisonous anti-Semitic garbage was disseminated in the 1930s and 1940s were such honourable and innocent people slandered and libelled so unjustly.

If, however, there was some interchange of arcane information between those two highly effective secret societies in the twelfth and thirteenth centuries, it greatly increases the likelihood that some genuinely ancient eldritch knowledge survived to be passed down to later secret societies. What timeless knowledge filtered through the fearless Islamic brotherhood who followed Hasan-e Sabah? Had it come from places like the Abode of Learning in Cairo, which had, perhaps, rescued vital fragments from the Alexandrian Library? What did the Templars unearth when they were digging so secretively in Jerusalem? Was it salvaged fragments of ancient learning that brought the indomitable Templars into contact with the resolute Brotherhood of Assassins in their Eagle's Nest?

If the Priory of Sion (lurking in the shadows on the fringe of the

Rennes-le-Château mystery in the Languedoc) is an ancient secret society and not just a twentieth-century invention, it may have been one of the channels through which the arcane secrets shared by the Templars and Hashishim eventually flowed. From the Priory, those secrets could well have trickled down through Illuminism and Rosicrucianism, until the dangerous political waves of Jacobitism broke over the British and European Masonic Orders in the early years of the eighteenth century.

Is there a sense in which the tragic defeat of the Scots at Culloden in 1746 can be interpreted as a grim battle between representatives of very different, but almost equally powerful, secret societies? William Augustus, the Duke of Cumberland, who commanded the victorious English army on that terrible day, was an English Mason. It has also been suggested that the leading Jacobite Masons, who brought the German Baron von Hund into their order, gradually faded from the scene and finally dwindled away altogether after the bitter defeat of the Jacobite hopes at Culloden.

If a hidden core of genuine old secrets had survived until the eighteenth century through the efforts of one or more of these secret societies, there is a strong possibility that some of those secrets were known to Sir Francis Dashwood and his Hell-Fire Club.

The popular picture of Dashwood, the fabulously wealthy eighteenth century rake and debaucher, usually centres on the legends of his irresponsible and uninhibited enthusiasm for sex and alcohol. But there seems to have been a great deal more than simple debauchery at the heart of the clandestine activities of the Buckinghamshire Hell-Fire Club which met at Medmenham Abbey.

It was by no means the first. Philip, Lord Wharton, had founded one in 1720 which met regularly in a Cornhill tavern called *The George and Vulture*. Their expressed objectives were "drinking, blaspheming, and gambling," but the landlord, for one, was suspected of being involved in Satanism and black magic. The idea of Hell-Fire Clubs caught on and spread so rapidly that a Royal Proclamation of 1721 officially banned them. Undeterred, they continued to flourish under different titles: the Demoniacs, the Edinburgh Sweating Club and the Dublin Blasters.

Twenty years later, Sir Francis Dashwood, already a member of the Dilittanti Club, and a great enthusiast for voluptuous Eastern art, began to meet with his friend Paul Whitehead and a few like-minded rakes in that same notorious *George and Vulture*, on the corner of St. Michael's alley.

Among the curiosities on display in *The George and Vulture* was a weird old "everlasting lamp" designed on Rosicrucian lines. It consisted of a large crystal sphere with a tail-biting golden snake around its circumference, symbolizing power and eternity.

If some small but useful insight into a man's character can be obtained from one typical example of his behaviour, Horace Walpole's anecdote concerning Dashwood's pranks in the Sistine Chapel is worth repeating. It was apparently the custom for pious visitors to the Sistine Chapel on Good Fridays to be given a small, innocuous, ceremonial scourge with which to beat themselves symbolically as a sign of penitence — the interior of the chapel being in darkness while this was being done. Dashwood smuggled in a large horsewhip, and plied it enthusiastically in all directions to the great consternation of every penitent within range of his powerful arm.

The group's other prominent members were as colourful in their individual ways as Dashwood was in his. Whitehead, the satirist, was thin, pale, and prematurely old. He was their official secretary, treasurer, and high steward. The fat and gouty Lord Melcombe Regis, formerly George Bubb Doddington, the politically powerful friend and adviser to Frederick, Prince of Wales, was another prominent member. John Montagu, First Lord of the Admiralty and Earl of Sandwich — from whom two pieces of bread with something in between allegedly took its name — was also involved.

Yet another member was John Wilkes (1725–1797), the outstanding hell-raiser, debaucher, journalist, and radical politician. He married Mary Meade, who was the heiress to Aylesbury Manor. This gave him a place among the Buckinghamshire gentry, and a base close to the ruined Abbey of St. Mary at Medmenham, where he and his fellow members of Dashwood's Hell-Fire Club used to meet. Wilkes's political techniques — although not much worse than those of most eighteenth century politicians — included bribing a ship's captain to land a party of those who were intending to vote against him in Norway instead of Berwick, which was where they had originally planned to disembark on their way to the polls.

He and his former Hell-Fire friend, Sandwich, became bitter political enemies and on one occasion Sandwich declared that Wilkes would either die of venereal disease or on the gallows. Wilkes instantly replied: "That depends, my Lord, upon whether I embrace your mistress or your principles!" With the help of another notorious Hell-Fire Club member, Thomas Potter, Wilkes wrote an obscene parody on Pope's famous *Essay on Man*. Potter and Wilkes called their version *Essay on Woman*.

Thomas Potter, son of the Archbishop of Canterbury, seems to have reacted as violently as Crowley did against the religious atmosphere in which he was brought up. Rising to the political heights of Paymaster General and Treasurer for Ireland, he was also Secretary to Prince Frederick, and a frequent visitor to Doddington's establishment at La Trappe, as well as to

Dashwood's home at West Wycombe Park. Potter's many debaucheries included the seduction of the Bishop of Warburton's wife, and some curious sexual adventures in graveyards!

Charles Churchill, the poet, was a member, as was George Selwyn, the MP, who had been expelled from Hertford College, Oxford, for worshipping pagan gods and demons and allegedly drinking toasts to them in blood. His macabre tastes in entertainment took him to France in 1757 to witness the execution by torture (involving red-hot pincers and molten lead) of Robert Francois Damiens who had unsuccessfully attempted to kill Louis XV.

The Earl of March, William Douglas (known affectionately to his fellow members of the Hell-Fire Club as the Piccadilly Goat), was noted first for his fine string of thoroughbred race horses and second for his private harem of nubile young women.

The seemingly hermaphroditic D'Eon de Beaumont was the only member who was registered both as a brother *and* a sister of Dashwood's strange Order. Declared probably male by post-mortem examination, and legally buried as such, D'Eon had happily switched genders on several occasions during his long adventurous life — having been a fencing master, a Captain in the Dragoons, and a female secret agent.

One deep and lasting friendship, which is a mile away from the personality patterns set by most of Dashwood's associates, was the one he formed for Benjamin Franklin, the great scientist and statesman, who was living in England in 1757 and again in 1762. Somewhere in the Thames between Marlow and Cookham lay the almost microscopically small Round Tar Island, which Dashwood either leased or rented. Records show that when he visited Buckinghamshire, Franklin was referred to as "Brother Benjamin of Cookham," which rather suggests that he may have stayed briefly on Round Tar Island. Old maps indicate that — small as it was — some sort of dwelling was erected on it for the use of Dashwood and his friends.

A very uncharacteristic aspect of Dashwood's life surfaced during his close friendship with Franklin: the two of them collaborated on a new prayer book, a volume of such genuinely high liturgical quality that it is still in use by some worshippers in the United States, where it is referred to with great respect as "Franklin's Prayer Book."

All of this seems to suggest that the mystery of Dashwood's intricate personality is a deeper and more profound problem than appears at first glance. How much of Rasputin's religious zeal was genuine, and how much of his strange charismatic power over women was only the other side of his fanatical religious coin? Instead of thinking of men like Dashwood, Crowley and Rasputin as essentially hypocritical or contradictory, might it not be more constructive to re-examine their apparently paradoxical motivations with a view to locating a possible nexus between their unbridled sexual behaviour and their spiritual, psychic energy? The whole concept of Freudian *libido* with its awesome behavioural implications would seem to suggest that such a connection may well exist. When certain types of volcanoes erupt, their lava flows in opposite directions — but the heat and energy of those diverging lava streams comes undeniably from the same dynamic source.

The alterations which Dashwood and his followers made to the old Cistercian Abbey, which he leased at Medmenham, provide significant clues as to what probably went on there. When Sir Francis acquired the place, it was derelict and was reported to have had a strange, sinister atmosphere. It is highly likely that the twelfth-century abbey was erected over much older pagan foundations, close to the river, possibly over the remains of a Roman Temple which had served the religious needs of some of Caesar's soldiers during their occupation of Britain.

With Dashwood's practically limitless financial resources — and those of his followers — the neglected, overgrown trees were cut back, a weird sham-Gothic tower was added, walls and ceilings were decorated with paintings, and the grounds were filled with statuary.

It seems more than coincidence that Dashwood did at Medmenham what the equally mysterious and enigmatic Bérenger Saunière did at Rennes-le-Château a century later. Saunière also built a strange watchtower, filled his church with statues, and covered its walls with unusual, symbolic paintings. The question inevitably arises: were Dashwood and Saunière both in touch with some, strange, ancient, secret society — the Priory of Sion, perhaps — which supplied them with arcane information or instructions about the curious decor that enhanced both Medmenham and Saunière's church of St. Mary Magdalene? A further, seemingly minor coincidence, is that the Cistercian Abbey at Medmenham was also dedicated to St. Mary.

It was characteristic for ancient, pagan, sacred sites, shrines, and temples, which were taken over by the expanding Christian Church, to be dedicated to St. Michael, because it is the Archangel Michael who overcomes Satan in the final battle described in the Book of Revelation. The tower on top of Glastonbury Tor which is dedicated to Michael is a case in point.

May it not also be the case that some pagan holy places dedicated to female deities, goddesses like Isis, Angerona, Aphrodite, or Hera, were deliberately dedicated to one of the St. Marys after the early Christian Church took them over? The symbolism inherent in St. Mary Magdalen would be particularly apt, and her statue is situated prominently in Saunière's Church at Rennes. Much pagan worship, especially that of the ancient Mediterranean agricultural fertility cults, and Eastern Tantrism, had a significant sexual component. Temple prostitutes, or in some cults priestesses who were available as sexual partners for the worshippers, played an important part in these rituals. In early Christian tradition St. Mary Magdalen was herself a reformed prostitute — so who better to take over as patron saint of a former pagan shrine where sacred priestess-prostitutes had worked in times past?

Water was also of great significance in the arcane mysteries of the ancient secret societies, fragments of whose teachings had percolated through to Dashwood's group. The proximity of the river was both convenient for transport and a source of relaxation and pleasure, but its moving waters almost certainly had occult significance as well. Some evil entities were believed to be unable to cross running water, so it offered a partial defence, or an emergency escape route, if any of the Medmenham conjurations went diabolically wrong and something which Dashwood and his minions could not control escaped from one of the Hell-Fire Club's pentagons.

Walpole's contemporary descriptions from his *Journals of Visits to County Seats* are illuminating: " . . . it was impenetrable to any but the initiated."

Two highly significant statues guarded the ends of the upstairs drawing room. The first was Angerona, the benign Roman goddess, with power to alleviate sadness and pain. She was also a goddess of secrecy. The second was the far more powerful and formidable Horus, sometimes called Harpocrates. Depicted as either a falcon, or a man with a falcon's head, Horus was the son of Isis and Osiris. When the evil god Seth murdered his royal father, the infant Horus was protected by his mother until he grew to his fully developed godhood and was able to avenge Osiris by overcoming Seth in a terrible battle which lasted eighty years, and cost Horus his left eye.

As Harpocrates he is portrayed as a helpless, naked child protected from Seth by his mother, Isis, and hidden — like the biblical Moses — in the papyrus reeds of Khemmis in the Nile Delta. The child Horus has his finger to his lips for silence as far as the Greek and Roman sculptors were concerned, but in North African non-verbal communication, the symbol of a finger on the lips merely indicated childhood. The silence and secrecy interpretation would certainly have been as appropriate for the eighteenth century "Monks and Nuns" of Medmenham as it would have been for the safety of the child Horus hidden among the papyrus reeds to keep him away from Seth until the great day came. As Harsomtus or Har-mau, Horus is seen as the great unifier who brought the kingdoms of Upper and Lower Egypt together as one nation.

In essence, Horus was the Egyptian sky-god, their deity of light and goodness, the traditional enemy of evil. Did Dashwood and his colleagues feel in special need of his protection because of the strange and dangerous ceremonies and rituals they were practising at Medmenham?

According to Walpole's account, Rabelais' famous *"Fait ce que voudras"* ("Do what you will") was inscribed over the door, and this principle accorded harmoniously enough with the philosophies of both the Marquis de Sade and Aleister Crowley.

In addition to the strange building work, decorations and statuary he undertook at Medmenham, Dashwood hired Cornish miners to extend some natural local caves into a labyrinth — apparently designed on broadly Tantric patterns symbolising mystical sexual energy. This would seem to link whatever was being practised in Dashwood's abbey and caves with the Palaeolithic concept of a great universal goddess: and this idea of the great universal goddess connects powerfully with the modern Gaia hypothesis.

In the course of his 1970s researches into the feasibility of life on Mars, James Lovelock examined the possibility that the Earth's oceans, atmosphere and climate are regulated by the life processes taking place within the whole biosphere. These continuous adjustments, which all living things carry out together, maintain the homeostatic balance which keeps Earth hospitable and pleasant — so that, in effect, the living things which *make* the environmental adjustments can go on existing *because* of them. Lovelock's hypothesis was named after Gaia, the Greek word for the Earth goddess who gave birth to the Titans.

Elizabeth van Buren, one of the most mystical and sensitive of the Rennes-le-Château researchers, is on record as saying that Rennes is "a Gateway to the Invisible." Theories have been put forward that certain mysterious locations like Rennes may be contact points — the "eyes" or "ears" of Gaia herself — through which perceptive human beings can contact their supra-consciousness, the living mind of the entire biosphere. Is this what the Palaeolithic priests and priestesses were able to accomplish to some degree? Could it partly explain the sympathetic magic of ancient cave art and timeless Tantric designs? Was this the real secret behind Dashwood and his Hell-Fire Club?

The most successful espionage agents have often hidden their real activities under the surface roles of actors, musicians, sales people, circus performers, and sporting personalities. Who would suspect that solemn, serious, and effective magical and religious practices of great antiquity were taking place under the colourful cloak of drunkenness and debauchery which Dashwood and his friends cultivated as their public image? The fictitious, but typical, Sir Percy Blakeney in *The Scarlet Pimpernel* novel could easily have been one of Dashwood's drunken revellers. He hid his serious purposes very effectively under just such a cloak.

Another fascinating aspect of Dashwood's caves is the underground river located one hundred metres down, which he referred to as the Styx. The Inner Temple of the whole subterranean configuration lay beyond this mysterious river.

With death rates and life expectancies as they were in the eighteenth century, and considering their persistently reckless and indulgent lifestyles, Dashwood and almost all his libidinous colleagues reached a good age. Only Tom Potter — whose strange habit of sleeping on graves may well have contributed to it — died in his early forties. Benjamin Bates, for example, was barely two years short of his century; Douglas, Earl of March, was eighty-six; Wilkes survived until he was eighty-three, and Dashwood himself — who was still busily fathering illegitimate children — lived well into his mid-seventies.

Paul Whitehead, who had pre-deceased Dashwood by several years, had made arrangements for his heart to be placed in the Hell-Fire Club's mausoleum. His beckoning ghost was reported to have been seen by numerous witnesses, including Dashwood's sister, Rachel, shortly before Dashwood's death.

The authors' great friend, Simon Probert — who is a very sensible, practical, and intelligent professional man with a funeral-directing practice in Penarth, near Cardiff — visited the Dashwood sites recently accompanied by his gifted clairvoyant and psychic friend, Pamela Willson. Up to the time of their visit, Simon had not said anything to Pamela about the history of the caves, Medmenham Abbey or the mausoleum.

Between the church of St. Lawrence and the mausoleum, however, Pamela reported seeing a spirit form, although Simon was unable to see it. As soon as Pamela entered the caves she felt extremely disturbed and reported a sensation of icy coldness. She also had a strange psychic feeling that she was being suffocated: and it seemed to her that a number of human sacrifices had almost certainly taken place there in the remote past. Simon himself felt that the caves seemed sinister and atmospheric, and projected a menacing atmosphere.

In Dashwood's time, it was widely believed that there were a number of secret chambers concealed within the labyrinth, their entrances known only to Dashwood himself and his privileged inner circle.

The riddle of Sir Francis and what he and his friends really did at West Wycombe and Medmenham remains unsolved, but the hidden truth is something much more profound than the immoral antics of a gang of high-spirited Regency rakes.

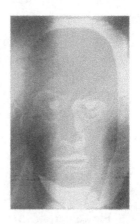

Chapter 17
Grey Owl

Things are not always what they seem — and neither are people. On August 17, 1987, Prisoner Number 7 committed suicide by hanging himself in Spandau prison. According to the prison register he was ninety-three-years old; his name was Rudolph Hess; and he had once been Hitler's Deputy-Führer. Inexplicable medical evidence, however, showed that Number 7's body bore no traces of the wounds which Hess had received in World War One. Whoever he was, the Old Man of Spandau was *not* Rudolph Hess.

Fedor Kuzmich was supposedly a remarkable old Russian monk with strange powers of spiritual healing. He died at the age of 87 in 1864. A thorough investigation and brilliant piece of analysis by Colin Wilson in *Unsolved Mysteries: Past and Present* points strongly to the possibility that Fedor Kuzmich was in reality Tsar Alexander I. The Tsar was supposed to have died at Taganrog on December 1, 1825, having caught malaria in the Crimea, but not many of the people who knew him recognized the body lying in the coffin as his. Years later, however, two former palace servants thought they had recognised Kuzmich as the Tsar. Wilson was almost certainly correct about Alexander's strange change of identities.

There are many more famous and confusing dual-identity cases such as those centring on Princess Caribou, the Tichborne claimant, and the Grand Duchess Anastasia.

The celebrated Canadian Indian, pioneer conservationist, and ecologist known as Grey Owl was actually born in Hastings, Sussex, England in 1888. His real name was Archibald Stansfield Belaney. As a teenager, he left home in 1906 to start an amazing new life in Canada as an entirely different personality called Grey Owl, the supposed son of an Apache mother and a Scots father (the Scots father was an ingenious idea to explain his otherwise anomalous blue eyes).

He worked in Toronto for a short while before moving out to the Temagami district in northern Ontario, where he met and married Angele Egwuna. Angele was an Ojibwa girl who taught him how to survive in the wild, where he lived as a trapper, hunter, forest ranger, and guide.

He volunteered to join the Canadian Army during World War I and served with great gallantry and effectiveness as a sniper behind enemy lines. Gassed and wounded in action, he went back to Hastings to recuperate. While there he married Ivy Holmes, a girl he had known prior to leaving for Canada in 1906. Although he later left her, and returned to Canada alone, she altruistically decided to keep the secret of his strange double identity. One other person knew Grey Owl's secret, but he too kept an

Grey Owl — the wise "Canadian Indian" who was really born in Hastings in England.

oyster-like silence for years. This man was Britt Jessup, a journalist on the staff of the *North Bay Nugget*. His editor considered that Grey Owl was doing such excellent work saving the Canadian beavers and defending the wilderness, that his cover must not be blown.

Twenty years later Grey Owl met Anahareo, a Mohawk girl from Mattawa on the Ottawa River. Under her influence, he gave up his trapping and hunting to become a conservationist and ecologist. In need of extra income, he began writing and publishing his ecological ideas, and his books brought him to the attention of the Dominion Parks Service. Their ideology coincided largely with his, and he was offered the post of official naturalist — the first ever to be appointed by them.

In 1931 he and Anahareo moved into a log cabin beside the lake in Riding Mountain National Park taking with them Jelly Roll and Rawhide, their two pet beavers. They moved after a while to the Prince Albert National Park where they settled beside the Ajawaan Lake.

During their time there, Grey Owl produced three books entitled: *Pilgrims of the Wild*; *Sajo and Her Beaver People*; and *Tales of an Empty Cabin*. These books, together with a number of films about him and his famous beavers, drew many visitors to his lakeside home, known, appropriately enough, as Beaver Lodge.

Having lectured successfully in Canada, Grey Owl toured England in 1935 and 1937, giving two or three lectures a day to publicize his books and his ecological philosophy. Usually dressed in his traditional Indian buckskins when he appeared in public to give his lectures, Grey Owl consistently promoted the cause of wildlife preservation and the importance of keeping the wilderness pure, clean, and natural.

It says a great deal for Archie Belaney's cool nerve and self-confidence that he even gave a lecture as Grey Owl in his old hometown of Hastings, speaking to the audience as if English was a language he had learnt with some difficulty.

Such was Grey Owl's fame and popularity as a lecturer, that he was called to Buckingham Palace where he gave a private performance for George VI, his queen, Elizabeth — now the Queen Mother — and the young princesses Elizabeth and Margaret.

Sadly, the hectic pace of these lecture tours ultimately proved too much for him, and when he got back to his home near Lake Ajawaan in 1938, he was exhausted and seriously ill. He died of pneumonia on April 13 that same year, at the age of 49.

Are there psychological explanations for his behaviour? Like the rest of us, Archie "Grey Owl" Belaney was a curious mixture of the good, the bad, and the indifferent. His work as a conservationist and ecological pioneer was outstandingly good. The gentle, protective care he showed to all animals — and to beavers in particular — was admirable. His far-sighted concern about the environment was erudite, statesmanlike, and years ahead of its time. He deceived people about his ethnic origin in order to accomplish his purposes — to further his ideals as well as to further his personal ambitions — and Grey Owl's conservationist ideals were undeniably good. Perhaps in his case a worthwhile end justified the questionable means. As Christ said on one occasion: "Let him who is without sin cast the first stone." And nobody did any stone-throwing that day. Archie liked a drink, perhaps more than most: but that's a very minor fault — if it can be regarded as a fault at all. There were plenty of lads in Dashwood's gang who drank more in a day than Grey Owl drank in a week. His saddest characteristics were the erratic, unpredictable responses he gave to the loyal women who loved and helped him so much during the various stages of his chequered career. Each of them seems to have deserved better treatment than she got. But Christ also said: "Judge not, that ye be not judged," and those women in his life who apparently had least reason to forgive Grey Owl, did not condemn him either.

He was a dreamer and an idealist; a restless, quixotic, mercurial character. His ne'er-do-well father had given Archie little or no help or support during his childhood and formative years. He had no role model there, and perhaps a man without a role model feels the need to try out a few for himself — Canadian Indian, hunter, trapper, guide, soldier, conservationist, ecologist, writer, lecturer, and husband. ...

The Greeks and Romans believed that great works of art and literature were the result of inspiration by one of the Muses: powerful, invisible semi-deities that took over the human artist or writer and produced their brilliant work through him or her. Madame Blavatsky believed that her *Isis Unveiled* was inspired in this way by Koot Hoomi and Morya. In a similar way, mediums believe that they have been taken over temporarily by the spirits of the dead who wish to communicate with the living. Algonquin shamans and medicine men, and many other North American and Canadian Indians, are strongly aware of the possibility of possession by the spirits of ancestors, or other supernatural entities. A warrior believed that on appropriate occasions he could be empowered by the spirit of his totem animal — an idea which finds parallels in the old Norse concept of the berserker.

Another theory that can be suggested alongside possession is *reincarnation*. It's a controversial area, of course, but one that's worth considering. Did the wise and powerful spirit of a dead Canadian Indian return to earth at Hastings, England, in the body of Archibald Stansfield Belaney in 1889? There are several cases of apparent reincarnation — especially in India, Tibet, and the East — that are well documented and difficult to explain away. Many readers will have had personal experiences of déjà vu which they find difficult to explain. Most of us have found ourselves at one time or another in a strangely memorable room, an old cottage, a walled garden, a stately home, a derelict castle, a decorated Palaeolithic cave, or a quaint old European town with narrow cobbled streets and houses built centuries ago. We have felt that the place in question was disconcertingly familiar — although we were absolutely certain that we had never visited it before during this present life. Do such examples of déjà vu provide evidence that perhaps we visited it long ago in a previous incarnation? Did a real Scots-Apache Grey Owl live and die in the great Canadian wilderness long before Archie Belaney was born?

Whatever the true explanation for his amazing changes of character, personality, and lifestyle, the mysterious man who was both Archie Belaney and Grey Owl has left a significant legacy to conservation and ecology.

Chapter 18
Who is Melchizedek?

In Genesis chapter fourteen, verses eighteen to twenty, there is an account of how a singularly mysterious character named Melchizedek, who is described there as the King of Salem and a Priest of the Most High God, comes out to meet Abram (later known as Abraham) in the Valley of Shaveh — a term denoting a flat valley, which was also the King's Valley. We can allocate the historical Abram an approximate date between 3000 and 2000 BC, which places this first recorded appearance of Melchizedek between four and five thousand years ago.

Abram had felt that he was called by God — whom he probably thought of as Yahweh — to leave his home in the ancient Chaldean city of Ur in Mesopotamia (probably Ur Kasdim or Tall al-Muqayyar, also known as Mughair, the same place as Kaldu mentioned in the ancient cuneiform tablets found at Mari) in search of a Promised Land. He ultimately became the founding patriarch of both the Arabian and Jewish peoples through his two sons, Ishmael and Isaac. As was the case with many Egyptian Pharaohs and their royal wives, Abram's wife, Sarah, was also his half-sister — and it was she who was the mother of Isaac. Ishmael was Abram's son by Hagar, Sarah's slave girl.

Abram's rank and importance are abundantly clear from the many biblical references to him, as well as the records of him in other sacred texts.

He was, in fact, honoured by the supreme title of "the friend of God." Yet despite his undeniable rank and spiritual status, he *receives* a blessing from Melchizedek and humbly *gives tithes* to Melchizedek as though to his rightful and acknowledged superior. The vital question which that raises has to be carefully considered if Melchizedek is to be properly understood. Melchizedek gives bread and wine to Abram along with his solemn blessing. Bread and wine are, of course, the central symbols of the Christian mass, representing the body and blood of Christ himself (to whom some Christians also give the title of Great High Priest).

The Messianic Psalm 110, verse four, also refers to Melchizedek, and describes the promised Messiah as "a priest forever after the order of Melchizedek." In chapters five, six and seven of the lengthy, scholarly but rather legalistic Epistle to the Hebrews in the New Testament, careful reference is made to these Old Testament passages about Melchizedek. He is without human parents. He has no genealogical line of descent — and just as his life had no beginning, so neither does it have an end. He has the temporal power of any great earthly ruler, combined with the spiritual authority of the highest possible order of priests.

Perhaps there's a clue in another enigmatic quotation from the ancient and intriguing book of Genesis. Chapter six, verse four, says that there were giants on the earth in those days, and that "the daughters of men" (presumably meaning normal human females) had children by "the sons of God." These "sons of God" were quite definitely *not* normal, terrestrial human stock. According to the Genesis account, their hybrid children became, "mighty men which were of old, men of renown."

Was Melchizedek in any way connected with these mysterious "sons of God" who intermarried with human women? And what exactly does the phrase "giants on the earth" mean? Does it necessarily refer only to straightforward physical size, or could a "giant" be an *intellectual* giant like Leonardo da Vinci, Newton, or Socrates?

Melchizedek was a benign being as well as an immensely strange and powerful one. He was a contemporary of the so-called gods of ancient Egypt: could he have been one of them under another name? It is Thoth who springs immediately to mind, Thoth who was otherwise known as Hermes Trismegistus, or Hermes the thrice blessed. Thoth (alias Hermes) was the scribe of the gods, and custodian of the priceless Emerald Tablets on which the power-spells of the Egyptian gods were written and upon which to a substantial extent their power depended.

Imagine a scenario in which Hermes Trismegistus (Thoth) and Melchizedek are one and the same benign and immensely powerful superior being. Ancient Hebrew legends tell how Abram and his sister-wife, Sarah, are travelling through the wilderness when she pauses and looks delicately and discreetly for a suitable cave which offers sufficient privacy to act as a restroom. Having located one, so the legend continues, she finds that it's already occupied by Hermes Trismegistus, who is lying motionless in what appears to be death, a very deep sleep or a strange state of suspended animation. Beside him lie the priceless Emerald Tablets. According to the legend, Sarah picks them up, and instantly Hermes begins to stir. The terrified girl races from the cave. It is possible that she took one or more of the Emerald Tablets with her. Were they, perhaps, one of the sources of Abram's many later successes?

Theologians and biblical historians, textual analysts and Church Fathers, as well as brilliant Jewish academics, have argued ingeniously for centuries over who Melchizedek really was, and where he might have been before he met Abram in Shaveh. Some of the Cabalistic, Talmudic, and Rabbinical writers suggested that he was a survivor of the flood, and was in fact Noah's son, Shem. They argued that Shem as the first lord of the land of Canaan had a perfect legal right to bestow it upon whom he chose. His extreme age would also have given him precedence and a status even higher than Abram's. But this does not accord with his having no earthly family. If Melchizedek was the patriarch Shem, he was clearly the son of Noah, whose ancient lineage was perfectly well known. The records left by Epiphanius maintain that the Samaritans also believed that Melchizedek and Shem were one and the same person.

Jewish scholars in the first century AD worked long and hard on the old sacred texts — a process known as *midrash* or "searching the scriptures." Part of this process was the mingling of *haggada* or "story-telling" with their legal and moral teachings — similar to the technique of modern preachers who frequently like to enliven their sermons with stories and anecdotes. Part of a long oral tradition at first, these stories and legends were eventually committed to writing and became part of the Talmud. Some of them seem wildly far-fetched: the Queen of Sheba had donkey's hooves; the infant Moses was able to talk on the day he was born; Cain, the first murderer, had a twin sister; Moses's brother, Aaron the High Priest, once locked the Angel of Death inside the Tabernacle; Solomon's good friend and ally, King Hiram of Tyre, who supplied materials for the Temple at Jerusalem, entered Heaven without dying first. There will be enough meat on the great sea monster, Leviathan, to feed all the holy men and women who go to Paradise when they die. Along with these stranger myths, legends, and fables, the Talmud also includes significant references to Melchizedek's immortality.

According to Jerome's writings, Origen and Didymus both held the theory that Melchizedek was an angel, visiting the earth for a specific purpose (to bless and assist Abram) in much the same way that Gabriel had visited Mary at a later time. Jerome also had his own theories about the location of Salem.

An early religious group calling themselves the Melchizedekians maintained that their mysterious leader was what they referred to as a "Power," "Virtue," or "Influence" of God. Another early religious thinker, Hieracas, and his followers thought that Melchizedek was a manifestation of the Holy Spirit. Ambrose had a theory that Melchizedek was the Son of God in human form. Other theories of this kind, from similar religious thinkers of this early period, have suggested that Melchizedek was perhaps Ham or Japheth (Noah's other two sons) or one of their descendants. Some of these early scholars also thought that he might have been Job — but after all his troubles and the great restoration that followed them, Job's eventual death is clearly recorded at the end of the book that bears his name. Melchizedek's life neither begins nor ends.

The author of the Epistle to the Hebrews is clearly an expert on Jewish Law, religious regulations, and customs. Priests were drawn from the Tribe of Levi, yet this scholarly author makes it abundantly clear (Hebrews, chapter seven, verse six) that Melchizedek was not a Levite: Melchizedek's priesthood was something altogether older, more powerful, and more mysterious.

The second part of the Melchizedekian problem is the precise geographical *location* of his ancient Kingdom of Salem. The biblical account of Abram's journey places it somewhere between Hobah and the plain of Mamre. In his time it may well have occupied the land on which Jebus and later Jerusalem were built. On this theory, Shaveh becomes the valley east of Jerusalem through which the River Kidron flows. In Psalm 76, verse two, Jerusalem and Salem are identified as the same place. Evidence from the ancient Targums favours the idea of Salem and Jerusalem being the same location, and Josephus argued that Shaveh was close to Jerusalem. In the Book of Joshua, chapter ten and verse one, there is a reference to a king of Jerusalem named Adonizedek, a name so etymologically similar to Melchizedek, that it seems probable there was a dynastic connection between them. If Melchizedek was one of the inexplicable "sons of God" who took human wives, then Adonizedek could possibly have been a remote descendant. If he was, he lacked his great ancestor's wisdom and power. Joshua overthrew him and his four allied Canaanite Kings, and buried all five of them in the cave of Makkeda. He then sealed up the entrance, and, according to ancient tradition, their bones still lie there. The second part of the name, "zedek," actually means "righteousness," and is considered by some linguistic experts to be synonymous with "Jerusalem." The connotation being that Jerusalem, the Holy City, is also Zedek, the City of Righteousness.

Saint Jerome had a completely different idea — and there are occasions when Jerome is well worth listening to. His real name was Eusebius Hieronymus and he was also known by the pseudonym of Sophronius. Born in Stridon in Dalmatia in 347 he died in his mid-seventies in 419 or 420 at Bethlehem. He was a tireless biblical translator and Latin scholar and is probably best remembered for his Latin translation of the Bible, the version known today as the Vulgate. Jerome thought Salem and Jerusalem were entirely different locations. He believed that a town near Scythopolis or Bethshan which was still known as Salem in his day was the Salem of which Melchizedek had been king when he encountered Abram. Extensive ruins in Jerome's Salem were said to be the remains of Melchizedek's Palace.

Professor Stanley thought that Abram and Melchizedek had met on Mount Gerizim, and Eupolemus had a theory that they were together on Mount Argerizim, the Mount of the Most High.

The evidence is not conclusive either way, but on balance Jerusalem seems to have the stronger case.

Archeologists have discovered the remains of a Chalcolithic or Early Bronze Age settlement — dating back some five to six thousand years — on a hill to the southeast of the city. There was also a very early settlement just to the south of the Temple Mount, which gives researchers cause to wonder just how much secret information the Templars had when they were digging there. A very early form of the name is given as "Urusalim," a word which some scholars think suggests a western Semitic origin. If they are correct the meaning would then be "founded by Shalem" or "founded by God."

At one period in its history, the ancient city seems to have been an outpost of the Egyptian empire because the old Tel-el Amarna correspondence contains a plea for help from the Ruler of Jerusalem, one Abdi-Kheba, to Pharaoh because the city is under attack from enemies described as "Hapiru" or "Habiru" — the old word for Hebrews.

Archeology has done much to rescue Abram/Abraham from the quagmire of myth, legend, and tribal symbolism to which some earlier scholars consigned him. When the biblical evidence in Genesis is aligned with Islamic and Jewish accounts and then reinforced by modern archeological findings like those at Mari, a powerfully historical and personal Abram emerges.

The excavations by the banks of the Euphrates at Mari, one of the oldest cities in the world, uncovered thousands of cuneiform clay tablets. Some of these formed part of the official archives; others were legal documents; some were religious texts and yet others were simple correspondence.

His original name, "Abram" or "Avram," meant either "God is exalted" or "the Father is exalted." When the extra syllable was added to create the name "Avraham" or "Abraham," the meaning changed to "Father of the Multitudes" or "Father of the Nations."

Abraham emerges from these studies as basically a good man, but he is not without those human weaknesses which provide some of the strongest evidence for his real, historical existence. He has a deep and sincere desire to serve his God. He sorts out the problems over where to graze the flocks with his nephew Lot in a statesmanlike way instead of going to war with him. He is a merciful and caring man: he prays compassionately for the inhabitants of Sodom and Gomorrah. He is a quick and effective warrior as his rescue of Lot demonstrates. But he is also capable of a major piece of deception when he tells Pharaoh the half-truth that the desirable Sarah is his sister (rather than his wife as well) and allows her to be carried off to Pharaoh's harem. His fear was that if a monarch as powerful as Pharaoh really wanted a particularly attractive girl, a minor obstacle like a husband who was still breathing inconveniently could easily be surmounted by two or three loyal and determined Egyptian soldiers.

So who was the mighty but mysterious Melchizedek to whom Abraham deferred?

A supernatural being, parallel, perhaps, to Tolkien's mysterious and powerful Gandalf in *Lord of the Rings*? A manifestation of some aspect of God himself? An angel, or archangel? One of the mysterious "sons of God" who married human wives, or one of their semi-legendary offspring who became "mighty men of old"? A survivor from the Flood? Job or one of the other ancient patriarchs? An extra-terrestrial, perhaps? Someone like Madame Blavatsky's Mahatmas, Koot Hoomi, and Morya, or even, perhaps, the time-defying Count of Saint-Germain? A survivor from Lemuria or Atlantis, or a refugee from that more than half-suspected, highly advanced civilization that may once have flourished on the continent currently shrouded by Antarctic ice? Thoth, or Hermes Trismegistus, from the ancient Egyptian pantheon — whoever and whatever they really were?

There can be little doubt that the real and historical Abram met the equally real and historical Melchizedek But whom did Abram really encounter — where did he come from originally, and where is he now?

Chapter 19

Hermes Trismegistus

Myth, legend, fable, and tradition claim that Hermes Trismegistus, alias Thoth, the scribe of the gods of Egypt — and possibly alias Melchizedek as well — is a benign, immortal being of great wisdom and power. To some of his disciples, including the Hermeticists — and there are still plenty of them around — he is a supernatural entity, semi-spirit, semi-deity. To others he is an angel or archangel. To a different group he is an extra-terrestrial, an alien whose extraordinary powers are technological rather than supernatural. Others see him as a Tolkienian Man of Westernesse, of the same ancient and powerful race as Aragorn in *Lord of the Rings*. Myth, legend, fable, demi-god, angel, alien, or antediluvian survivor: whatever his real origin, Hermes Trismegistus presents a tantalizing riddle for researchers to ponder.

In old Egyptian, Hermes, or Thoth, is known either as Djhuty or Djhowtey. The Egyptian priests regarded him as one of their moon-gods. They credited him with having inspired humanity to write, to count, to think, to study and to learn: Thoth was always regarded as a god of wisdom and knowledge — especially secret, magical, arcane, alchemical knowledge. Many of his followers credited him with being the inventor of writing, or, at least, the bringer of writing to our Earth. This literacy task was the joint responsibility of Thoth and the goddess Seshat. She and Thoth worked on it together, for the benefit not only of the human race but of their fellow gods and demi-gods in the Egyptian pantheon. He was also credited with being the god of languages and communication. As the supreme linguist, he was the interpreter of the gods as well as their scribe.

It has been suggested that if the old gods of Egypt needed an interpreter in the first place, there must be a striking similarity between their work and the functions of the EU or the UN, where skilled interpreters are practically as important as high-status political representatives: the ambassadors, government ministers, secretaries of state, premiers, and presidents who make the decisions.

If the strange-looking gods of ancient Egypt (almost invariably represented as animal or bird-headed humanoids) genuinely possessed those alien features because they were extra-terrestrials from many different worlds, it would certainly explain their pressing need for an interpreter like Thoth!

The ancient Egyptian Thoth-worship originally had its headquarters in Khmunu (the "City of Eight"), otherwise known as Hermopolis, in what was then Upper Egypt. The town is called al-Ashmunayn today. A German archeological expedition worked there from 1929 to 1939 and succeeded in

Hermes Trismegistus, alias Thoth, the scribe of the gods of Egypt. Many believe that his ancient Emerald Tablets hold the Keys of Power.

uncovering portions of the Temple of Thoth as well as extensive Greek and Roman ruins. Al-Ashmunayn is situated on the banks of the Nile, and lies to the south of al-Minya. At Tunah al-Jubal, on the west bank, there's a fascinating labyrinth of catacombs and subterranean passages — almost a miniature underground town in itself. The High Priest of Thoth during the reign of Alexander the Great was Petosiris, and his body, too, lay buried in that same labyrinthine necropolis. These dark convoluted ways are reminiscent in some respects of the great Labyrinth on Crete which Daedalus and Icarus constructed for King Minos to house his fierce, bull-headed Minotaur. Is there a link between that dangerous, animal-headed anthropoid and the weird-looking, animal-headed pantheon of ancient Egypt? If so, what might that link be?

In the great battle between Isis, Osiris, and Horus on the one hand and the evil god Set, or Seth, on the other, Thoth played a major role in guarding and helping the vulnerable Isis during her vitally important pregnancy. Without his protection, Horus would not have been born to avenge his murdered father, and Seth's evil would have triumphed.

Another of Thoth's tasks in Egyptian mythology was to weigh the hearts (in a moral and ethical sense, rather than a physical one) of those who were being judged by Isis and the rest of the pantheon. He was assisted in this task by Mayet (sometimes rendered Ma'at). Like the personification of Wisdom in the biblical Wisdom Literature, Mayet represented cosmic order as opposed to chaos, truth against falsehood, and justice versus injustice. Her father was Ra, the sun-god, and she was invariably associated with Hermes/Thoth, mainly because he was the god of wisdom, writing, language, and learning — indispensable instruments for bringing order and harmony out of chaos. Ma'at had the disconcerting habit of appearing in two places at once in the Judgement Hall, as though she were two distinct goddesses rather than one. It was almost as if she had some sort of doppelganger, which came to assist her in the work of judging and weighing alongside Thoth. The hall where all this took place was called "The Hall of Double Judgement" because of the two figures of Ma'at that were frequently visible there. One theory attempts to explain this double symbolism by suggesting that Ma'at's twinned appearance is intended as a timely but tactful reminder to her judgemental fellow gods that there are two sides to every argument.

Ma'at always travelled in the bows of the sun-god's great ship, her father's great ship, as it glided across both the aerial heavens and the darkness and gloom of the underworld. She was also regarded as the personification of the Order which overcame Chaos at creation. This Egyptian teaching of the primeval battle between Order and Chaos is very close indeed to the opening words of St. John's Gospel, where he describes Jesus as being there with God at the very beginning of creation. In St. John's words: "without Him was not anything made that was made."

Thoth too was closely linked with creation. His city — the "City of Eight" — derived its name from the belief that Thoth called four gods and four goddesses into being in the very beginning: they were the pantheon of eight who gave the city its name.

In a symbolic sense, Ma'at (Order) invariably accompanied each new Pharaoh, whose task it was to bring order, justice, and wisdom to the United Egyptian Kingdom. This again has biblical echoes. It is certainly reminiscent of the Hebrew King Solomon's humble and unselfish prayer for wisdom at the start of his reign so that he would be able to rule his people wisely and well for their benefit rather than for his own.

Like all Egyptian deities, Thoth/Hermes Trismegistus had certain animals which were sacred to him. The ibis and the baboon featured prominently in his cult, and countless mummified specimens of both have turned up in burial grounds at Memphis and Hermopolis. When he himself was shown with a non-human head, it was almost invariably the head of an ibis that surmounted his shoulders.

Hermes Trismegistus is always associated with the mysterious Emerald Tablets. Traditionally, these contain the ancient wisdom which is said to be the source of all power, and of Hermetic philosophy and alchemy.

Hermes was believed to have carved them himself, and placed them in the King's Chamber of the Great Pyramid attributed to the Pharaoh Cheops — but now widely regarded as being much older than his period. Was it, in fact, a huge, ancient, and mysterious structure to which Cheops merely added his name and a few modifications in the hope that posterity would accept it as his work?

Taken at face value alone, the inscriptions on the Emerald Tablets of Hermes Trismegistus purport to be the relatively simple alchemical instructions for preparing the Philosopher's Stone — the magical compound with the power to transmute base metals into gold. But those who have studied alchemy more profoundly are interested in what they believe to be the deeper meaning of Hermes' inscription on the Emerald Tablets. They claim that the change referred in that inscription is something infinitely greater than monetary wealth. According to these alchemical experts, the Philosopher's Stone can change everything for the better.

Just as enzymes act as catalysts in the biological processes of digestion and respiration in a living organism, so, these higher alchemists would claim, the Philosopher's Stone is the magical, universal catalyst through which, in Aristotle's words, "The whole of Nature strives towards Perfection."

According to this higher alchemical theory, the Stone, properly understood, not only changes lead into gold, or water into wine, it changes the whole of life — and our perception of it. With the aid of the stone, human consciousness itself can be enriched and expanded into something totally beyond our present comprehension — very much along the lines of what Gurdjieff taught.

This is the amazing claim made by the Hermeticists about what the Emerald Tablets of Trismegistus can really achieve. If it is that important, we all need to know more about what the fabulous inscription says. We can no longer be certain, of course, at this distance in time, what — if anything — Hermes himself actually carved there, but there are Latin versions going back at least a thousand years. They vary and overlap to some extent, but most of them can be broadly translated as follows:

> All that follows is absolutely true and free of all deception. As above — so below. Everything which is below corresponds to everything which is above. This correspondence is necessary in order to achieve the Miracle of Unification, the Wonder of the One Great Thing. All things have come from the One, through the will, thought, and meditation of the One. All things, both above and below, must naturally follow from this One First Thing.
>
> Its parents are the Sun and Moon. The Wind was carried through its bellows. The Earth provides its nourishment. It is the Parent of everything which is truly perfected and completed throughout the whole Earth. Its strength is demonstrated when it turns towards the Earth. The Earth must be separated from it gently, delicately, and with great skill using the power of Fire.
>
> Rising to Heaven it returns again to Earth, taking its power both from below and from above. This will provide you with the Glory of the Earth, yes, of the whole world. All things will be clear to you, and your understanding will be perfect and complete. Herein is the ultimate Power above all other Power: it can overcome everything fine (i.e. it is so small that it is finer than the finest things, and so can penetrate everywhere). It can pass through all solid matter, however dense and strong it may be. This is how the world was created. By applying this primal pattern great things can be achieved. Therefore my followers call

me Hermes the Thrice Great, the Thrice Powerful, because I understand and control the three Great Wisdoms upon which the whole world depends. Those who understand what I have carved here will know that I have completely explained the Solar Operation.

At first glance, the brutally honest — if somewhat bewildered — response to Hermes' ancient Emerald Tablet Inscription (as broadly translated above) is that it is meaningless, pseudo-mystical Jabberwocky. But if at the basic "lead-into-gold" level the sun is accepted as the symbol for gold, and the moon regarded as the symbol for silver, some sort of basic transmutational process begins to emerge. The reference to the wind in the bellows would seem to suggest a metallurgist's forge where the bellows were essential to raise the temperature sufficiently to melt the metals on which the work was being done. Earth would then refer to the base metals and their ores, which the alchemist was hoping to convert into something much more precious in his bellows-driven furnace. The reference to separating things with great skill and delicacy might mean fractional distillation: a vital part of many modern refining processes. The rising to heaven and descending to earth again gives the impression that a retort is being used to distil something: is it vaporized metal which is being distilled? If it is, how were the necessary temperatures reached and sustained in the primitive forges then available? Unless, of course, our century is badly underestimating the technology and the intelligence of those who compiled and studied the oldest versions of the Hermetic texts millennia ago. The next reference is to the glory of the Earth, which this alchemical knowledge will provide. What does Hermes mean by "the Glory of the Earth"? Bearing in mind the date of the Hermetic Emerald Tablets, their phraseology and innuendo need not be too far away from those used in New Testament times. During Christ's temptations in the wilderness, he was shown all the kingdoms of the world, and told that all of them — and their contents — could be his if he worshipped Satan. The material wealth, power, and luxury of the earthly kingdoms — i.e. their temporal "Glory" — may well have this same meaning for the author of the Hermetic texts. The gold provided by the transmutation process will enable the successful alchemist to buy his or her way to limitless terrestrial power.

If the order of the Emerald Tablet text is followed carefully, it looks as though the promised "completeness of understanding" comes after material wealth and luxury have been acquired. In considering the flowering of ancient Greek philosophical and mathematical thought, it's relevant to remember that the philosophers and mathematicians who achieved it had the luxury of time at their disposal in a way that few of us enjoy today. The tablets may be suggesting that — after the acquisition of sufficient material wealth to buy the luxury of time, the alchemist can devote himself, or herself, to those higher studies which are the true reward of the mysterious art. When the tablets promise "all things will be clear to you" they could be suggesting that total freedom from the financial necessity to-work-in-order-to-live gives the devotee time to study the deeper Hermetic teachings. Material wealth provides the opportunity to study alchemy's philosophical and metaphysical dimensions: its microcosmic-macrocosmic interface — as above, so below — the part of it which sets out to explain the meaning of the cosmos and its curious inter-relationship with humanity.

The tablets then tell of an "ultimate power," something that parallels the secret of creation, the power of turning will into substance, of changing mind into matter. There is a strange force whose very smallness means that it can penetrate everything: nothing can bar its way. Was Hermes Trismegistus explaining sub-atomic theory, the infinitesimal world of quarks and neutrinos, electrons and protons, millennia before contemporary nuclear physics began tentatively to explore it? Were the closely guarded inner secrets of Atlantean science on those Emerald Tablets? Were they nuclear secrets — and do they still lie buried beneath the ice-sheets of Antarctica?

The tablets refer to three Great Wisdoms, and relate them to the triple power and triune nature of Hermes. What might they be? If the secrets of the tablets are being decoded correctly, then the first secret is the secret of material wealth. The Hermeticists understood well enough that there is insufficient time for essential study, personal development and contemplation if a person's energies are largely absorbed by the necessity of working-in-order-to-live. So they believed that at its shallowest, most superficial level alchemy provided the wealth that bought freedom and time for thought and study. The second secret seems to have been the integration of humanity and the greater universe: the vital role of the observer-controller in the wonders of the cosmos: "as above — so below." It is in this second area that the power of mind over matter, of will over substance, comes into its own. This is the domain of magicians and shamans, wizards and witches, wonder-workers and thaumaturgists of every kind. This is the dynamic, mental crucible from which incandescent, molten miracles are poured into the physical world.

If the tablets have been correctly interpreted and decoded, the third zone houses the proto-nuclear and proto-sub-nuclear mysteries. Here dwells the quintessential enigma which seems to lie at the innermost heart of Hermeticism: the secret power that pervades and penetrates all material objects because of its incredibly minute size.

The first secret looks like being the key to the counting house, the provision of wealth so that the alchemist can proceed to what is really important. Having obtained her freedom using this first key, the Hermeticist can study and meditate in order to understand and utilise the power of mind over matter — what Paracelsus, Dr. Dee, Crowley, and even Tesla would have recognized as the secret at the heart of any effective magic. The third enigma which seems to be translated from the inscriptions on the Emerald Tablets is apparently a reference to the ability to access the dynamism within the atom. This is what the Hermeticists would apparently regard as that alleged secret power which dwells in "particles so fine" that they can dance through the energy shells surrounding an atomic nucleus, or leap triumphantly upon that nucleus itself — as a mountaineer stands upon a peak she has just conquered.

G.R.S. Mead was a scholarly theosophist who actually knew Madam Blavatsky. His writings on Hermes Trismegistus include the intriguing idea that certain important truths and ancient secrets are not learnt, neither can they be researched in any normal way: they are already buried in the deepest strata of the subconscious and simply *remembered* by the enlightened few in moments of higher consciousness.

There is, of course, another, totally different theory about the Emerald Tablets, which regards the crystals themselves, rather than their inscriptions, as the centre of the Trismegistus mystery. Perhaps, like Pentium processor chips, or CD-roms, discs, and tapes where vast amounts of information are stored, the real Hermetic secrets are preserved within the emerald crystals themselves. It has been conjectured that the crystals take the form of a rectangular base-board into which smaller crystals can be slotted and arranged in distinct configurations to produce varying patterns which in turn project distinct and divergent forms of energy. This crystal energy is then said to be able to affect both the operator and the material objects which he, or she, is trying to influence, forming a dynamic interface between the operator and the cosmos — "as above — so below."

A further very speculative development of the theory suggests that the use of this emerald crystal power was known in Egypt at the time of the Jewish Exodus. When Moses led his people out, having privileged access to Egyptian secrets through his adopted mother, he took the priceless Emerald Tablets with him. According to this theory, the discovery that they were missing was believed to have prompted Pharaoh to launch his charioteers suicidally across the treacherous bed of either the Red Sea, or the Sea of Reeds. It was further speculated that the Emerald Tablets were perhaps stored in the Ark of the Covenant and accounted for some of the miracles associated with it. They might also have been the mysterious Urim and

Thummim — the stones of divination which were used by the early High Priests to ascertain the will of Yahweh.

After many vicissitudes, the Emerald Tablets were allegedly hidden below Solomon's Temple in Jerusalem, where they were found in the Middle Ages by the Knights Templar, and became an important factor in the Templars' spectacular rise to power and their many military triumphs. When Philip IV attacked the Templars in 1307, the precious Emerald tablets were said to have been spirited away to Sinclair's Orkney Kingdom, where refugee Templars were welcomed and protected. It was also believed that the Tablets were taken for safety to Nova Scotia by Sinclair and the surviving Templars, where they were concealed below the amazing system of shafts and flood tunnels on Oak Island, near Chester in Mahone Bay.

Wherever they come from — the stars, the subconscious, or the delusions of bygone ages — the secrets of Hermes Trismegistus and his legendary Emerald Tablets are well worth further study.

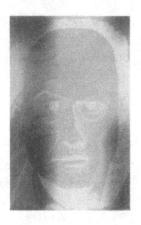

Chapter 20

Wilhelm Reich: Tantraism, Taoism, and Orgone Energy

Wilhelm Reich was born in Galicia in 1897. He died, hated and reviled, in Lewisburg Prison, Pennsylvania, on November 3, 1957. He was, arguably, one of the most tragically misunderstood men who ever lived. What went wrong for a man who had started out as a brilliant, pioneering psychologist, and who might — with a bit more luck — have ended up in the Social Scientists' Hall of Fame alongside Jung, Freud, Pavlov, Skinner, and Malinowski?

Reich had a traumatic childhood. As a precocious twelve-year-old, the son of wealthy parents, he discovered that Mrs. Reich was having an extramarital affair. Wilhelm told his father. His mother promptly committed suicide. A few years later, his father died the same way. The effect this must have had on the boy's mind can only be guessed at.

Nevertheless, Wilhelm graduated from Technical High School in 1915 with top grades in all subjects.

Perhaps it was a desperate search for stability and order in a universe that had dealt him two devastating emotional blows which motivated Wilhelm to consider a military career. He served in the Austrian army on the Italian front and rose to the rank of lieutenant. After demobilization, he studied medicine in Vienna. Former soldiers were given the privilege of completing the six-year course in four years, which meant a great deal of pressure and extra work. Reich handled this with no problems. It wasn't long before he joined the Psychoanalytical Society there, and became one of Freud's outstanding pupils. By the age of twenty-two, young Reich had already decided that human sexuality was the great driving force behind all individual and social behaviour. In reaching that decision Wilhelm was not only carrying Freud's well-known concept of the libido a stage further, he was updating and Europeanizing the far older teachings of the Tantrists and Taoists.

There is rather more to Tantraism than what its opponents and persecutors condemn as its sexual excesses. The original word in Sanskrit simply meant part of a woven design, like the warp and weft on a loom. Tantrists see life as a set of spiritual aspirations through which physical things — including sexual activity — are woven.

Their great mother goddess, Shakti, is regarded in much the same way as Palaeolithic peoples thought of the Earth Mother. Her consort is the god Shiva, and the two of them represent the opposite polarities on which the entire universe rests. Two of the most positive and acceptable aspects of Tantraism are the absence of the caste system, and the equal social status of men and women.

Tantraism teaches that there are seven energy zones, called *chakras*, within the human body. They're located in positions ranging upwards from the base of the spine to the head. Stated in its briefest and most basic form, the Tantrist endeavours to unite the lowest chakra, known as kundalini, a symbolic snake representing the goddess Shakti, with the highest chakra, called sahasrara — symbolized as a lotus with a thousand petals situated in the highest part of the head. When kundalini reaches sahasrara, the god and goddess, Shiva and Shakti, are united, and the Tantric worshipper who has achieved this goal is in tune with the balanced powers of the universe. In theory at least, such a fulfilled worshipper should be able to operate successfully (to work magic) on any part of the universe, or on any living thing within it — including the operator's own physical body.

The ancient Chinese Taoist beliefs are strangely similar in some ways. They are concerned with balancing *yin*, the feminine principle, with *yang*, the masculine one. Like the Tantrists, Taoists used sexual techniques to achieve this balance at the basic, physical level — but they also developed a much more advanced system which can best be described as a form of "internal alchemy." Where the Tantrists attempted to move kundalini from the lowest of seven chakras to sahasrara, the highest, the Taoist topography of the human body consisted of just three divisions. Based on their interest in alchemy, the Taoists saw the body itself as a kind of alchemical laboratory, or workshop. At the lowest level of the central column was a forge, or furnace, sometimes depicted as a cauldron. This has strange echoes of the magical cauldron of the Celts with the power to restore life to the dead — because the Taoists were also vitally concerned with immortality and the alchemical Elixir of Life.

The lowest Taoist crucible contains raw, primitive, and immensely powerful sexual energy known as *ching*. Taoists regard it as situated in the lower part of the abdomen. Above ching, in the central furnace located behind the solar plexus, just below the thorax, is *chi'ai*. Difficult to describe and explain, this same chi'ai energy is an integral part of several advanced martial arts systems. It's a type of kinetic dynamism, or vital movement energy. It takes the martial artist's hand through wood or stone. It strikes an opponent like a lightning bolt — over and above the ordinary physical momentum of the blow.

In the highest fire-chamber of the three, glows *shen*. This is the true personality, the soul, the sentient awareness of self and being: it is both luminous and illuminating, an incandescent spiritual entity.

Taoists aim to combine the three forms of energy into something new: *ching-chi'ai-shen*. During this supposed mystical union, there is a physical counterpart during which blood and other bodily fluids flow. One medieval Taoist described it as "the marriage of the dragon and the tiger from which an immortal being is born." Alchemically, he regarded the dragon as mercury and the tiger as lead: which is particularly interesting in view of the Taoist fascination with the bright red mineral known as cinnabar, symbolizing blood. Cinnabar is actually mercuric sulphide (HgS) which occurs naturally. It can be produced in the laboratory by passing sulphuretted hydrogen through a solution of any mercuric salt. Subliming the black precipitate formed by that reaction produces the familiar blood-red vermilion pigment. Subliming a simple mixture of mercury and sulphur has the same effect — but as they say on responsible TV shows: "Don't try this at home!"

There can be little doubt that these processes were frequently repeated in Taoist and other early alchemical workshops. In consequence, many alchemists shortened their lives significantly instead of achieving the longevity they sought via the elixir. The dangers of working with mercury vapour were only dimly understood, but more than one dying alchemist had enough sense to recognize the correlation between his work and his terminal illness, and to leave notes warning his successors of the hazards of the craft.

There are significant parallels between Wilhelm Reich's 1957 tragedy in Lewisburg and the deaths of some of the early alchemists: in particular, his apparent failure to understand the medical consequences of exposure to radium runs alongside their failure to understand the consequences of exposure to mercury vapour.

173

Reich graduated as an MD from the University of Vienna's medical school in 1922, then worked as a lecturer, writer, and administrator in various psychoanalytical organizations. Until 1930 he was an active member of the Socialist Party in Austria. Then he quarrelled with them, moved to Berlin, met Arthur Koestler, and joined the Communist Party. At one time the two men served in the same party cell. Many years afterwards, Koestler recalled a book which Reich had written. It was entitled *The Function of the Orgasm*. Wilhelm had based it in part on the research that Bronislaw Malinowski, the great social anthropologist, had recently done.

In order to understand Reich better, it is necessary to examine some of the formative influences which helped to mould the man. Malinowski's powerful intellect and highly respected anthropological research made a big impact on Reich during the inter-war years in Berlin.

Malinowski himself was born in Krakow, Poland, on April 7, 1884. He never enjoyed robust health and died on May 16, 1942, when he was only fifty-eight. His father was Professor of Slavic Philology at Krakow's Jagiellonian University, and his mother was also an expert in languages.

Malinowski achieved his doctorate in 1908, and was at that stage primarily a philosopher, physicist, and mathematician. An important formative influence on him was Frazer's *Golden Bough*, which triggered his interest in religion, magic, and anthropology. Malinowski carried out important research among the Mailu people in New Guinea, and then in the Trobriand Islands. All the time his research results were shepherding him closer to the widely respected sociological theory of functionalism, which is a fitting academic memorial to him. In essence, Malinowski's central idea was that in all types of civilization, every custom, idea, belief, and material object had to perform a function which was important to that society.

Malinowski's books on the sexual behaviour of the Melanesians and other cultures he had studied were published in 1927 and 1929. They were two of the launching pads for Reich's own later theories. As a Freudian-Marxist, Reich founded a group which became known as — Sex-Pol — the Institute for Sexual Politics. In *The Function of the Orgasm*, Reich outlined his theory that the problems of the Proletariat were mainly caused by sexual frustration, and that only when they overcame this would they be able to organize a successful revolution.

The Kremlin wasn't impressed. Apparently Reich's work wasn't sufficiently Marxist to impress Stalin and his minions. Frustrated and disappointed, Reich left the Communist Party. By 1934 he had quarrelled with Freud as well. He left the International Psychoanalytical Association: he could no longer accurately be described as a Freudian-Marxist. But what was he?

Wilhelm Reich: Tantraism, Taoism, and Orgone Energy

One of his books contained a searing attack on Fascism and Nazism, which he regarded as the sadistic projection of neurotics who were sexually repressed. When Hitler came to power in Germany, Reich left. Travelling by way of Sweden, Denmark, and Norway, Reich reached the United States in 1939 and worked as an associate professor in Manhattan at the New School of Social Research. He acquired a publishing interest in Greenwich Village and issued English translations of his books. He also set up his Orgone Institute in Forest Hills, Long Island. Another of his establishments — the Orgone Energy Observatory — was opened at Orgonon near Rangeley in Maine.

From his original, semi-Freudian, psychoanalytical theories about sexual inhibitions and repression and the importance of the orgasm, Reich expanded his Orgone concept until it became bio-chemical and cosmological. It would be difficult to establish the precise point in his theorizing when it slipped over the razor-edged crest of brilliant, imaginative thinking and became farcically obsessive instead. It was as if a man riding a maverick idea had been galloping towards what looked to him like a fascinating, exciting, and worthwhile objective, but had failed totally to see that he was in reality thundering towards the edge of an intellectual precipice with jagged boulders at the bottom. The smash when it came was reminiscent of the *Titanic* ripping herself open on the fatal iceberg.

Once Reich left psychoanalysis for biochemistry and physics, he was exposed to the merciless and deadly accurate criticism of hard scientists who believed in gathering data, then creating and testing hypotheses and demanding that any experiment which a colleague conducted could be repeated objectively in another laboratory. For something allegedly so powerful and all-pervasive, Orgone energy was surprisingly shy.

Reich claimed, for example, that in such unlikely substances as sterilized soot he had observed things that he described as "bions." In his opinion these bions were energy vesicles — halfway between living and non-living matter. Reich was convinced that they would turn into protozoa (simple but genuinely living single-celled organisms) in favourable circumstances. Any serious biologists who were shown his microscopic photographs of these bions were equally convinced that there was nothing to them at all: they were merely tiny pieces of inorganic matter whose apparent "movements" were easily explained by perfectly natural and well-understood physical causes.

Reich was especially keen on what he described as radiating bions. In 1939 he thought he had actually created these "sapabions" from ordinary beach sand which had been thoroughly sterilized first. He concocted the prefix "sapa" from the first two letters of *sa*nd and *pa*cket. Not surprisingly, no established micro-biologists went along with Reich's conclusions about his supposed sapabions. What strange radiation were these minute quasi-creatures giving off? Reich soon had an answer for that. It was some hitherto undetected form of cosmic energy — and it was the most important thing yet discovered, he thought. For him, it was the basic force behind the universe. It was the Taoist mystery of the perfectly combined *yin* and *yang*. It was the long, difficult, Tantric climb through the seven chakras until kundalini was eternally united with sahasrara. Reich called it Orgone energy and life for him was never to be the same again.

He was so enthusiastic about his miraculous discovery that everything else now had a far lower priority. Orgone energy ruled Reich's world, and impertinent intruders such as logic, reason, empirical tests, and common sense were no longer welcome there. He and his staff began building Orgone energy accumulators. Reich had decided that this new energy he had discovered was blue. He used his theories to explain the blueness of the sky, and the heavy metallic, greyish-blue of thunder clouds. His Orgone energy accumulators looked rather like old-fashioned army sentry-boxes — but with seats in them. They were built from alternating layers of organic and non-organic materials, a structure which Reich believed would greatly increase their power. Volunteers (often patients) would sit inside these strange little multi-layered cabinets which vaguely resembled outhouses or Victorian bathing machines at British seaside resorts. The abundant literature which Reich disseminated at this time suggested that the Orgone energy generated and amplified in the boxes would cure a vast range of diseases — several of them fatal, and incurable by orthodox medicine.

Reich believed that Orgone energy could be combined with radiation from radium to create something even more powerful. He was working on various theories to the effect that the benign, creative influence of Orgone could neutralize the morbid effects of nuclear radiation from atomic bombs. In January of 1951, he set up his ORANUR project. The acrostic was formed from "Orgonomic Anti-Nuclear Radiation." Having acquired lethal quantities of radium, Reich introduced it to one of his Orgone rooms. Geiger counters reacted dementedly. Project workers became seriously ill. Buildings at the centre had to be closed down. Reich decided that the problem was being caused by DOR (Deadly Orgone Radiation).

Another of his controversial inventions was an orgonomic cloud-buster device, which he believed aimed a stream of Orgone energy at clouds and dispersed them.

He was also keenly interested in UFOs, and, needless to say, developed a theory that some models at least were Orgone-powered. Earth, he theorized, was at the centre of a huge space battle between benign forces who were replacing our vital Orgone and bad guys who were stealing it.

Wilhelm Reich: Tantraism, Taoism, and Orgone Energy

Because of the medical claims made for the therapeutic powers of Reich's Orgone energy accumulators he inevitably came into conflict with the FDA (the United States' Food and Drug Administration) who decided against Reich's claims about Orgone. He was technically jailed for contempt of court when he refused to discontinue his work.

After his death in prison one of his devoted followers used to dress in Orgone blue and sit in semi-darkness for lengthy periods trying to contact Reich's spirit with a ouija board.

Reich was undoubtedly a mystery. Whatever else he was, he was not a charlatan in the sense of being a deliberate cheat or fraudster. He genuinely believed in his own theories — however improbable they seemed to others, and however difficult they were to support with acceptable, objective proof. Orthodox science generally dismisses Reich's Orgone energy, but a few lingering doubts remain. His fanatical enthusiasm for his work may have blinded his once powerful intellect to its obvious failures and misconceptions — but if there is one nugget of truth hidden below the fallacies, it's worth digging out. Some of what he said merits the courtesy of re-examination, and the man himself undoubtedly deserves a little more human sympathy than he has received so far.

Chapter 21

Francis Bacon

"What is truth?" said jesting Pilate; and would not stay for an answer. (From Bacon's Essay on Truth)

The mystery of Francis Bacon begins with his birth itself. It has frequently been suggested that he was the secret child of Queen Elizabeth I — and that theory cannot be lightly dismissed. According to this scenario, the unsavoury Lord Robert Dudley, Earl of Leicester, arranged for the murder of his wife, Amy Robsart, in 1560. He was said to have been Queen Elizabeth's lover for some time before that, and it was alleged that he married her secretly as soon as Amy was dead. Elizabeth was supposedly already pregnant when this clandestine royal wedding took place in the home of Lord Pembroke. The strictly exclusive, high-security guest list included Sir Nicholas Bacon, the Lord Keeper, and his second wife, Anne Cooke, who was Chief-Lady-in-Waiting to Elizabeth. Anne was the daughter of Edward VI's tutor, and her sister was married to William Cecil, the Lord Treasurer. These supposed conspirators were a decidedly well connected, politically powerful, wealthy, and influential group.

The plan was that Anne Bacon would simulate a well publicized pregnancy, while the Queen would do everything possible to keep her real one concealed. When her majesty was "indisposed" for a few days around

Was Francis Bacon the secret son of Queen Elizabeth I? If so, who was his father — Essex, or the dashing young Sir Francis Drake?

January 22, 1561, the new-born Francis was smuggled out of the palace with Anne, who promptly announced that she had just given birth to him in private at her home in York House. Elizabeth, with characteristic toughness, got back on her feet as quickly as possible, and carried on as if nothing had happened.

Dudley's character is the weakest part of this hypothesis. He was the fifth son of John Dudley, Duke of Northumberland, who had been virtually running the country during the latter part of the short life of the boy-king, Edward VI. The failure of the conspiracy to get Lady Jane Grey on the throne after Edward's death saw Robert Dudley imprisoned in the Tower. However, as soon as Elizabeth I came to power in 1558, his career took off. Conventional history records that despite all his anxious endeavours to marry Elizabeth, she not only rejected him, but actually recommended that he should marry Mary Queen of Scots instead. By 1571 he was having a protracted affair with Lady Sheffield, but discarded her in 1578 and married Lettice Knollys, who had previously been the wife of Walter Devereux, Earl of Essex.

In 1585, Dudley made a hopeless mess of commanding the six- or seven-thousand-strong force which the Queen had sent to Holland in his charge. In 1588, Elizabeth, who never quite seemed to reconcile her otherwise shrewd judgement with Dudley's manifest incompetence, appointed him as lieutenant-general of the land forces massing to resist the Armada at Tilbury — if it got that far. It was fortunate for England that Drake and his incomparable seamen deprived Dudley of the opportunity of staging yet another of his embarrassing debacles.

Francis bore little or no physical resemblance to his alleged father, Sir Nicholas Bacon, but he did resemble Dudley, as can be seen from Leicester's portrait among Hilliard's miniatures. As a boy, although Francis had no official position and no formal title, he was always welcome at Elizabeth's court. When old Sir Nicholas died in 1579, he did not provide for Francis in his will: was he assuming that the Queen would provide for her son? When young Francis went to Cambridge, he didn't attend Sir Nicholas's old college, Corpus Christi, which would have been usual, but went instead to Trinity — founded by Elizabeth's father, Henry VIII. Was Francis attending the college his grandfather had established?

If Francis Bacon was Elizabeth's son, not Anne's, was Dudley the father? There is another possibility. Some minor doubts exist about Drake's precise date of birth. Generally reckoned to be 1544, there is a slim possibility that it was as early as 1540 — which would have made him a lusty young twenty-year-old when Francis Bacon was conceived. If Dudley was ostensibly Elizabeth's effete, courtly favourite, Drake was undeniably her awesome, swashbuckling, privateer-adventurer friend. If the dominantly charismatic Elizabeth had ever succumbed to an illicit lover, he would have been an ebullient, macho man like Drake — not a bumbling incompetent like Dudley, no matter how well his good looks and gentility camouflaged his failures.

The theory that Francis was Elizabeth's son is further strengthened by the fanatical Protestantism of the Bacons. The mid-sixteenth-century was a period of agonizing religious controversy and sectarian hatred. Sir Nicholas and Lady Anne would have realized better than most that if the truth about Elizabeth's son had become public knowledge it would have rocked the throne. To Protestants as obsessive as they were, anything would have been preferable to the risk of a Catholic monarch replacing Elizabeth — so they loyally played out their charade, and the Queen's secret child grew up as the son of Nicholas and Anne.

As a young man Francis became interested in psychic phenomena, as well as in science and philosophy. Macaulay's *Essay on Bacon*, written in 1837, records how Francis examined a strange old vault in St. James's Park because there was an unusual echo in it. He also paid very careful attention to the performances of travelling conjurors and jugglers to try to determine whether they just used skillful trickery, or whether there was anything genuinely paranormal about their displays.

In 1573, Francis and Anthony (who was ostensibly his younger brother) went to Cambridge together. They studied at Trinity under the celebrated Dr. Whitgift, who was later to become Archbishop of Canterbury. At that time there was bitter, chronic, and rancorous theological controversy between Whitgift on one side and Cartwright's Calvinists on the other. Francis became a highly critical participant observer of the weaknesses of sixteenth-century academia. In *The Advancement of Learning* he complains with acerbity that the "excellent liquor" of knowledge is spoilt by the constant bickering of those who should be leading the university's teaching and research. He was sickened and repelled by their narrow Aristotelian framework, and the prodigal ways in which gifted minds wasted their time with trivia. Had Bacon lived four centuries later it would have seemed to him as if Einstein and Newton were working out the millionth decimal place of π to amuse themselves instead of working on gravity and relativity.

When Francis left Cambridge he became a member of Gray's Inn, which was then as much a training ground for Elizabethan courtiers and politicians as it was for learned advocates. A trip to France with Sir Amyas Paulet interrupted Bacon's work at Gray's, and according to some chroniclers it was on this trip that the secret of his true identity was revealed to him. Amyas was the newly appointed ambassador to France, and, as such, had many knowledgeable and observant friends in high places. Someone in the know might have informed him deliberately and told him to pass the information on to Francis, or it might simply have slipped out over too many glasses of Amontillado. Conversely, it could well have been one of Bacon's rivals who was circulating a complete fabrication in the hope that Bacon would be foolish enough to believe it and — even more foolishly — try to do something about it. This French visit went on until 1579, but Francis went back again in 1582.

His younger "brother" Anthony, however, was there for considerably longer and seems to have had an intriguing role as a sixteenth century espionage agent. He suffered from gout and chronic lung disease, but despite his infirmities he was a sensitive, intelligent, rather suspicious man, with a great deal of natural curiosity about what was going on around him and what it might mean. That creates an interesting parallel between Francis Bacon and Fouquet, the immensely powerful finance minister of Louis XIV of a later century. Each had a younger brother who worked undercover and kept a low profile, and each rose to great political heights and then fell again.

Ben Jonson, one of Bacon's many friends and admirers, and a man who knew him better than most, wrote of him: "Thou standst as though a mystery thou didst."

One of the greatest mysteries about Bacon was the seemingly irreconcilable mixture of contradictory opinions about him. The versatile and studious Mrs. Henry Pott, who founded the Francis Bacon Society in December 1885, collected and expounded on these comments at great length in her *Francis Bacon and his Secret Society*, published in 1895. She quotes Macaulay and Pope, who both testify to Bacon's meanness, but immediately balances their words against those of Baconian experts like Professor Fowler and Dr. Abbot who praise his open-hearted generosity. Campbell regarded him as a servile flatterer, as did Sortain. Spedding testifies that he was one of the few courtiers who would never stoop to servile flattery. Macaulay, Campbell, and Sortain accuse Bacon of being a selfish, intriguing, money-loving opportunist. Montagu, Dixon, and Storr all say that he was generous to a fault, and never cared about money, place or pomp for their own sakes. In one of his own essays, Bacon writes: "Money is like manure — no good unless it is spread."

Macaulay and Abbott both argued that Bacon's quest for wealth, power and fame was highly successful. Dr. Rawley in his *Life of Bacon* says equally clearly that it was not. Campbell, Devey, and Macaulay accuse him of marrying for money. Spedding and Hepworth Dixon both testify that he gave his bride double the amount of her dowry in return. Abbott regarded Bacon's pliable and conciliatory approach as a serious weakness.

Sir Tobie Matthew and Dr. Rawley both praise Bacon's patient, conciliatory personal style as an excellent and admirable characteristic — especially in so powerful a statesman. Macaulay, Campbell, and Storr detest his self-confidence and optimism. Storr, for example, refers to Bacon's "overweening self-confidence" as something abominable. Spedding counters this by describing Bacon as "hopeful, sensible, and amiable ... glowing with noble aspirations."

Abbott assessed Bacon as cold, calculating, and incapable of any really strong affection. Spedding described him as a sensitive man who felt kindness and its opposite very acutely. Campbell noted coldly that anything Bacon said about himself was not to be trusted. Abbott recognized that Bacon "committed his defects and infirmities to paper" with great frankness. Macaulay concluded that Bacon was only prepared to defend and assist his old friend Essex as long as it brought no harm his way. Montagu and Matthew both regarded him as staunch and loyal. Abbott sums him up as unloved, unloving and very short of friends. John Aubrey testifies that "all who were good and great loved and honoured him." Abbott says Bacon had no great feelings of sympathy or kindness towards birds or animals. Dixon describes his love of them, and there is a clear account of Bacon's giving five shillings to a washerwoman who rescued a bird from the Thames.

Carvalho's article in the *New York Herald* of October 5, 1874, says that Bacon knew little or nothing of human nature. Spedding and Dr. Sprat both regard him as a definitive expert on it. Campbell accused him of lacking boldness and moral courage: Hepworth Dixon evaluated him as politically bold and independent in matters which he felt were important. Craik and Rawley criticized him for having no sense of humour. Ben Jonson and Tobie Matthew both declared Bacon was one of the wittiest humorists they'd ever met. Fowler says he was not a truly religious man in any sense: Rawley says he was.

What is particularly significant about this selection of comments on his character is that friend and foe, supporter and detractor alike, frequently recognized similar characteristics in Bacon, but evaluated them as positive or negative depending upon each critic's overall assessment of his subject. Much the same thing happens in modern political exchanges: a good speaker on our side is described as a "great orator," or is said to be "fluent, convincing, and a formidable speaker." If she's on their side, she's only a "windbag," she's "got the gift of the gab" or she suffers from "prolixity."

Aesop's fable of the father and son with the donkey also sheds light on the widely varying judgements made on Bacon. Having bought the donkey, the men were leading it away from the market when someone commented that they were fools not to ride it. The son then got on its back. The next bystander said he was a selfish, lazy boy and he should allow his father to ride while he walked. They changed places. An onlooker commented that the poor, tired boy should be riding as well. He got up behind his father. The overloaded donkey began to stagger. This attracted the criticism that two great sturdy men like them should carry the poor little beast instead of forcing it to carry them. They attempted it. The inverted donkey fell off their improvised shoulder pole into a river and drowned. Aesop's meaning is clear. If Bacon had been aware of all that his critics had said, and had attempted to heed their advice, he could well have gone the same way as Aesop's hapless donkey.

Did Bacon write the plays and poems attributed to William Shakespeare? Like the comments on Bacon's character, the evidence is not only mixed but often contradictory. If he was the secret son of Queen Elizabeth I — and knew that he was — he would have had sound reasons for anonymity during the stormy and unpredictable years through which he lived. The Elizabethan court did not have much regard for poets, playwrights, or actors, and, accordingly, members of the court who had talents in those directions preferred to exercise them anonymously. There is also evidence that Bacon was a Rosicrucian and/or a Freemason, and one of the Rosicrucian rules insisted on an author's anonymity for at least a century. There's also the matter of the mysterious "Promus," which was Bacon's personal notebook. It contains a mass of words, phrases, similes, metaphors, proverbs, aphorisms, and colloquialisms which he seemed to think would come in handy one day when he was writing. Even in this age of the Internet and the word processor, many professional writers still rely on such note books.

The word "promus" actually means a storehouse, a large walk-in cupboard, a closet, a place where a miscellany of things can be kept safely until needed. Bacon's store contained two thousand entries in Latin, Greek, Spanish, German, English, French, and Italian. His own handwritten original is now in the British Museum, and appears to cover a period from 1594 to 1596. The indefatigable and painstaking Baconian scholar Mrs. Henry Pott published a copy in 1883. She also went to great lengths to provide examples of entries from the Promus that also appeared in Shakespeare's plays and poems. Because the Promus was a private notebook that was never intended for publication, it was practically unknown for over two centuries.

What does seem to be significant is that Bacon made little or no use of the ideas he had preserved in the Promus in any of the many works which he published under his own name: but example after example from the Promus *can* be found in the plays and poems attributed to William Shakespeare. Scholars who argue that William Shakespeare, the Bard of Avon, *was* the author of the works that bear his name, attempt to refute this Baconian argument by saying that the Promus merely contained common sixteenth-century material that would have been well known to both men. What they fail to explain is why anyone — least of all a man with Bacon's intellect — would bother to write down words and phrases that were already well known to him and his contemporaries.

What the Baconians argue is that there are so many examples of material from the Promus appearing in texts attributed to William Shakespeare, and that whoever wrote those works must have had access to the Promus. They pursue the argument by saying that William would not have had access to Francis's private notebook, so Francis must have written the Shakespearean material.

One of the most telling examples from the Promus is the Spanish word *albada*, which means "good dawning." As far as is known, the phrase occurs only once in any English play or novel. Its sole appearance is in Shakespeare in *King Lear:* "Good dawning to thee, friend" (Act II, Scene ii). The play was not published until well after the Promus had been compiled, and as far as is known, Shakespeare did not speak Spanish.

Another large segment of the Promus that apparently links it to Shakespeare's works, is the whole list of greetings which Bacon collected: good morrow; good soir; bonjour; good matin; and good day. When *Romeo and Juliet* appeared a year or so after the Promus entries were recorded, it contained several of these greetings — and so did a number of Shakespeare's later works. Mrs. Henry Pott analyzed them statistically and found:

"Good morrow" — 115 times;

"Good day" — 15 times;

"Good soir (evening)" — 12 times.

Other strange verbal coincidences between the Promus and the plays include: "To drive out a nail with a nail," in *Coriolanus* Act IV Scene vii; "A fool's bolt is soon shot," in *Henry V*, Act III, Scene vii; "Good wine needs no bush," in *As You Like It* (Epilogue). Wine-sellers traditionally had a bush as a sign outside their shops or taverns, just as barbers, boot-sellers, and pawnbrokers had characteristic trading signs to advertise their wares. The meaning of the aphorism is that the best products soon get known by word of mouth and need no sign to advertise them.

The *Manes Verulamiani* are an anthology of Latin poems written as obituaries to Bacon after April 9, 1626. Some of them contain the same words as were used on the Shakespeare monument in the church at Stratford. One, in particular, praises Bacon for his tragedies and comedies.

Francis Bacon lived at Gorhambury, less than three miles from St. Albans, where the White Hart Inn contains an amazing mural dating from about 1600. One theory is that it was specially commissioned for a Rosicrucian chapter meeting held in that room, and Bacon was believed to have been the leader of the English Rosicrucians at that time. It shows detailed scenes from *Venus and Adonis*, which was published in 1593. Leading historian and art expert Dr. Clive Rouse is on record as saying that this unique painting is of major importance. Adonis is a sun symbol, and the boar in the picture represents winter. There is also a boar (a visual pun on "bacon") in Bacon's crest. The house in the picture resembles Bacon's Gorhambury home in several respects, and the hill in the picture may be meant to represent Bacon's Mount, which Francis used as an observatory. It rises in Prae Wood, about a mile from Gorhambury itself. One of the horses in the mural appears to be carrying a red rose in its mouth. The rose is naturally one of the signs recognized by Rosicrucians as a symbol of their order, but it also ties in with the legend of Adonis and the boar.

The story tells how Venus was accidentally wounded by one of her son Cupid's arrows while they were playing together. As a result, the goddess fell in love with Adonis, a handsome young huntsman. Venus was so afraid that something dangerous would kill Adonis that she warned him never to hunt anything dangerous — especially the bear or the boar. "Be brave towards the timid," she said. "Courage against the courageous is not safe." Not surprisingly he ignored her cowardly advice and went in pursuit of a huge wild boar. He wounded it in the side, but the fearless and ferocious beast dragged out his spear with its teeth and charged unerringly towards him. Its huge tusks ripped the boy open, and he died in a welter of blood. Venus flew down and wept over her young lover's corpse, mingling nectar with his blood, until a blood-red flower grew in the place where he had died. This was said to have been an anemone in the original story, but in other versions it becomes the pheasant's eye (known in French as the *goute-de-sang*), the scarlet field-poppy, or the *rose*.

Another significant detail of this White Hart mural is the stump of a hollow tree, split as though by lightning at the base. There are Baconian scholars who associate this detail with *The Tempest*. Sycorax, the evil mother of Caliban the half-monster, had imprisoned the benign but mischievous spirit Ariel inside a cloven pine: Prospero, the master magician, reminds Ariel that it was his art which had freed him from the trap. Is this really a Rosicrucian mural? And is it trying to tell us that Bacon was not only the author of *The Tempest* but that he sees himself symbolically as Prospero? If Francis saw himself as Elizabeth's son, the rightful heir to the throne, and the future King Francis I, he would have sympathized wholeheartedly with Prospero, whose Dukedom had been usurped by his scheming, duplicitous brother — whom he had always treated well.

This raises the new question of *ingratitude* as a further clue to the possible Baconian authorship. Passage after passage in the works attributed to Shakespeare complains poignantly about ingratitude. Yet what did William Shakespeare have to complain of compared to what Bacon had to complain of? Robbed of his kingdom as Hamlet had been? Promoted and favoured, but never enough to match what he considered to be his true rank? Unjustly accused and wrongfully imprisoned? And what was it that Bacon thought that he had done to deserve generous gratitude? Was it that he had kept his royal birth a secret, first for his mother's sake — as long as she lived — and then for the sake of King James?

Baconians believe that further important clues to support their case can be found in the famous Northumberland Manuscript. This was said to have been discovered in 1867 in Northumberland House, and is now reported to be in Alnwick Castle. It comprises a manuscript folder in which Bacon's name appears alongside Shakespeare's. The manuscript is also interesting because of the odd little squiggle — rather like a tadpole — which some researchers have suggested is a representation of the hand mirror used by

Pallas Athena, or Minerva, the goddess of wisdom. This same hand mirror shape might also be meant to represent a symbolic, Rosicrucian rose insinuating its way into Bacon's story once more. It was a mirror which was used to slay the dreaded Gorgon; that is, to overcome an evil entity and then use its severed head — as Perseus did — to accomplish better things. Bacon's symbolism often involved the image of a mirror, and the importance of reflection — especially in *The Advancement of Learning*. In Bacon's writings, King Solomon the Wise (a vital figure in Freemasonry) was credited with putting forward the idea that God had formed the human mind like a mirror so that it was capable of reflecting all the wonders and mysteries of the universe.

In Greek mythology, Pallas Athena had no mother, but had sprung armed with her spear, straight from the head of her father, Jupiter. This symbolic springing from the god's head — from his creative mind, perhaps — carried within it the essential core of the theory of magic. Paracelsus, Crowley, John Dee, Blavatsky, and other classical magicians would have acknowledged the principle that a magician's thoughts possessed creative energy, and that — given the right conditions — such creative energy could find expression in the world of matter.

Pallas Athena's bird of wisdom was the owl, her sacred tree the olive. Pallas, according to Brewer, comes from a root word meaning to brandish, or shake — so Minerva brandishing her spear could easily be a coded allusion to shaking-a-spear or *Shakespeare*.

There is a polysyllabic giant of a word "honorificabilitudinitatibus" in *Love's Labour's Lost*. In Latin it can be hammered into an awkward anagram: "hi ludi F. Baconis nati tuiti orbi" which translates broadly as: "These plays, the children of F. Bacon (or born from F. Bacon) are kept safely (stored, or preserved) for the world."

Letters from Bacon to King James and the Duke of Buckingham in 1622 and 1623 contain references to his researches into — and work on — the history of King Henry VIII (his grandfather?). Bacon also applied to the Records Office in January of 1623 for material relating to Henry VIII. As far as is known, *The Historie of King Henry VIII* appeared in print for the first time in December of 1623. Did Bacon write it?

Baconian speculations also extend to the works of Edmund Spenser and Christopher Marlowe. Did Bacon write those as well? Bacon's younger brother Anthony was allegedly a secret service agent, and so was the mercurial Kit Marlowe, who was said officially to have died in a tavern brawl in 1593. There are speculations, however, that this was part of an Elizabethan secret service, identity-switch, cover-up job in order to get Marlowe away. In this account, another corpse was substituted and Kit was whisked off to France and later to Italy, where he supposedly continued to write for several years. Some theorists have suggested that it was Marlowe, hidden in Italy, rather than Bacon, who actually wrote the major portion of the works attributed to Shakespeare.

One interesting attempt to solve the Shakespeare problem was made through automatic writing via a medium named Hester Dowden in 1947, working with author Percy Allen. Claiming to be in contact with the spirits of various Elizabethan personalities, Hester reached the following solution. The authorship was *shared* among Edward de Vere, the Seventeenth Earl of Oxford, William Shakespeare of Stratford, Beaumont and Fletcher, who were already well-known dramatists, and Francis Bacon, who worked mainly as an editor and reviser.

Very few original manuscripts in the handwriting of Shakespeare, Marlowe, or Spenser are known to exist, and it seems just a trifle odd that almost all of them should have vanished so effectively. Baconians argue that the manuscripts are written in Bacon's idiosyncratic and easily recognizable hand, and have all been hidden away carefully for that reason.

On December 3, 1948, Dr. Burrell F. Ruth told students at Iowa State College that he believed that Bacon had set such great store by those original manuscripts and had arranged for them to be hidden "until the world became a better place."

It has been suggested that Bacon arranged for them to be concealed beneath the amazing subterranean flood-tunnel defence system guarding the Money Pit on Oak Island, Nova Scotia. His book *Sylva Sylvarum* contains details of how to create artificial water sources not unlike the Oak Island workings. It also refers to methods of preserving manuscripts in mercury, and among the many intriguing discoveries reported from Oak Island were some old stone jars which allegedly contained traces of mercury. In 1610, King James I had granted Bacon land holdings in Newfoundland.

Other suggestions are that the manuscripts were hidden at Rennes-le-Château in France because of its supposed Templar, Cathar, Rosicrucian, and Masonic connections. The secret vaults below Roswell in Scotland are another possibility. There is also said to be a mysterious chamber concealed beneath the river bed near the mouth of the River Wye in western Britain. Dr. Orville Ward Owen found what he believed was a Baconian cipher which led him to this underground store-room. When he examined it, it was empty, but he found what he believed to be Baconian symbols carved into the walls. Owen's theory was that it had once been Bacon's intention to store the handwritten originals in that chamber, but that he had changed his mind and decided on somewhere safer, farther away — Roswell in Scotland; Oak Island, Nova Scotia; or Rennes-le-Château in France, perhaps? If those hidden manuscripts are ever discovered, it is probable that — like the Dead Sea Scrolls — they will raise more questions than they'll answer.

Passing through Highgate in March, 1626, Bacon got out of his coach to collect snow to stuff a chicken to see how long the cold would preserve its flesh in an edible condition. He caught a chill which turned to a fatal bronchitis. He died on April 9, and was buried in St. Michael's Church in St. Albans.

Ben Jonson was right: Francis Bacon was indeed a man of mystery. His connections with the Rosicrucians, the Freemasons, and the enigmatic magician, Dr. John Dee, are areas of his intriguing life over which a veil still lies. The secrets of his birth and his possible Shakespearean authorship are only the first two steps on the Baconian Mystery Tour.

Chapter 22

Joe LaBelle and the Deserted Village Mystery

Some people just vanish individually — like Benjamin Bathurst, who walked around the heads of his horses and was never seen again. Others vanish in small groups. The famous mystery of the Nova Scotian-built *Mary Celeste* centres on a sturdy, seaworthy sailing brig found abandoned near the Azores in 1872 with no sign of her passengers or crew. They were never found, and no totally satisfactory solution was ever put forward.

It is strange enough when a handful of people vanish from their ship suddenly and without explanation in the middle of a vast ocean. It is infinitely more sinister and mysterious when the entire population of a thriving settlement vanishes from the land.

Joe LaBelle was a tough, seasoned Canadian trapper with over forty years' experience. A strong, confident, self-sufficient man, Joe was used to working alone. It was the depth of winter in 1930, and his sled was heavily laden with furs. His dogs were well-fed and pulling steadily, as they made their way back from the Aberdeen and Baker Lake area of the vast Canadian Northwest Territories, only 150 miles below the Arctic Circle. Joe's ultimate destination was Churchill, Manitoba, which lay on the western side of Hudson Bay. That was still a good three or four hundred miles southeast of Joe's current location.

There is a wise Chinese proverb: "A march of 10,000 miles begins with the first step." Intrepid men like Joe LaBelle with the strength and stamina of Spartan warriors know the meaning of that proverb. You take one step at a time. You don't allow the idea of the overwhelming duration of the entire awesome journey to weigh you down. You go from day to day, from one reachable resting place to the next. You take care of the here and the now, and you solve the immediate problems of food and shelter for yourself and your dogs. Eventually the longer journey takes care of itself. You just go on steadily and tirelessly putting the pieces of a huge jigsaw puzzle together one at a time. The whole picture will emerge in the end.

Joe was heading for an Inuit village on the shores of Lake Angikuni where he had many hospitable friends. They had helped him with food, shelter, and companionship many times in the past. He was assured of a good welcome there for himself and his dog team.

It was well after mid-day, but Joe calculated that he could reach the safety of the village before dark. He was looking forward to seeing his old friends again and catching up on their local news. LaBelle had a genuine respect and admiration for these village hunters. As one who knew many of the hazards of the frozen wilderness first hand, he admired the skill and courage of his Inuit friends. Inuit ingenuity in the past had invented the harpoon, the kayak, the umiak, dogsleds, stone oil lamps, and igloos in order to survive. Joe also appreciated their generosity and community spirit.

Inuit settlements tended to do without chiefs or any recognizable form of government. Their traditional norms and cultural mores demanded a high degree of sharing and co-operation. A successful huntsman would share his kill with the entire village, especially with those in need of food, knowing that the time would come when he would be grateful for another hunter's generosity in return.

As Joe approached the village he began to feel strangely uneasy. It was as if some sixth sense — the kind that survivors tend to develop in the wild — was warning him that something was wrong. He reached the crest and started the long gentle descent towards the cluster of dwellings. There was absolute silence. Normally, by the time he reached the crest, the dogs would have been barking loudly, and crowds of excited village children would have come running out to meet him. This time, nothing stirred.

LaBelle drove cautiously into the centre of the village, secured his dogs and began to explore. Like the team from the *Dei Gratia* who had boarded the deserted *Mary Celeste* almost sixty years earlier, LaBelle found evidence that whatever had happened to his Inuit friends must have happened fast. Wherever they'd gone, and however they'd gone, they'd gone suddenly. On the *Mary Celeste*, a half-finished child's garment had been found in Mrs. Briggs' sewing machine. In the empty Inuit village LaBelle found a half-stitched sealskin coat with the sewing needle still in it. In the partly flooded galley of the *Mary Celeste*, Oliver Deveau from the *Dei Gratia* had found the remains of food in the unwashed pots and pans. In the deserted village, LaBelle found cooking pots full of uneaten food — now frozen solid — dangling from their supports over the ashes where the cooking fires had burned out.

Joe began to experience a strange, frightening feeling of depression and foreboding. It was something uncanny. He sensed a terrible, negative atmosphere in what had once been a lively, happy, and friendly place. The situation recalls an incident we outlined in *The World's Greatest Unsolved Mysteries*, when two English schoolteachers had what seemed to be a weird time-slip experience in Versailles on an August afternoon in 1901. One of them wrote:

> [F]rom the moment we left the lane an extraordinary depression had come over me, which, in spite of every effort to shake off, steadily deepened.... [T]he sudden gloom upon my spirits became quite overpowering on reaching the point where the path ended. ... Everything suddenly looked unnatural ... unpleasant. ... [T]he trees behind the building seemed to have become flat and lifeless, like a wood worked in tapestry. There were no effects of light and shade, and no wind stirred the trees. It was all intensely still.

Joe LaBelle made two more sinister finds in the village. Inside every hut and every tent, the hunter's rifle stood in its accustomed place beside the entrance. An Inuit hunter's rifle was as vital to him as one of his limbs. There was no way a man would voluntarily have left his village without taking his gun. The dogs, which would normally have barked cacophonously when Joe's sled came over the snow crest, were lying still where their missing owners had tethered them: frozen solid. That was as bad an omen as the rifles. No Inuit would willingly have left his dog team to die like that.

Joe walked from the village towards the frozen shore of Lake Angikuni to explore the area where the hunters' canoes, kayaks, and umiaks were normally kept. They looked derelict and weather-beaten. It was clear to LaBelle's experienced eye that they hadn't been repaired or maintained for quite a while.

His next discovery was perhaps the most sinister of all. In the little community's sacred burial ground at least one grave had been carefully and deliberately opened, and the body removed. It is not Inuit custom to exhume their dead. The final resting places of dead ancestors are sacred and are respected as such. Joe wondered for a moment if animal predators had attacked the grave after the living villagers were no longer there to protect it, but that didn't seem possible: the stones that had once covered the grave were now stacked neatly beside the gaping hole.

It was a very strange and uneasy night that Joe spent in the empty village, his dogs on guard, his rifle loaded and close beside him. At first light he set out for Churchill as fast as his sled would cover the intervening snow. At the Royal Canadian Mounted Police Headquarters he made a full report and then returned with the Mounties to the deserted Inuit village. These closer examinations revealed that the villagers — assuming for a moment that they had travelled somewhere in the normal way and of their own accord — had not taken any of their heavy clothing with them. Hunters in a great hurry to deal with some emergency might have travelled light, expecting to return soon. The Inuit hunters might have gone without their heavy clothing, but the women and children? Never.

One wildly improbable theory is that some strange beast came from the lake to attack them, but the evidence left behind would have been very different. Men would have raced to the shore with rifles and harpoons. Dogs would have been released to help in the fight. Some at least of the women and children should have escaped while their men fought a savage rearguard action to protect the families they loved. There would have been signs of a desperate struggle everywhere: but there were none. All the circumstantial evidence left behind seemed to point to the villagers having been spirited away without a fight. And what kind of lake monster stacks the stones up neatly when it opens a grave?

Is it remotely possible that those Inuit villagers were the simultaneous victims of a time-slip of the kind that apparently touched Versailles briefly in the summer of 1901? When Joe felt a sensation like the one the English schoolteacher described in the beautiful, old Versailles gardens, was he experiencing the dying ripples of whatever massive time-distortion had hit the village so cataclysmically?

Another strange theory was linked to evidence given by the Laurent family. Armand and his sons lived in a lakeside cabin some distance from the mysteriously abandoned village. They told the RCMP that they had seen a strange, brightly lit object flying in the direction of the empty village some time before LaBelle discovered the tragedy and raised the alarm. Were the villagers the victims of a UFO abduction?

The RCMP hunted for months. The search went nation-wide across the whole of Canada. Hunters and trappers were asked to report anything that might provide the slimmest clue as to what had happened to the villagers. Despite all these efforts, and the grim determination and dedicated skill of the expert RCMP officers, no trace of the villagers was ever found. Just as with the *Mary Celeste*, something unknown simply caused everyone in the settlement to drop whatever he or she was doing and go.

Chapter 23

Sir John Sherbrooke, Captain Wynyard, and Others

If you work with mysteries for long enough, there's always a danger that you'll turn into one yourself. Every trade and profession has its characteristic hallmarks, which seem to draw its people together. Carpenters and candlestick-makers, soldiers and sailors, haberdashers and hairdressers, artists, writers, and actors.... Veteran unsolved mystery researchers eventually become just as clearly delineated and defined as other artisans. There's also a strange reciprocity between craftspeople and their working environment: "while we're making something, something's making us."

There are few members of the unsolved mysteries profession to equal our great Nova Scotian friend and colleague, George Young. His vast experience of the subject and his unfailing courtesy, enthusiasm, help, and advice have always been worth their weight in gold. For the facts in this chapter in particular we owe him a substantial debt of gratitude.

In 1940, when George was sixteen, he added a couple of years to his age and did his best to join the British army. A sternly selective recruiting sergeant with a moustache on which an Aberdeen Angus bull could have been fatally impaled, told him in no uncertain terms that King George VI could manage without him for the time being. Disappointed but undefeated, George went to the naval recruiting office instead. A small, elderly man in a resplendent uniform smiled and made him welcome.

Convinced at the time that this naval recruiting officer was a rear admiral at least, George discovered rather later that he was a pensioner chief petty officer who'd been specially recalled for recruiting service duties during the war. On learning that George was an electrical engineering apprentice in civilian life, and politely pretending to believe that he was eighteen, the navy took him on board. Training began in a naval infantry battalion, followed by service on destroyers. For part of the war he was on loan to the Royal Canadian Navy. When hostilities ended in 1945, he served with the Irish Regiment of Canada, an outstandingly good militia battalion. With the advent of the Korean emergency, he again served as an officer in the Royal Canadian Navy. In 1955 he left the service and went into engineering management and consulting.

We first had the pleasure of meeting George twenty years ago in connection with our on-site Oak Island researches in Nova Scotia, and he's been a tremendous help to us ever since. His knowledge of the ancient Ogham script is phenomenal, his nautical and engineering expertise are both exceptional, and his special interest in the interpretation of the inscriptions on old Canadian stones is second to none. It was George who put us on the fascinating trail of Sir John Sherbrooke's psychic adventure, and several others.

Sir John Coape Sherbrooke lived from 1764 until 1830, and was governor general of Canada from 1816 until 1818. The attractive township of South Sherbrooke in the southwest corner of Lanark County, which was first settled in 1821, is named after him. Like many other

The authors' great friend, George Young of Nova Scotia, expert investigator of the paranormal and renowned authority on Canadian mysteries, with Patricia Fanthorpe.

generals and politicians, Sir John kept a journal, and it is from this first-hand information that the evidence for his strange psychic experience comes. On the October 15, 1785, he was serving with the garrison on Cape Breton Island. His friend and colleague, Captain Wynyard, was in the room with him. It was precisely four o'clock in the afternoon, and both officers were sitting quietly reading. Sherbrooke suddenly glanced up from the page in the way that people do when they sense that someone has just entered the room. Sure enough, a man whom Sherbrooke had never seen before was standing silently in the doorway. Sherbrooke drew Wynyard's attention to the newcomer and was surprised by the strength of his friend's reaction. Wynyard went deathly pale and looked deeply shocked. As the two officers watched, the newcomer moved past them and entered a small windowless room, like a dressing room or large closet, situated at the far side of the room in which they had been sitting and reading. Sherbrooke observed that the figure seemed to glide, or almost to melt, through the door of this small room rather than open it in the normal way. As the figure passed them, the two officers noticed that the face had a very sad and solemn expression. Sherbrooke, always a fearless man of action, leapt to his feet and flung open the door through which the strange figure had just passed. The tiny room beyond was quite empty. He and Wynyard searched the whole place thoroughly, but not even a mouse was hiding anywhere within their quarters. Wynyard explained to Sherbrooke that he had reacted so strongly because the ethereal figure who had just crossed their room and vanished had borne an uncanny resemblance to his brother who was currently serving in India. Both men made a careful note of what they had seen, and of their fruitless search afterwards. In particular, they made certain of the time and date.

Information travelled slowly in the eighteenth century, and it was not until the following year that Captain Wynyard received the letter which he had been dreading: his brother had died in India on October 15, just when he and Sherbrooke had seen their paranormal visitor on Cape Breton Island.

There is an interesting corollary to the General's account. Many years later, he was walking in London when he saw a man who bore an uncanny resemblance to the weird apparition which he had seen in Canada in 1785. The General introduced himself and asked tactfully if his new acquaintance was by any chance a member of the Wynyard family as he, Sherbrooke, had had the pleasure of serving with a Captain Wynyard years before at the Sydney Garrison on Cape Breton Island. The man's name was not Wynyard, but he was a relative, and he distinctly recalled that one of his cousins had died of fever in India, while another had served in Canada and North America. Sherbrooke never saw him again, but he felt satisfied that this chance meeting in London had written the epilogue to the strange affair on Cape Breton Island so long ago.

Another weird account which falls broadly into the Wynyard-Sherbrooke category is the report that the ghost of Captain Matthew Webb was seen in Dawley in Shropshire, where he was born on January 18, 1848. This episode was so well known and widely reported that Sir John Betjeman, a recent Poet Laureate, made it the subject of one of his fascinating poems. Webb first won acclaim as a marathon swimmer when he covered the twenty miles from Blackwall Pier in East London down to Gravesend in Kent in four hours and forty-five minutes. That record stood for twenty-four years. On August 24 and 25 in that same year, Webb swam the Channel from Dover to Calais. It took him twenty-one hours and forty-five minutes. On July 24, 1883, when he was thirty-five years old, he attempted to swim the treacherous whirlpool rapids below Niagara Falls and was drowned during that courageous attempt. His ghost — wearing a bathing costume — was reported as being seen swimming in the canal near Dawley at the time when he died at Niagara.

Yet another Sherbrooke-Wynyard type incident was said to have occurred in 1828, although the date, the timing, and the other details are far less precise than in the Sherbrooke case. During an Atlantic crossing, a skipper heading for Newfoundland looked into the cabin next to his (just as Sherbrooke and Wynyard examined the room next to theirs) and saw a stranger standing there. Knowing that this was not a crew member, and having no passengers aboard, the captain was certain that he'd caught a stowaway. He sprang into the cabin to apprehend the man — only to find that it was empty. There was nowhere the stranger could have gone — a fact that again recalls the Sherbrooke case. What was very different, however, was that a message had been scribbled on the cabin wall: "Steer northwest." The captain was so impressed by the strangeness of the whole incident that he actually altered course in compliance with the unaccountable message. A few hours later, his look-out sighted a precarious floating wreck which looked as if it was about to go down at any moment. Clinging desperately to it was the man the captain had seen in his cabin a few hours before. After he'd been rescued, the survivor related that he had fallen into a deep, exhausted sleep, during which he had had a vivid dream of being rescued.

There are strange coincidences, or, perhaps, more accurately, inexplicable synchronicities, associated with the sinking of the *Titanic* and the tragic loss of 1,513 lives during the night of April 14, 1912. In 1898, Morgan Robertson wrote a disaster novel called *Futility* in which a huge "unsinkable" liner called the *Titan* struck an iceberg on her way to America and sank with terrible loss of life. In 1892, the great reforming journalist and editor,

William Thomas Stead, wrote a short story which had close parallels with the sinking of the *Titanic*. He was one of those who drowned when the liner went down. Professor Ian Stevenson wrote an article entitled: *A Review and Analysis of Paranormal Experiences Connected with the Sinking of the Titanic*, which appeared in issue 54/1960 of the *Journal of the American Society for Psychical Research*. He refers to such strange events as the recurring nightmares of Connon Middleton which led him to cancel his trip; the American woman who had a vision of her mother in a crowded lifeboat — the daughter having no idea at the time that her mother was on board the *Titanic*; and Mrs. Jack Marshall who watched the huge liner passing close by her home on the Isle of Wight. She said as she watched it go past that it would never reach New York.

There was also the tragedy of the *Waratah*, a Blue Anchor liner which vanished on its way home from Australia to the UK via Durban and Cape Town in 1909. A passenger named Claude Sawyer booked a passage from Sydney, Australia, to Cape Town. It was a nightmare voyage. The *Waratah* pitched and rolled ominously. The bath water was often at an angle of 45°, and passengers were occasionally flung across their cabins by the erratic movements of the ship. Sawyer dreamt of a strange figure with a sword in one hand and a blood-stained rag in the other. He saw this weird figure three times, and the dream convinced him that he had to get off at Durban if the ship got that far. To his great relief, it did. He immediately booked a passage with the Union Castle Line instead, sent a wire to his wife to say that he was unhappy with the *Waratah* and had changed ships. He also told the Union Castle manager of his dream. Claude had made a very wise decision: the *Waratah* never reached England, and her precise fate remains unknown. Sawyer did have one more dream, and it occurred before the *Waratah*'s loss was known. In this later nightmare, he saw a great wave break over her. She rolled over to starboard and plunged into the depths.

The psychological explanation might well be that Claude Sawyer's subconscious processed the dramatic environmental data which was causing him so much justifiable anxiety, and then projected it as a warning dream. There are, of course, other explanations involving psychic phenomena and precognition.

George Young met a great many other engineers and members of associated professions while he was working as an engineering consultant and manager in Nova Scotia after the end of the Korean emergency. Bob Gregory worked with a firm of architects and engineers in Halifax, and his main duties were to supervise and inspect work which his company had designed and which was being undertaken for them on site by independent general contractors. It was Bob's regular practice to leave Halifax on a

Monday morning, and check on the Antigonish County projects on his way to Sydney, where he would spend the rest of the week before heading back to Halifax on a Friday evening.

One of Bob's projects was a small school in St. Andrew's, which lay just a few miles to the east of Antigonish. The contractor was hoping to be able to use gravel from a local riverbed to mix his concrete, and he wanted to meet Bob to ensure that the material was up to the standard required in their contract. Accordingly, an appointment was made for eleven o'clock on the next available Monday morning.

Bob and the builder were soon riding down to the river in the contractor's half-tonner, along dirt roads which Bob was certain that he had never been on before. The builder was driving, which gave Bob ample opportunity to look around and enjoy the scenery. A strange little octagonal building on the right attracted his attention. It was very old and dilapidated. Bob thought it looked rather like a badly neglected Victorian summerhouse, or a gazebo, and its windows were boarded up.

"Can we stop here a minute?" asked Bob. The sight of the old summerhouse had given him a very odd feeling. (Was this anything like the strange sensation which had affected the two English schoolteachers who seemed to have gone back in time during their visit to Versailles in 1901, or the weird experiences of Joe LaBelle at the Inuit village in 1930?) The contractor brought the half-tonner to a gentle halt on the unpaved road and looked at Bob enquiringly. It was several minutes before he could explain his request.

"The sight of that odd little octagonal building seems to have triggered something in my mind," he began. "I'm certain that I've never been down this road before, but I have the strangest feeling that I know exactly what's round the next bend. There'll be a split-level house with a back section that runs almost down to the riverbank. It's got green windowboxes full of red geraniums, and there's a road that goes off to the right. Close to that corner there's another house with a row of spruce trees running from front to rear." As the truck moved off again, the houses and scenery were exactly as Bob had described them.

Is there any kind of rational, everyday explanation for these strange déjà vu, or time-slip, experiences, or are we inevitably thrown back on the paranormal? Psychologists postulate a type of crypto-amnesia in which the subject is totally unaware of certain memories, until a stimulus — like the sight of the strange old derelict summerhouse — brings them into consciousness. Subjects then tend to describe the experience as déjà vu, or are otherwise totally unable to account for their detailed knowledge of what they think they have not previously seen. One of the English schoolteachers at Versailles was also particularly impressed by a summerhouse, although, in her case, it was circular rather than octagonal: "In front of us was a wood," she wrote, "within which, and overshadowed by trees, was a light garden kiosk, circular, and like a small bandstand."

In the controversial Bridey Murphy "reincarnation" case, careful research apparently disclosed that, as a very young girl, the subject — who believed that she had lived a previous life in Ireland — had in fact learnt a great deal about Irish culture from an elderly Irish neighbour who had also allegedly taught her some traditional Irish songs and dances. If these memories of what the old neighbour had taught her had been totally submerged and inaccessible in the normal waking state (crypto-amnesia), then the subject on recovering them under hypnosis might well have concluded that they were from a previous incarnation.

On this crypto-amnesia hypothesis it could be argued that Bob had actually been on that Victorian summerhouse road long before, perhaps as a child, but had lost all accessible memory of it.

When we were lecturing in Lowestoft in East Anglia in the 1970s, we met a very interesting man named Turner who had some intriguing accounts of apparent paranormal phenomena to share with us. One of these had certain parallels with Bob Gregory's adventure in St. Andrew's. In the Turner account, during the nineteenth century a girl who had never previously visited the area went to look at a house in Scotland and felt that she knew what lay round the next corner. When she reached it, everything was as she had described it in advance, and she explained her odd precognition to herself by recalling that she had dreamed of this large old house and garden.

She reached the front door and knocked. The butler who opened it for her was flabbergasted. For several minutes he lost that coolly detached self-control for which nineteenth century butlers were justifiably renowned. Then he apologized profusely for staring at her. "I'm so sorry, Madam, please forgive me," he blurted, "but you are the lady who haunts this house."

If probable future events — such as her visit — had somehow cast their teleological equivalent of a shadow backwards into that girl's present, could that have led her to dream of the Scottish house? And to dream of it so vividly that something akin to astral projection made her visible to the occupants while her actual physical body was many miles away?

We still do not understand the complex mental and physical mechanisms by which perception operates, nor how the eye and brain can co-ordinate to give us workable pictures of our external environment, pictures to which we can make relevant and effective responses.

It may be that there are subtle differences in people's teleological focus — the psychological, perceptual equivalent of long and short sightedness as it affects normal optical vision. If most of us "see" only the instant "now" without the benefit of any depth of teleological focus which would enable us to look further into the future, then we will be aware only of what the infinitesimally small present instant contains. Just occasionally, however, short-sighted people rub their eyes and find that for a moment they can see rather better than before. Unfortunately, the improvement passes as soon as the hand is moved again. Is it possible that so-called déjà vu and time-slip experiences occur in a parallel way? Does something like the derelict summerhouse, which Bob Gregory felt was his stimulus, act like the psychological equivalent of physical eye-rubbing as far as our perceptions of time are concerned? If we normally perceive only the present instant, but some freak event enables us temporarily to experience more of what surrounds it, are we then able to describe something in the present which we would normally regard as "the future"?

Consider the model of a pinhole in a sheet of opaque metal. If we are well back from the pinhole we can see very little through it. If we place an eye close to it, we can see considerably more of what lies on the other side of the opaque metal sheet. Using this explanation, the derelict summerhouse got Bob's eye closer to the teleological pinhole. It's also interesting to compare this teleological pinhole idea with the technique used by the Brahan Seer, who was said to have looked into the future through his special "fairy-stone" with a hole through it.

Something very strange undoubtedly happened to Bob Gregory that Monday morning in St. Andrew's. Its precise nature and cause are wide open to debate.

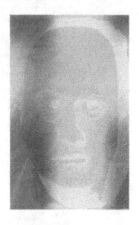

Chapter 24

Philip of Warwick: A Toronto Mystery

There are three basic theories about the strange, psychic powers of the human mind. The first is that they may seem convincing but are actually entirely illusory — so-called "strange mental powers" do not really exist at all. The second is that some psychically gifted individuals still possess faint residual traces of paranormal powers that nearly all human beings once had — and needed — in pre-literate societies aeons ago, but which most of us no longer possess in useful quantities today. The third theory is that paranormal mind powers are as real as reinforced concrete — and potentially far stronger. The great majority of us do have them — although like height, weight, and physical strength, they tend to vary considerably from person to person.

If we accept this third theory as a working hypothesis, we begin to ask precisely what potential powers we possess, what we can learn to do with them, and how they can be exercised, developed, and strengthened.

We start by looking at hypnosis, suggestion, and auto-suggestion. Efficient, professional, medical hypnotists can often assist their patients to exercise improved control over bodily functions, pain thresholds, tension, and stress. Medical hypnosis can be used for painless dental surgery, to help with childbirth, and to overcome numerous psychosomatic conditions.

Sufficiently determined subjects can sometimes use their powers of auto-suggestion to overcome addictions, to battle on for long periods without sleep or food when vital tasks have to be completed, and to perform feats of strength which would normally be considered as superhuman.

The powers released by hypnotism, suggestion, and auto-suggestion do not have to be direct in the sense that the subject says: "I will do this. I can do that." Very often, the effectiveness of mental powers in this area seems to be increased through an intermediary. The subject believes that a particular talisman, a certain spell, a special ritual, a holy place, or a unique person has the power to accomplish the desired objective. By making contact with this intermediate person, or object, the subject's own mental powers are, perhaps, concentrated, focussed, and amplified.

Over eighty percent of the accounts of biblical miracles have faith as a central proviso. This is not for one moment to deny the existence of some genuine, external, objective power residing in the holy person, sacred site, or religious object, but only to suggest that both may be needed.

Perhaps the example of resonance is useful in this context. By operating on the exactly the right frequency, certain sounds or vibrations can resonate with a wine glass, a suspension bridge, or even a building, and destroy it. Perhaps it is necessary for two or more minds to operate simultaneously: the healer and the patient; the saint in heaven and the pilgrim praying by her tomb; the seer and the client who has come for a Tarot reading; the medium and the circle of eager sitters at the seance.

There are also many and varied accounts of telekinesis to consider: from Uri Geller's modern spoon and key bending, or his remarkable clock and watch repairing, to the suggestion that so great were the powers of the Elizabethan magician, Dr. John Dee, that he raised the storm which destroyed the Armada. Can a human mind really move solid matter merely by the force of non-physical will? Irrefutably conclusive proof that this can be done on any significant scale is still awaited, but there are numerous examples in the literature which are difficult to refute. Levitation of the kind practised by Daniel Dunglas Home in Connecticut in 1852, in front of witnesses like F.L. Burr, the tough, no-nonsense editor of the *Hartford Times*, is difficult to explain away. St. Teresa of Avila, who died in 1582, and St. Joseph of Copertino, who lived from 1603 until 1663, were also apparently able to levitate on numerous occasions, and they were also seen by many reliable and reputable witnesses.

Telepathy and teleportation may also fall within the range of these inexplicable mental powers. What about the strange visions of the past, the future, of some distant part of this earth — or even further afield — that are frequently reported? If there are alternative universes and parallel time tracks — the worlds of "if," as they are sometimes called — is the mind able to see them by some inexplicable remote-vision process? Or is it the astral body that makes these strange, lengthy journeys and then relays information back to the mind just as the physical body does?

Do these mysterious powers of the mind also enable it to survive bodily death, to remain integrated and aware of itself long after the physical brain has ceased to function? What are we to make of the many carefully recorded cases of near-death experiences where the subject has subsequently made uncannily accurate reports of what he or she saw in the operating theatre while the surgical team was resuscitating a body which had temporarily ceased to function? What of those commonly described journeys along a mysterious tunnel towards a realm of exquisite light and colour, where radiantly happy groups of long dead friends and relatives were waiting to welcome the newcomer?

Strangest of all, perhaps, is the creative power of the mind. Madame Blavatsky believed that she had created a "tulpa," or thought-form, during her Tibetan pilgrimages. According to her account, it was extremely difficult for her to dispose of it afterwards. Did some ancient Jewish magicians occasionally succeed in creating and activating a "golem" — an animated thing of clay like a cross between a robot and Frankenstein's monster, but far more terrible than either? What of the Greek sculptor Pygmalion whose beautiful statue came to life?

Should we, perhaps, be looking for the paranormal creative powers of the mind which may be the real, but mysterious, dynamic forces behind the anecdotes, myths, and legends?

What if the tale of Aladdin's lamp, or the myth of the genie sealed in the bottle by Solomon the Wise, are really intended as symbols of a potent psychological truth? If so, the genie represents the almost unlimited power of the mind. The imprisoning lamp or bottle represents the common-sense strictures and inhibitions of the everyday world of normal consciousness: the switch is in the "off" position simply because we cannot accept that our great paranormal mental powers are really there. Once we begin to believe in them, we can start to use them, and, like an athlete's muscles, the more we use them, the more powerful they will become. Symbolically, the genie is imprisoned in the lamp, or bottle, until we accept the reality of its existence. It's a catch-22 situation. We cannot utilize the genie's enormous powers until we believe in it: and we cannot believe in it until we see convincing evidence of its enormous powers. The immense psychic energy dormant in the subconscious cannot be liberated until the conscious mind lives and acts as though it was there and accessible. A hint which some exponents of paranormal mind power recommend is to treat your subconscious as a distinct personality. Regard it as a totally loyal and supportive partner or ally, but one who is far stronger than your conscious mind. Give your subconscious a name, and keep that name a strict secret between the two of you. Guard it more jealously than the PIN of your credit card, or your password on the Internet. Then talk to your subconscious friend as if he or she was a real, physical presence. Ask him, or her, for help to accomplish whatever task you're undertaking. Some researchers who have experimented along these lines have found it surprisingly effective.

The borders between physical reality, virtual reality, and the thought-form universe created by the powers of the mind seem at times to be dangerously thin and fragile. Phenomenologists would regard the differing realities as an infinitely graduated continuum rather than as definitive either-or, black-white, positive-negative states of being. In L. Ron Hubbard's *Typewriter in the Sky*, a character named Mike de Wolf is friendly with Horace Sackett, who writes popular pulp fiction. Somehow Mike gets transported into the story which Horace is writing and finds to his dismay that he's cast in the role of the villain. Knowing what happens to the bad guys in Horace's stories, Mike is extremely anxious to get out again. The problem of disentangling his two "realities" is a tricky one, and even through the medium of fiction Hubbard succeeds in posing deep metaphysical questions about the mind's interpretation of experiential data, and its response to the questions about the nature of being.

One of the most interesting experiments in the use of creative paranormal mind powers took place in Toronto over a quarter of a century ago. Dr. George Owen and a group of his friends from the Toronto Society for Psychical Research decided to invent the history of an imaginary person whom they called Philip. Paracelsus, among other magicians, always said that when magic failed to work it was because the mind of the magician had not gone into sufficient detail while mentally creating the effect which it hoped to achieve. Owen and his colleagues avoided that problem with commendable thoroughness. They placed their imaginary Philip in turbulent seventeenth-century Warwickshire, in England. They found and photographed a stately home of the kind he would have lived in — which they referred to as Diddington Manor, although that was not its real name. They even sketched him and kept the portrait in the room where they were conducting their on-going experiment.

Like most traditional ghost stories, Philip's imaginary history was emotional and dramatic. He had endured miserable years of loveless marriage with a cold-hearted wife named Dorothea, finding brief but intense happiness with his young gypsy mistress, Margo. Dorothea had found out about Margo, and spitefully denounced her as a witch. In an age when the odious Matthew Hopkins plied his foul, sadistic trade as a witchfinder, the innocent Margo had inevitably gone to the stake. It says little for Philip's character — real or imaginary — that he had been too timid to defend her. Any man worthy of his name would have cut his way through her accusers and either succeeded in rescuing her or died honourably fighting beside her. In one lesser-known variation of the Arthurian romances, Lancelot arrives with only minutes to spare before his adored mistress, Guinevere, is due to be burnt at the stake for her adultery with him. There are no doubts in his mind about what has to be done: if nothing but her accusers' blood can quench their spiteful, self-righteous fire, then so be it. The triumphant Lancelot — champion of champions — gallops away through a sea of his enemies' blood with his beloved Guinevere safe and sound behind him. It was poor little Margo's tragedy that Philip of Warwick was no Lancelot. After her death, gripped with hopeless melancholy and remorse, he paced the battlements of Diddington like Hamlet at Elsinore before succumbing to his own inconsolable misery and guilt and leaping to his death.

The Toronto group tried to create Philip as a "shared hallucination" and apparently succeeded beyond their wildest dreams. They were encouraged by the reports of three English researchers, Brookes-Smith, Hunt, and Batchelor, whose articles had appeared in the journal of the London-based Society for Psychical Research in 1966 and later. Their work suggested that traditional psychic phenomena such as rapping and table turning could be produced by psychokineses — human mind-power alone — without bringing disembodied spirits into the equation. They also suggested that certain states of mind, or social atmospheres, were more likely to produce PK phenomena than others. As a result of their work Hunt, Brookes-Smith, and Batchelor recommended that no individual member of an experimental team should allow himself, or herself, to feel personally responsible for any phenomena which were produced. No one should feel, or express, any surprise when the phenomena appeared, and the likelihood that phenomena would occur had to be accepted without question by everyone working in the experimental group. (This is just another way of saying that you really have to believe in the mind-genie before he can get out of the bottle.) Rather surprisingly, the English experimenters from the sixties had also found that a jovial, light-hearted atmosphere was more likely to release PK powers than a solemn, serious one.

Within a few weeks, the Toronto team found that the table was beginning to move on its own in the way that tables had done in Victorian seance rooms. Philip answered every question with one knock for "yes" and two for "no" in accordance with the traditional spiritualists' knocking-code method. Audiometric analysis indicated that these knocks had totally different acoustic profiles from the sounds made by striking the seance table with a hand, a ring, a pen, or a cigarette lighter.

There were eight experimenters in the Toronto research group, and when they greeted Philip in turn, there was a short, sharp, answering rap under the hand of the speaker. On at least one occasion, lights which had been specially arranged around Philip's portrait began to flicker strangely. On another occasion, the table rose into the air with all four of its legs clear of the floor.

Philip's character and knowledge of his invented life history tended to vary depending upon which members of the group were present during any one experimental session. He usually got the broad outlines of his invented life history more or less correct, but some of his knowledge of seventeenth-century history wasn't always accurate. On some occasions he would extend the life story the group had made up for him.

At other times Philip, would be asked to go to the room above "to see what George was doing." On these occasions, George, who was working in the room immediately above the one where the Philip group were working, would distinctly hear one of Philip's characteristic raps, but the main group in the room below did not hear it.

It is perfectly clear from the reports of their work that the well-organized Toronto group were fully aware the whole time that Philip was "unreal," that he was just a composite PK phenomenon which they had in a sense constructed. They found that when the sense of his unreality, or artificiality, was uppermost in their minds, his signals became weaker and it was almost necessary to perform mental acrobatics — what George Orwell of *1984* fame might have called "doublethink" — in order to reinforce him.

The Toronto experiment itself deserves far wider publicity and the excellence of the experimenters' work deserves greater acclaim and recognition than has yet been directed towards them. Its implications are extremely important, and the need for further work in this field cannot be emphasized strongly enough.

Chapter 25

Louis Cyr, Edouard Beaupré, Thomas Hickathrift, and Robert Hales: Giants and Strongmen

Tradition tells that Thomas Hickathrift, the giant of the East Anglian Fens, was born in the second half of the eleventh century. The old books say "during the reign of William the Conqueror." His father was a poor day labourer who lived in a cottage beside the marshes around the Isle of Ely. He was reputed to be strong enough to do the work of two men. This same area was also the home of the great Anglo-Saxon hero, Hereward the Wake. He and his followers had expected that King Sweyn II of Denmark would launch an invasion, and they planned to join him against William's occupying Normans. Hereward's men, aided by an advance party of Danish sailors, took Peterborough Abbey by storm to keep its treasures out of the clutches of Turold, the newly appointed Norman abbot. Unluckily for Hereward and his hopes of liberating Britain from the Normans, Sweyn changed his mind, made peace with William, and recalled his highly effective Danish fighting sailors. Left with nothing but his own resources, Hereward nevertheless put up a stubborn and protracted struggle against the Normans. He and his men established themselves on the Isle of Ely, which became a noted refuge for other fugitive Anglo-Saxons, including Morcar, Earl of Northumbria.

William was a resolute opponent as Harold had discovered to his cost in 1066, and his determined, methodical approach eventually broke through

Hereward's defences. When the Isle of Ely finally fell to the Normans, Hereward himself escaped.

The account of his dramatic death may have grown in the telling, but a good case can be made for the substantial truth at the core of the romantic tradition. An uneasy, fragile truce had been established between Hereward and William, although neither had any real trust in the other's word. The popular version of Hereward's grand finale tells how twelve hand-picked Norman men-at-arms — the best of the best — were sent to assassinate him in one of the old Saxon long-halls. Hereward, who was then well over fifty, grimly barred the door to prevent their escape, swung his great, two-handed Saxon battle axe, and challenged the lot of them together to take him down if they could.

It turned into one of the bloodiest, most desperate — and most glorious — hand-to-hand combats in history. Hereward, dying of his wounds, but still, miraculously, on his feet, leaned on his great axe and smiled down grimly at the corpses of the twelve would-be assassins: silent and still on the blood-drenched floor of his long-hall. With a final, magnificent laugh, Hereward ordered them to save the best fireside seat in hell for him — adding that it wouldn't be empty for long.

One of the most difficult tasks confronting folklorists and serious students of mythology and legend is untangling and analysing the many different strands. Medieval minstrels, troubadours, and storytellers

Ancient carving on the church wall at Walpole St. Peter's, showing the giant Thomas Hickathrift celebrating one of his many victories.

borrowed liberally from the exploits of one famous hero to augment the gallant deeds of another: and during this borrowing process, the stories grew in the telling. Some great feat of Charlemagne's tended to be grafted on to Arthur, Lancelot, Galahad, Roland, Harold, Beowulf, Eric the Red, or Richard the Lionheart. Daring escape stories slid from Robin Hood to Hereward the Wake. Somewhere below the colourful exaggerations and interchangeable characters lies a core of historical fact. Because Hereward and Thomas Hickathrift were contemporaries, stories of their courage and fighting prowess have adhered first to one and then to the other. Legend never gave Hereward Hickathrift's prodigious size: but two heroes from the same era and the same Fenland location were certain to have shared interchangeable heroic incidents.

When Hickathrift's father died, the boy became lazy and seemed content to sit at home eating prodigious meals while his mother did the work which provided them. The first improvement in Tom's character came when she sent him to a neighbouring farmer to beg for a bundle of clean straw to replenish the bedding in their cottage. The kindly farmer said he could have as much as he could carry, and was amazed when Tom walked away with a bundle that would have been too heavy for six normal men to lift.

Once the news of Tom's great strength had travelled around the Isle of Ely's hamlets and villages, he was in great demand. Typical of many incidents was the story of the tree. Hired by a rich woodsman to retrieve a felled tree from the forest and place it on a cart ready to be taken to the owner's yard, Tom watched smiling while four normal men equipped with a pulley sweated and strained mightily, but failed to raise the great log. When they were exhausted, Tom lifted it easily enough by himself on to the woodsman's cart. Asked about wages for the job, Tom said he'd like some wood for his own fire. Told he was welcome to as much as he could carry, Tom plucked up a tree considerably larger than the log he had just lifted on to the cart, threw it lightly over his shoulder, and trotted home with it, easily outpacing the six horses dragging the cart he had just loaded for the woodsman.

There seems to be something deep in the human psyche which needs Superman, Captain Marvel, the Gods of Olympus, Tom Hickathrift, and the rest. Perhaps it is a response to the frustrations of everyday life: the wish to be able to uproot the stubborn tree with one hand. Some theologians would suggest that there is an instinct to search for the one true omnipotent, omniscient, and omnipresent God, which leads the human mind to look in unlikely places for feats of strength and endurance far beyond the normal. That argument would suggest that an interest in legendary giants, gods, and other assorted super-beings may be considered as a rung on the ladder leading to the Divine.

At village fairs, Tom always won the cudgel fighting, wrestling competitions, and other country sports and games — he threw the hammer six furlongs into a river on one occasion.

Hickathrift was offered a regular job as a drayman by a King's Lynn brewer, where his honesty and trustworthiness soon led to promotion to the post of the brewer's chief assistant. One day, Tom's shortest road from King's Lynn to Wisbech, where he was scheduled to make some deliveries, lay through a marsh that belonged to a particularly hostile and aggressive giant — an ogre far bigger than Tom. The brewer advised Tom to take the longer, safer route, but Tom had other plans. The marsh giant duly appeared, armed to the teeth, and angrily ordered Tom off his land. Having no other weapon at hand, Tom pulled a wheel from his cart to use as a shield, and drew out the sturdy axle to use as a club (the wheel and axle later became Hickathrift's insignia). After a fight reminiscent of Hereward's performance against the twelve Norman assassins, Tom knocked the giant to the ground and decapitated him with his own sword — as David did to Goliath of Gath. (This detail may well be a typical heroic-story transfer from the biblical narrative.)

Tom acquired the dead giant's lands and treasure, and became known as Master Hickathrift in consequence. Some of his later exploits included kicking a soccerball so hard that it was never seen again — a feat that would be especially valuable during a World Cup penalty shoot-out!

Despite his formidable reputation, Tom was once attacked by four burly highwaymen, who must either have been acutely myopic or suffering from severe learning difficulties. They were buried side by side in the nearest churchyard. Being wealthy, and a good citizen, Tom generously paid for their funerals to save the Parish any unwarranted expense. It can safely be assumed that he gained more than he spent from the spoils which he had rightfully removed from the bodies of the highwaymen — reminiscent of Ali Baba's ransacking of the cave belonging to the Forty Thieves. (Another heroic-story detail transfer, perhaps?)

Tom met his match only once. He fought to an honourable draw with Henry Nonsuch, a fighting gypsy tinker from Lincolnshire. Like Robin Hood and Friar Tuck, the two heroes fought each other to a standstill with quarter-staffs. Tom was so impressed that he invited Henry home with him, and the two great warriors became inseparable friends.

Shortly afterwards the sheriff of Ely fled to Tom's house for refuge because of an insurrection. On orders from the King, Tom and Henry set about the rebels, with predictable results. Tom picked up a big miller, who was one of the leading insurgents, and used him as a club. Not to be outdone, Henry knocked the head off the rebel nearest to him so hard that it flew like a cannonball and killed their leader. The grateful Sheriff reported all this to the King, who promptly knighted Tom and settled a pension of forty pounds a year on the fighting tinker.

Tom's mother died and he went in search of a wife. A beautiful, wealthy young widow from Cambridge took his fancy, but a rival suitor tried to murder him to eliminate the competition. Foolishly going for Tom with a sword, the spiteful rival ended up on a roof when Tom kicked his backside. The villain then hired a team of local hitmen, who hadn't actually met Hickathrift previously. On encountering Tom in person in a tavern, and hearing a few tales about him from his friend Henry, they took the hit money swiftly back to their employer and prudently declined the commission. Tom married the nubile young widow and they lived happily ever after in the best medieval fairytale tradition.

Only once was Tom lured out of his blissful, wedded retirement, and that was to help the King to deal with an invasion of lions, bears, dragons, and giants. Henry came along just to make up the numbers, and the two great Fenland warriors dealt with the invaders with their customary lethal efficiency. A grateful King made Tom lord governor of the Isle of Thanet to add to his other titles and distinctions.

Despite the many obviously fictional, ballad-type elements in the tale, it seems likely that Hickathrift was an actual person, possibly a royal champion or king's bodyguard, and there is also likely to be a grain or two of historical reality in the famous fighting tinker from Lincolnshire.

The grave of Thomas Hickathrift in the Churchyard at Tilney All Saints.

Several significant elements can be analysed in the story. Like John Ridd in Blackmore's *Lorna Doone*, Hickathrift rises from obscurity and poverty to fame, rank, and fortune. Although as physical as Beowulf, Hickathrift does not suffer and die like the model epic hero of fiction. Tom lives and prospers, which suggests that he is a man of flesh and blood, not a stereotypical epic hero. Many details of his story resemble the classic Cornish tale of *Jack the Giant Killer*, but Hickathrift and Henry Nonsuch are East Anglian Fenmen, not Cornishmen. They are not social reformers like Kett of Wymondham or Robin of Locksley. It never occurs to them that rebels might sometimes have a just cause, or a fair grievance. They never consider the possibility that the invaders of Thanet may have had some legitimate claim to the territory. Henry and Tom are unthinking, unquestioning Establishment men. Hickathrift also has one or two elements of Paul Bunyan in him — yet there are few, if any, etiological features attached to his story. He has strong sporting overtones, as does Henry Nonsuch: they enjoy games like wrestling, quarter-staffing, and football. Tom also lifts and carries prodigious loads.

There are some elements of German and French folk heroes in Hickathrift, as well. In some ways, he is an early, low-key Fenland Hercules, but he lacks the ingredients of quest and epic which are found in many more developed stories. His basic simplicity may well be an argument in favour of his historical core. He has no real purpose except his own interests, but he is not selfish. He does not exploit others. He is not mean or ungenerous. It is gratifying for him to use his great strength, and he uses it because he enjoys using it. His help is given willingly, but not discriminatingly: his mother, his employer, a friend, a neighbour, the sheriff, the King — all benefit from it.

If Hickathrift demonstrates no great intellectual capacity or strength of moral purpose, he has no great wickedness either. He will flatten a human opponent, a tree, a dragon, or a bear with equal unconcern. He harbours no grudges. Henry proves that he is Tom's equal with a quarter-staff, and Tom accepts it sportingly enough. Hickathrift is essentially a country hero. There is an underlying rurality about his uncomplicated directness. He seems to be totally lacking in introspection.

All of this argues more for his historical reality than for his being an ethereal creature of myth or legend.

Compare Tom Hickathrift with the undeniably historical Canadian giant, Edouard Beaupré, and similarities begin to emerge which add weight to the argument for Tom's historicity.

Edouard Beaupré was born on January 9, 1881. He was the eldest son of the twenty children who made up the family of Florestine Piché and her husband, Gaspard Beaupré. Edouard was the first infant to have his baptism recorded in the register of the Church of St. Ignatius in the newly established Parish of East Willow Bunch. A copy of that certificate dated 1904 still hangs in the town museum today. From a birth weight of around fourteen pounds, Edouard's toddler years were fairly normal but he began to grow rapidly after the age of three. At nine, he stood well over six feet tall, and he reached seven feet before he was eighteen. In 1902, when he was just twenty-one, Edouard stood at eight feet two and a half inches. Part of the Beaupré genetic mystery was that Gaspard and Florestine were only slightly above average height, and Edouard's nineteen brothers and sisters were all normal size.

Despite his enormous stature — or maybe because of it — Edouard was a very quiet, gentle character. He was intelligent, thoughtful, and fluent in French, English, Cree, and Sioux. He also had a well-developed streak of practical, day-to-day philosophy. One of his favourite sayings was: "There's a new day coming tomorrow — but today is today." He loved horses, was an expert with a lasso, and greatly enjoyed the life of a young ranch-hand, becoming the firm friend and companion of such famous scouting and cowboy heroes as Johnny Charbrand and John Savary. His enormous size prevented him from following the ranching career he longed to follow. Friends found him the tallest horses available, but his feet still trailed on the ground, and his four-hundred-pound body weight was too much for the strongest mount to carry for long.

Edouard's strength matched his phenomenal size. His gentle nature and sympathetic intelligence often brought him in to separate and pacify men who were quarrelling and fighting. If teased about his height, Edouard gently lifted the joker up on to a nearby roof and refused to lift him down until he promised to stop.

Always kind and helpful, one of Edouard's real-life exploits was very similar to some of the stories told about Tom Hickathrift. When on a visit to Moose Jaw, he pulled a wagon out of a swamp and rescued the struggling horses. His generosity to his impoverished family was legendary. Realizing that he couldn't achieve his ranching ambitions because his size prevented him from riding a horse, he went on tour with André Gaudry and another friend, Albert, who was the son of Jean-Louis Légaré, founder of Willow Bunch. Their show took them as far as Winnipeg, Montreal, Rhode Island, Buffalo, Minnesota, Chicago, and California. All the time, Edouard sent money home regularly. One regular demonstration of his massive strength was to lift an eight-hundred-pound horse shoulder high. This is reminiscent of Milo, the great Greek strongman, who developed his muscles by lifting a small calf day by day as it grew, until he was strong enough to lift a fully grown bull.

When travelling by train, Edouard could reach his cases down from the rack without standing up. When staying in hotels, his bed had to have the end removed: trunks and an extra mattress were then added to the foot.

There are two accounts of Edouard's wrestling contest against the almost unbeatable French Canadian, the great Louis Cyr, undoubtedly one of the strongest men who ever lived.

Born in 1863, Louis weighed a full three hundred pounds, although he stood only five feet ten and a half inches tall. He had a massive sixty-inch barrel chest and almost unbelievable biceps. Accounts of his great feats of strength include being able to lift a barrel full of cement on one arm, and pushing a loaded railway freight wagon up an incline. He once lifted a platform with eighteen men standing on it. His most famous triumph was on December 10, 1891, when four huge dray horses failed to pull his massive arms away from his chest. He always ate prodigiously to keep up his colossal strength, and the general opinion was that his huge appetite contributed to his early death at the age of forty-nine.

According to the account given by Beaupré's family and friends, Edouard and the mighty Louis Cyr first fought an informal contest, which Edouard won. According to the official records of their second, formal match in Montreal's Sohmer Park in 1902, Louis won. Sadly, by the time that contest took place Edouard was already seriously weakened by the tuberculosis that was destined to contribute to his tragically early death two years later.

It was actually a lung haemorrhage that killed him on July 3, 1904, while he was working at Barnum and Bailey's Circus at the St. Louis World's Fair. He was just twenty-three years old.

The strange adventures of his mummified corpse are almost as curious as the sad young giant's life. Because his family were too poor to bring him back from St. Louis to Willow Bunch, a kind-hearted Willows Bunch citizen named Pascal Bonneau went to help. He rescued the body from a promotional exhibition in a store window and brought it back to Montreal. It was displayed in the Eden Museum for a while, then transferred to a freak show attached to the Montreal Circus. The show went bankrupt, and Edouard's body was stored in a warehouse.

Found by children in 1907, it was transferred to the medical faculty at the university and used for research. After this it was mummified and placed on display in a glass case in the university — rather like the body of Jeremy Bentham in its glass cabinet in the foyer of University College, London.

Jeremy was born on February 15, 1748 and died on June 6, 1832. He went to Oxford University at twelve, and began studying law at Lincoln's Inn when he was fifteen. Of only average physical size, Bentham was an intellectual giant of the first magnitude. He was a pioneering social scientist, a tireless administrator and a truly magnificent reformer. He maintained that good government should have four objectives: subsistence, abundance, security, and equality. Bentham also believed in guaranteed employment and a minimum wage. One of his unorthodox theories concerning prison reform advocated using a glass prison called a *Panopticon*, in which the prisoners were in full view of the warders the whole time. It's mildly ironic, therefore, that his preserved body is said to be observed every five minutes by a video camera, and updated pictures of it are reported to appear on the Internet. He even has his own e-mail address: *j.bentham@ucl.ac.uk* — which is pretty impressive for a man who's been dead since 1832.

A Quebec rock band, Beau Dommage, wrote and performed a song about Edouard called *Le Géant Beaupré*. The lyric suggested that Edouard's enormous ghost might roam the halls and corridors of the university. In the course of their medical research, the university specialists suggested that a possible cause for Edouard's supernormal growth rate was a tumour in his pituitary gland which stimulated it to produce an excessive and constant stream of hormones.

In 1967 an article in the *Canadian Medical Association Journal* described measurements that had recently been taken on the giant's body, which had by that time shrunk considerably. A doctor friend showed the article to Ovila Lesperance, one of Edouard's nephews, the son of his sister Josephine. After a number of lengthy delays, Cecile Gibouleau, Ovila Lesperance and other members of Edouard's family succeeded in having his ashes returned to Willow Bunch where they were laid to rest near a life-sized, fibreglass statue of him at the town museum.

Another real-life giant — as authentic as Edouard, and as strong as Louis Cyr — was Robert Hales, the Norfolk giant, who lies buried at West Somerton near Yarmouth in England. Born in 1820, Robert died in 1863, while only in his forties, and his tomb still stands in the graveyard of St. Mary's Church. At his best he stood seven feet eight inches high and weighed 452 pounds. He had a sixty-four inch chest and a sixty-one inch waist. His ancestors were believed by some researchers to have been Patagonians originally, although the Hales family had farmed in the area for several years. Robert spent his early life as a sailor. Then, like Edouard and Louis, he earned his living as a showman. He visited the United States and also appeared before Queen Victoria. Later on, he became landlord of the Craven Head Tavern in London where his great size attracted many customers. Like Edouard, Robert was a gentle, generous, and good-natured man who did much to help those in need.

One of the most interesting aspects of the mysteries connected with giants — real or legendary — is the source of their giantism. If the Genesis record is reliable, and there is no logical reason to doubt it at this point, there were giants on the earth in those days. Have their genes managed to surface again here and there over the centuries? Or, are there other medical causes such as the faulty pituitary gland which seems to have made Edouard grow so much?

St. Mary's Church in West Somerton, England, where Robert Hales, the Norfolk Giant, lies buried.

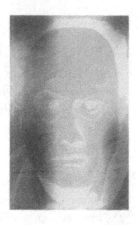

Chapter 26

Jonathan Downes and the Owlman

Jonathan Downes was born in Portsmouth in 1959, but spent an exciting and interesting childhood growing up in Hong Kong. Ancient Chinese mysteries and a dazzlingly diverse range of exotic wildlife laid the foundations for the later studies of cryptozoology which made him famous.

The caring and compassionate side of his nature was clearly revealed during the years he spent as a nurse with the mentally handicapped before becoming a professional writer and musician in the 1980s, with seven books to his credit so far.

A major landmark in his life was his founding of the Centre for Fortean Zoology in 1992 where research into many mysterious, bizarre, and aberrant animals is conducted and co-ordinated. Jonathan's speciality here is the investigation of zooform phenomena — defined as paranormal entities which appear in animal form. Many ancient myths and legends refer to "Shape-Shifters" — strange beings like werewolves and werebears with the power to assume other forms either at will, or when certain conditions prevail. Werewolves, for example, are affected by the full moon; swan maidens change shape at dusk and dawn. Scottish legends tell of people — often witches — who have the power to turn into hares.

The three missing lighthouse keepers of Eilear Mor in the Flannans were said to have been transformed into huge black birds by the mysterious magic lingering in the bleak and sinister granite.

Jonathan has searched for lake monsters in Loch Ness, pursued sea-serpents and birdmen in Cornwall, and chased big cats over miles of west country moorland. He's also been to Latin America on the trail of the grotesque, vampiric Chupacabras.

His many hobbies include drinking tequila, radical polities, Scott Walker's music, and a whole library of books which he reads voraciously. He also thinks Harpo Max is the funniest man who ever lived. Jonathan lives in Exeter with two cats, an elderly dog, and a two-toed amphiuma. His zodiac sign is Leo with Scorpio rising — which may account for some of the mystery that continues to surround him.

His excellent books and albums include *Riding the Waves, The Chicken Sleeps Tonight*, and *The Owlman and Others* (the latter published by Domra Publications 1998). Jonathan's fascinating quest for the mysterious Owlman dates back to 1986 when he was given a copy of Graham McEwan's book *The Mystery Animals of Britain and Ireland*. Like many other researchers into cryptozoology, Jonathan had previously worked on the almost instinctive premise that the weird and wonderful creatures which interested him most had to be pursued in the world's remotest and loneliest places. McEwan's book hinted that they weren't that far away after all.

Co-author Lionel Fanthorpe (left) in concert with Jonathan Downes, the famous international cryptozoologist.

One of the interesting reports which McEwan had collected referred to a strange, feathered humanoid that had been sighted at Mawnan Smith, just outside Falmouth in the south of Cornwall.

Sally Chapman and Barbara Perry, who were both fourteen at the time, saw the Owlman during the night of July 3, 1976 while they were camping in the woods near Mawnan Old Church. Sally said that what she had seen resembled a huge owl with pointed ears. The thing, which was as big as a man, had red, glowing eyes like something from a horror film. Sally's first reaction was to think that some practical joker had dressed up in a weird costume to try to frighten them. She and Barbara just laughed: the incongruous apparition looked more humorous than frightening. Then it amazed them by taking off into the air and they were able to see its feet clearly for the first time. The feet were also incongruous but not in the least amusing: they were lethal pincers, like something from a blacksmith's shop or a medieval torture chamber. Barbara reinforced Sally's description. She recalled that the sinister pincer feet were black and that the feathers covering the creature were grey.

Each girl made an independent sketch of the Owlman. Any experienced police officer, lawyer, or judge will agree that when the evidence of two or three witnesses agrees in every minute detail there is reason to suspect collusion or fraud. If evidence differs too widely, there is also room for reasonable doubt, but when the major points coincide substantially and only the details differ, it is probable that reliable witnesses are corroborating an honest account of something that really occurred. This was the case with the sketches of the Owlman which Sally and Barbara made.

Their evidence was supported by a letter to the local press after their sighting had become widely known. The writer and her sister reported seeing the Owlman one Sunday morning among the trees near Mawnan Church above the rocky coast. They described the feathers as silvery grey and the forbidding pincer feet as reminiscent of big, black crab's claws. They, too, wondered whether someone in a well-designed costume was playing a practical joke, but were baffled by the bird-like way in which the Owlman took off into the air.

Further sightings were reported in 1978.

Before Jonathan began his investigations, the colourful Tony "Doc" Shiels had also investigated the Owlman of Mawnan Woods. American author, Mark Chorvinsky, once described Tony as "a magical wolf amongst Fortean sheep." He's a truly wonderful character, a great showman, a musician, and well up in conjuring and wizardry. Doc received a phone call from Ken Opie, who told him that his teenaged daughter had seen the Owlman during the first week in June. She described it as a demon-like monster flying up through the trees near Mawnan Church. Three French girls staying in a Falmouth boarding house that August also reported to their landlady that they had seen something frightening like "a very big furry bird with a gaping mouth and round eyes."

Jonathan managed to contact another witness, a young man called Gavin, who gave him his account of a sighting made in Mawnan Wood shortly before 10 p.m. on a July evening. When he saw the Owlman it was standing about fifteen feet off the ground in the branches of a large conifer. As he shone his torch over it, he guessed it was approximately five feet tall. The feet had two large black toes like pincers of the type which other witnesses had described.

Jonathan became fascinated by the Owlman reports and interviewed Gavin on numerous occasions over a period of years. The results were always consistent and Jonathan became convinced by Gavin's evidence that some real phenomenon had been lurking in the branches of that pine tree in Mawnan Wood when Gavin's torch beam settled on it.

One particularly intriguing response was the Owlman's reaction to Gavin's torch. The creature's head came forward — a gesture that could have signified aggression, curiosity, or both — and its odd, bird-like legs went back. It then took off swiftly and vanished.

Gavin's teenage girlfriend was with him at the time and both he and Jonathan noted later that every Owlman sighting was either made by a teenage girl or by someone in the company of a teenage girl.

This ties in with much of the well-known literature on poltergeist cases where a teenager, frequently — but not necessarily — an unhappy or disturbed one, is a member of the household in which the poltergeist is being manifested.

There is, perhaps, cause to suspect that the Owlman is more likely to be what Jonathan calls a zooform phenomenon, or a phenomenalist entity, than a solid creature of flesh and blood. The witnesses did not imagine it in the sense that they deliberately made up their strange stories, but an experience can seem real to an honest witness without actually having much — if any — physical substance. Rainbows, sunsets, the aurora borealis, and shimmering mirages in the desert, for example, are all observable phenomena that can be shared objectively by large groups of perfectly sensible and reliable witnesses.

There is also the possibility that strange apparitions such as Owlman could be thought forms like Madame Blavatsky's tulpa, or Philip of Warwick, whom the Toronto experimenters created. But if it had no independent, objective externality to act as the skeleton, or framework, around which the thought form could grow, why did it appear in such similar outline to all who reported it? Is there any mileage in a theory which suggests that thought-forms or tulpas might grow like stalactites and stalagmites in a cave, or coral on a reef? The first observer deposits the basis of the idea, or one small part of one component, and later creative thinkers add to it.

There is, perhaps, a link here with the experiments performed on sponges by marine biologists. If a sponge is thoroughly disintegrated in a device like a liquidizer and then allowed to settle in a saline solution, the widely diffused pieces will reassemble themselves into the pattern of the original sponge. Does that happen because of some original, invisible blueprint? Are the instructions somewhere in the sponge's genes? Does each individual cell contain a location sensor which is able to identify and then refasten itself to its former immediate neighbours? If the invisible blueprint theory is valid, does something similar account in part for the creation and subsequent observation of thought forms such as the Mawnan Wood Owlman? Did a powerful character with a vivid creative imagination, someone like Tony or Jonathan, perhaps, inadvertently lay down the original invisible blueprint for Owlman, and did the creative energy of the later teenage witnesses build up that outline into something much more solid-seeming and observable?

Dr. Owen's Toronto group certainly had a good blueprint for Philip. They had a sketch of him, pictures of the manor house in which he had lived his imaginary life, and an outline plot of the tragic events which had led to his death and Margo's. Madame Blavatsky riding with her party of pilgrim monks had a clear mental picture of a Tibetan monk in her mind before she set out to create the tulpa monk — who later escaped from her control and began to assume an almost sinister aspect.

There is another strange aspect to Jonathan's persistent investigations of the bizarre Owlman phenomenon. Tim Dinsdale, who spent years in similar persistent, patient, and painstaking study of the Loch Ness Monster, experienced a run of bad luck which seemed to be statistically significant at a level well above random chance.

A conversation between Jonathan and Doc Shiels raised the same connection between runs of bad luck and close observation and study of certain types of monster phenomena. Shiels called it "psychic backlash" and actually gave Jonathan a word of warning about it.

Madame Blavatsky was dogged by ill luck and poor health, and so was Crowley. No more than coincidence, perhaps — whatever coincidence really is — but certainly sufficient grounds for serious thought and further investigation. In Jonathan's case he told us that during his intense involvement with the Owlman phenomena his marriage broke up, he suffered serious financial difficulties, and he lost two cars and several computers.

His related studies over many years have included UFO sightings, mysterious animal mutilations, teleporting cattle, and the invidious and ubiquitous "Men in Black." Jonathan himself sees a connection between them all and now regards the Mawnan Wood Owlman phenomenon as only one tip of a large and sinister psychic iceberg. He could well be on the track of something very significant here.

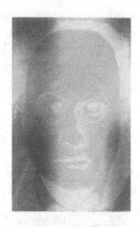

Chapter 27

Modern Men and Women of Mystery

Research into the paranormal and the unexplained frequently brings investigators together, and some of the greatest pleasures and privileges which the profession provides are opportunities to enjoy the company of fascinating and gifted people.

It was as a result of our Barbados vault investigations (see *The World's Greatest Unsolved Mysteries*) that we first met our friends Simon Probert and Pamela Willson. Like us, Simon has been interested in researching all aspects of the paranormal for as long as he can remember. He has some peripheral telepathic ability, and a number of his dream visions have linked with subsequent events, although they tend to be somewhat indistinct and lacking detail. They don't occur often, and he reports feeling rather disturbed and distressed afterwards. He also instinctively feels that the universe is a far stranger place than most people suspect, and that what has been revealed so far is only a grain of sand at the edge of a vast desert. He shares Colin Wilson's view that humanity is on the brink of a great evolutionary leap forward in terms of regaining the use of extrasensory powers.

Pamela Willson has been a sensitive and gifted clairvoyant since birth, being able to "see pictures" for as long as she can recall. Having grown up with her psychic talents, she took it for granted at first that everyone else had the same ability. As a youngster she never discussed it with her parents

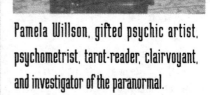

Talented psychic investigator Simon Probert.

Pamela Willson, gifted psychic artist, psychometrist, tarot-reader, clairvoyant, and investigator of the paranormal.

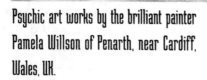

Psychic art works by the brilliant painter Pamela Willson of Penarth, near Cardiff, Wales, UK.

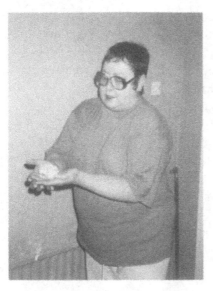

Bremna Howells of Landare, Wales — alias talented novelist and psychic Rosie Malone, specialist in hypno-regression — holding a stone which the authors recovered from the Chase Vault in Barbados.

or anyone else. It was about twenty years ago when she consulted a tarot reader that she was made aware that she had her unusual gifts. The reader told her "You see pictures, don't you?" and Pamela replied, "Yes, everyone does." The tarot reader then assured her that most people don't. In addition, Pamela is a very fine natural psychic and occult artist, who has executed many spirit drawings for people. When she is painting her work just seems to flow on to the canvas. She has also acted as a psychic consultant to members of the National Youth Theatre on a number of occasions.

With her many psychic talents and a wealth of experience on which to draw, Pamela is certain that "spirit will present not when you want, but when it wants." She feels that contact with the spirit world is rather like picking up a telephone into another dimension. Whether the intermediate instrument is a crystal ball, a bowl of water, or a piece of jewellery belonging to the enquirer, paranormal communication depends upon the reader's own psychic ability and development. Among the many enthusiastic letters of thanks and recommendation which Pamela has received over the years are comments like:

> " ... Accurate and perceptive ... in depth and detailed.... " Diss, England.
> "I was amazed at what you were able to tell me.... " Grangetown, Cardiff, Wales.
> " ... Thank you for the healing you have been sending out to my dog.... He is much friskier and more mobile..." Southgate, London, England.

"Thank you for the Tarot readings.... This knowledge has been a great comfort to me.... " Crouch End, London, England.

"I listed all of your prophecies for my own record and was astonished at the remarkable accuracy of them...." Oldham, Lancashire, England.

"Everything which you stated in regard to the person in the photograph proved to be 100% correct." High Barnet, Hertfordshire, England.

"As time goes by I can definitely relate your readings with day to day events in my life." Elstree, Hertfordshire, England.

"It all seems to be coming together following the pattern predicted by the cards." Northwest London, England.

Bremna Howells, who has written *Wicca: The Craft* and other interesting books under the penname of Rosie Malone, is also a naturally gifted psychic, psychometrist, and clairaudient who discovered her paranormal talents very early in life, just as Pamela did. We first met Bremna many years ago during one of our lectures on the Rennes-le-Château mystery, and during the subsequent discussion she came up with a fascinating theory about Saunière and his attractive young housekeeper, Marie Dénarnaud, performing a magical ritual known as *The Convocation of Venus*. Bremna was also a great help to us in connection with psychometrizing Colonel Fawcett's signet ring.

Her psychic experiences began when she was a young child with the customary imaginary friends associated with that stage of development. Bremna's two psychic companions were Sarah and Oas. Sarah gradually faded, but Oas remained with her as a permanent spiritual guide. She describes him as Nepalese, but unusually tall and thin. Bremna says that his Mongoloid features are augmented by a very thin, drooping Chinese Mandarin-style moustache.

In the days when the public enjoyed unrestricted access to Stonehenge, Bremna was taken there by her parents as a small girl. Wandering around examining the great trilithons, she placed her hand on the Heelstone and immediately fainted. When she recovered she explained to her father that she had seen "horrible pictures in her head of people being killed with long, gold knives." She went on to describe these ceremonial knives as having their crosspieces, or hand guards, in the shape of a new moon, or crescent.

By the time she was a young teenager, she realized that she was able to do things which most people could not. She began scrying using mirrors. She saw at first what seemed to be turbulent water reflected in the glass; this gradually cleared and was followed by a series of pictures. One such vision which she recalled clearly during our interview was a Templar Knight, standing with his head resting on the hilt of his long sword and leaning forward. She noticed particularly that he was standing in an unusual manner with most of his weight on one foot. In another of her visions she was swimming with dolphins, who were talking to her.

Her psychometric powers were demonstrated to us when she felt the strange energy emanating from the stone we had retrieved from the floor of the Chase vault in Barbados in which the coffins had moved mysteriously during the early years of the nineteenth century. Another of her remarkable psychometric demonstrations involved a pebble from the beach at Dunkirk.

Having taken an academic interest in the Old Religion to begin with, Bremna felt that in order to understand it more completely, it needed to be studied from the inside. She suspects that more women than men seem to be psychically gifted and wonders if this has anything to do with gender differences in brain chemistry. She is convinced that her long-term spiritual companion and guide, Oas, advises her of what is safe to investigate and warns her away from what is dangerous. Her current studies are being directed towards hypnotherapy and regression.

Another fascinating and gifted psychic-investigator friend is Terry le Riche Walters of Wokingham in Berkshire, England. Terry's book *Who on Earth am*

Terry Walters, psychic healer and clairvoyant. Author of *Who on Earth am I?*

I? gives a very interesting and readable account of his work, which the dynamically talented Ken Seddington sums up aptly and succinctly as: "Incredible stories — credible man."

Over the past half century, Terry has reported his experiences of many strange phenomena: alien visitations and telepathic contact with them, remarkable psychic healings, exorcism, and strange associations between ancient Egypt and the stellar universe. Terry's philosophy is centred on his belief that there is a paranormal, invisible energy waiting to be tapped. He feels that most people are too busy pursuing material advantages to realize what is going on close beside them in this vitally important invisible universe. He is confident that if only we took more time over it, we could all learn a great deal from each other just by listening carefully and attentively. He feels that in the beginning the concept of love and respect for others was a dominant social motivation, but that gradually the pursuit of money and power has displaced it. Terry's major concerns are currently with investigating the how and why of his psychic predictions when events occur in the way that he foretold.

One of the most striking of his healings took place in 1986 when Mandy, a close friend of Terry's teenage daughter, Angela, was suddenly struck down by a severe form of meningitis. Terry himself experienced the same blinding headache as the patient must have been suffering in the intensive care ward in the Atkinson Morley Hospital in southwest London. Just before dawn, Terry had an out-of-the-body experience in which he paid a psychic visit to the ward where Mandy seemed to be experiencing breathing difficulties with the tracheotomy tube of the respirator. In this strange astral sphere he seemed to be advising Mandy to pull the tube out, which he saw her do in the vision, and her breathing then improved significantly. When Terry later telephoned the hospital and spoke to Sister Francis, whom he already knew, she confirmed everything that he had seen during his astral journey and described how Mandy had removed the tube. Sister Francis also reported that there had been a slight improvement, and asked Terry to continue praying for Mandy, which he did. The following day, at around 4 a.m., Terry again experienced an astral travel incident in which he returned to the ward and saw Mandy's eyes flicker open. He also saw that she was able to move her right arm. He telephoned the hospital again, and Sister Francis confirmed what he had seen on the astral plain.

Terry's daughter, Angela, told him a few days later that her friend Mandy was now safely home again. They arranged to call to visit her, and she told Terry that she had seen him and heard his voice when his astral entity had visited her in the intensive care ward.

Another of Terry's amazing — yet totally credible — exploits concerns

Kevin Carlyon at Stonehenge — High Priest of the White Witches and expert in many forms of benign magical ritual.

his strenuous psychic battle with a huge, shimmering, bear-like creature in a remote cottage in Wales. Although Terry's own psychic powers and charismatic personality were more than a match for his sinister, eldritch opponent, he felt that the evil entity posed a terrifying threat to the family and friends who were with him, and whom he had to protect. The account of his astounding paranormal struggle in that sinister, old Welsh cottage was fully confirmed by the testimony of a family friend, Isabel Mattick, a former mayor of Bracknell, and a borough councillor, who was one of the party staying in the cottage with Terry and his wife at the time.

Largely because of the negative PR generated by characters like the execrable Matthew Hopkins, the timorous King James I, and the brilliant but biased author of the plays bearing Shakespeare's name, witches — even white ones — have not got a very positive image. But unknown to most people, their friends, neighbours, local bank clerks, nurses, and police officers could well hold magical beliefs. Kevin Carlyon is currently recognized as the High Priest of British Witches. This thirty-nine year old has practised white magic for over twenty-five years, and leads the largest coven in Europe with almost one thousand members.

Like the other modern men and women of mystery in this chapter, Kevin first became aware of his paranormal gifts when he was five years old, after beginning to have remarkably vivid dreams about school friends and members of his family. These varied from innocuous forecasts of what a classmate had in his lunch tin, to more serious predictions about a friend falling out of a tree and breaking his left arm.

As Kevin grew older he began to understand, as Terry Walters did, that his considerable paranormal gifts could be used to heal and defend those who needed his help.

After leaving school in 1976, Kevin went into the printing profession. In 1986 he founded The Covenant of Earth Magic, but found that so many people were asking for his help that it was difficult to fit everything in alongside a full-time career in the printing industry. In 1994 he went full time into his psychic work. Kevin describes his Earth Magic as a science of the mind, the power of positive thought via ritual to bring about a desired objective. What Kevin and his group practice is a thousand light years away from the popular horror-film image of evil magicians flying in on broomsticks to participate in orgies, and the sacrificing of goats, chickens, and teenage virgins.

Kevin's ideas can be summed up as a belief in a Force of Nature — apparently neutral in itself — something like Bernard Shaw's concept of the Life Force, or the Force in *Star Wars*, which Kenobi and the Jedi used for good, and Vader and the Emperor used for evil. Kevin's group, like the Jedi, will have nothing to do with the Dark Side.

One of Kevin's most interesting environmental magical projects took place in 1989 at Kitts Coty, an ancient Stone Age burial ground near Maidstone in Kent, England. Over two hundred participants joined Kevin in a ritual designed to protect the ancient sacred stones from a proposed rail link. At the time of writing, Kevin reports that the stones have not been disturbed.

The famous "haunted car" at Eastbourne, which the authors worked on with Kevin and Sandie Carlyon.

David Everson, who experienced a major miracle of spiritual healing and has had several strange paranormal experiences.

When asked to sum up his views on White Witchcraft or Earth Magic, Kevin said: "Even though we have so many scientific marvels about us, there is still one subject that baffles everyone — the paranormal. To me it is a fact and a way of life. It is not my goal to prove the existence of supernatural powers. I know they exist and can be tapped into. My goal is to use them to benefit others."

One case on which the authors themselves worked with Kevin and his partner Sandie, concerned an allegedly "haunted" car at Eastbourne on the south coast of England. This vehicle carried the licence plate "ARK 666 Y." Many strange tales were told of its earlier history. It was alleged that a suicide by carbon monoxide exhaust fumes had taken place inside it, that one of its front wheels had inexplicably caught light, and that it had apparently been the cause of a dangerous lightning strike that had hurled the owner back against a wall, and sent sparks crackling from his shoes. It may have been no more than an odd coincidence, of course, but as Lionel came back from Eastbourne by train late that night — after sprinkling this "unlucky" car with holy water and using a prayer of protection and exorcism over it — his train apparently went over a log which vandals had placed on the line near Swindon, which caused a delay of more than an hour.

David Everson from Thornton Heath in Surrey is a very interesting character who certainly qualifies as a rare man of mystery, and one whose heart-warming story is a pleasure to include in this collection. David was kind enough to write to us to say that he enjoyed our *Fortean TV* programs on Channel 4 on British television, and to tell us two remarkable stories of the paranormal.

Now thirty-five years old and single, David was raised as a Catholic and educated at a Catholic School in Croydon. Always true to his own faith since boyhood, David has nevertheless maintained a tolerant and interested attitude to life's other possibilities — what he refers to as its "tangents" — and that's a very healthy and sensible attitude to adopt. While studying Catholicism in depth, he also read around Taoism and Amerindian religion and culture. In Dave's own words: "The voyage of discovery is amazing."

In July of 1992, when David was only thirty, he was diagnosed as having non-Hodgkins' lymph cancer. After chemotherapy he relapsed so badly that his weight went down to seventy pounds, and a tumour behind his left eye blinded him on that side. His only hope of survival was a bone marrow transplant, and before that could be undertaken he needed more chemotherapy on an already shattered body. Despite these traumatic medical problems, his faith never faltered.

As he lay alone in his separate hospital room one night, with only his fighting spirit to keep him going, Dave wasn't sure whether he blacked out or not, but somehow he suddenly found himself walking through the countryside. The colours, however, were brighter and more intense than he had ever seen them before in the real world. Dave compared them to the old Technicolor movies from the fifties. In his dream, vision, or out-of-the-body experience — whatever it was — David saw a fairground roundabout with people riding it. He heard the sounds of happy laughing voices and music. As David drew closer to the roundabout he recognized the riders: one was his mother, who had died in 1984; another was an uncle who had also passed over. There were numerous other friends and relatives on that carousel, all of whom had left this earth. They all looked very happy to see him, but as he went to join them on the roundabout, they said: "David, it's not your time to ride — but you're going to be OK." They smiled and gave him a cheery thumbs-up sign. He left the ride and watched it slowly fading away. Then he saw himself walking slowly back to the hospital and getting back into bed. In the air above his bed was a vision of the Virgin Mary enveloped in pure white light. She looked at him, smiled and disappeared. David came to again in bed, unable to stop crying. His spirit was soaring. He felt totally elated, and stronger than he had ever felt in the whole of his life up to that amazing moment.

The very next day the doctor in charge of David's treatment wandered into his room on an unplanned visit accompanied by a group of his students. To the doctor's amazement, David was out of bed with his back to the door so that he had not seen them enter. He was wearing his headset and dancing to a piece of Jimi Hendrix music. Turning to face the door, David stopped because the medical group on their rounds had startled him. The doctor stopped dead in his tracks and exclaimed: "My God! I don't believe what I'm seeing!" Then he took David in his arms and embraced him like a long lost friend who has come safely home against all hope.

The bone marrow transplant was effective, although David had a slight relapse in 1994. When he wrote to us in 1997, he had been clear of all cancer for three years, and the vision in his left eye was fully restored as well. He was well on the way to resuming the management work which he had been enjoying before the medical problem hit him. Up to a hefty 180 pounds, he also took a motorcycling course successfully and says how much he loves biking and rock and roll music. In his own truly uplifting and inspiring words, he has faith in God and faith in himself, and his thirst for life is unquenchable. When we wrote back to him to say how truly delighted we were to hear his wonderful news we said:

Miracles of divine healing do take place, not only in the Palestine of Christ's days on earth, but here and now in Surrey, in Cardiff, in any place that God in His wisdom selects. There is so much about these mysteries of healing that we can't yet explain, or understand properly, but reading your ideas carefully, we're of the opinion that faith in God and in oneself is at least as important as surgery and medicine. We're not very well versed in computer technology, but we know from friends who are experts that there are superficial codes and deeper, more powerful pathways which they call machine code. This machine code gets to deeper levels of the computer and does things at a fundamental level which the surface codes, like spreadsheets or word processors, cannot reach. Is it possible, do you think, that the human mind and body also have these two types of communication? When we use what Jesus Himself called "faith" of the strongest and deepest type, the kind that can move mountains, defy gravity over water, turn water into wine, and raise the dead — then we're using machine code. When we take an aspirin to alleviate a headache after a stressful day at the office, we're using a superficial code like a word processor package. To a man or woman who really believes in that earliest Christian sense in the power of the mind attuned to God's will, there are no limits whatsoever. Which brings in some more metaphysical speculation of the kind that we're sure appeals to you as much as it does to us: believing as we do that God's love is infinite, and His power immeasurable, it must be totally in accordance with His will for health to be sustained and for healing to take place.

David recounted two other fascinating experiences for us in addition to his detailed account of his own amazing recovery. The first of these took place shortly after his mother's death in 1984. As he was walking upstairs he felt something which he described as like a warm, gentle breeze that apparently passed right through his body. He also smelled his mother's favourite perfume which was very distinctive. He was absolutely convinced that she was there in spirit. About six months later, he had gone out clubbing with his friends and they were returning in a taxi. Just before he was due to be dropped off, his friend John, who was in the taxi with David, glanced up and saw someone looking out of a lighted window in David's home. "Your Mum's still awake. She's looking out of the window," said John. David looked up, and saw that she was. He remembered that she'd always done that years ago, because he was the youngest and she'd always tended to worry if he was home late. "So she is," he said calmly to John, who had no idea that she had been dead for several months. David didn't tell John about his mother's death until a month or so after the incident in the taxi. The fact that they had both seen her so clearly was powerful evidence for the soul's survival.

Steve Andrews of Ely, near Cardiff, Wales, is a talented poet, as well as a gifted musician and singer-songwriter. His impressive songs and music to date include *Sound of One*, *Dive in Deep*, and *From Venus with Love*. Some of his equally impressive verse appears in an anthology entitled *Visions of the Mind*. An Initiated Bard of the Free Gorsedd of Bards of Caer Abiri, otherwise known as Avebury, where an ancient and mysterious stone circle stands,

Steve Andrews of Ely near Cardiff, Wales, talented musician, singer-songwriter and poet, who has had many psychic adventures.

Steve is also a Quest Knight and Bard of the Loyal Arthurian Warband. This is a mysterious druidic order whose leader is styled King Arthur Pendragon. His followers believe him to be a reincarnation of the original Arthur, whom they regard historically as a Celtic Chieftain rather than a Romano-British Warlord.

Steve has been fascinated by the wonders of nature since childhood, and is equally interested in what he describes as "supernature." He regards this vitally important supernature as an extension, or continuation, of ordinary nature, but one that humanity has tended to lose touch with. Like Pamela, Bremna, Kevin, and Terry, Steve has had many strange psychic and paranormal experiences over the years, including sightings of what he believes to have been UFOs.

Steve would regard himself as a conspiracy theorist: he is convinced that the general public are not being told the truth about UFOs, nor about several other very curious and enigmatic subjects. His theories of the true nature of the cosmos are basically multidimensionalistic. In Steve's own words: "I believe that, just as we can see life expressed on this planet in a fantastic multitude of ways, it is the same throughout Creation — which has very, very many dimensions as well as the ones we know about. I believe all life is spiritual in essence and part and parcel of an infinite creative spiritual whole which many people call God, or express as a deity. This spirit is constantly and forever experiencing itself via all its creations. I believe that spirit cannot die but that the material body can change form, or is recycled, while the spirit continues. All life is sacred, but I believe that life as we perceive it is an illusion because we are unable to sense its complete reality as we operate within only a minute fraction of our sensory range. Everything is part of everything else and is linked together, but like a jigsaw on an infinite scale we have to find the right pieces to see it fit together."

Another of Steve's research areas is alternative medicines, and he has recently investigated an unusual fungus-tea called *Kombucha*, for which powerful healing claims are being made. It's a brownish, rather slimy substance that looks like the alien invaders in a "B"-grade science fiction film. It's also known as Russian Mother, Manchurian Elixir, and Kvass. According to Steve's research, it was first used medicinally during the Tsin Dynasty in 212 BC. Technically, Kombucha is neither a fungus nor a lichen, but a weird symbiotic mixture of numerous yeasts and bacteria. This strange culture feeds on sugar and tea, and users allow it to brew and ferment until its strange ingredients turn into what they claim is a health-giving elixir. Steve reports that orthodox medical experts have already expressed interest in Kombucha and are of the opinion that it could well contain active ingredients which may be worth testing and putting through clinical trials in due course.

One of Steve's most interesting and exciting investigations took place in the late seventies and concerned an allegedly haunted house in the Gabalfa area of Cardiff in Wales. A family who were keenly interested in psychic phenomena had recently moved out of the house after holding regular seances there, during which they claimed to have contacted the spirit of Elvis Presley. (We featured a similar incident in one of our *Fortean TV* shows in which a devoted Presley fan in Holland had a statuette of Elvis which appeared to weep occasionally.) The Gabalfa family were dedicated Presley devotees and had constructed a shrine to him in the house.

The middle-aged couple who followed them as tenants reported that they had seen a ghost, as a result of which the husband had a heart attack — fortunately this was not fatal, but, understandably, they moved out as soon as they could. The local church authorities were approached for help, as was a neighbouring spiritualist church. The press soon took an interest as well. The house belonged to the local authority, who felt that the best way to return it to normality would be to advertise for volunteers to spend the night in it to show that it was perfectly innocuous. Steve and his friend Colin Sutton were among those who volunteered. What they noticed most were unnatural cold spots in the premises, and an unusual smell — which Steve described as "like musty aftershave" — that came and went.

Steve recalled that some of the reporters who arrived to write up the story had been unwilling to enter the house, even though he had reassured them that it was perfectly safe to do so.

Steve pursued his enquiries by contacting the original, psychic family who had set up the Presley shrine in the first place, and examined some interesting examples of automatic writing among their large collection of Presley memorabilia. The local council's idea of having volunteers sleeping in the house seemed to have discouraged whatever was causing the disturbing phenomena, as there have been no further reports of any trouble.

This small sample of modern men and women of mystery serves as a timely reminder that this present moment, the priceless here and now in which we find ourselves, is every bit as exciting and interesting as the era of the Sphinx and the pyramids, Stonehenge and Avebury, Roswell and the Philadelphia Experiment. Unexplained enigmas surround us today. We have to hunt them down with that infallible net: an honest, open, critical, and enquiring mind.

BIBLIOGRAPHY

Andere, Mary. *Arthurian Links with Herefordshire.* Great Britain: Logaston Press, 1995.

Ashe, Geoffrey (Ed.). *The Quest for Arthur's Britain.* London: Granada Publishing. 1972.

Bacon, Francis. *Essays: The Wisdom of the Ancients and The New Atlantis.* London: Odhams Press Ltd., 1950.

Betjeman, John. *Collected Poems.* London: John Murray, 1988.

Blashford-Snell, John. *Mysteries: Encounters with the Unexplained.* London: Bodley Head, 1983.

Bord, Janet and Colin. *Mysterious Britain.* Great Britain: Paladin, 1974.

Boudet, Henri. *La Vraie Langue Celtique et le Cromleck de Rennes-les-Bains.* Nice, France: Belisane, 1984 reprint.

Bradbury, Will (Ed.). *Into the Unknown.* United States: Readers Digest, 1988.

Bradley, Michael. *Holy Grail Across the Atlantic.* Toronto: Hounslow Press, 1988.

Briggs, Katharine M. *British Folk Tales and Legends: A Sampler.* London: Granada Publishing in Paladin, 1977.

Brookesmith, Peter (Ed.). *Open Files.* London: Orbis Publishing, 1984.

Carrington, Richard. *Mermaids and Mastodons.* London: Arrow Books Ltd., 1960.

Cavendish, Richard (Ed.). *Encyclopaedia of the Unexplained.* London: Routledge & Kegan Paul, 1974.

Clark, Jerome, *Unexplained.* United States: Gale Research Inc., 1993.

Cohen, Daniel. *Encyclopaedia of Ghosts.* London: Guild Publishing, 1989.

Dixon, G. M. *Folktales and Legends of Norfolk.* Minimax, 1983.

Dunford, Barry. *The Holy Land of Scotland.* Scotland: Brigadoon Books, 1996.

Dyall, Valentine. *Unsolved Mysteries.* London: Hutchinson & Co. Ltd., 1954.

Eysenck, H.J. and Sargent, Carl. *Explaining the Unexplained.* London: BCA, 1993.

Encyclopaedia Britannica: Britannica Online: http://www.eb.com.

Fanthorpe, Lionel and Patricia. *The Oak Island Mystery.* Toronto: Hounslow Press, 1995.

Fanthorpe, Lionel and Patricia. *Secrets of Rennes-le-Château.* USA: Samuel Weiser Inc., 1992.

Fanthorpe, Lionel and Patricia. *The World's Greatest Unsolved Mysteries.* Toronto: Hounslow Press, 1997.

Flem-ath, Rand and Rose. *When the Sky Fell: In Search of Atlantis.* Toronto: Stoddart, 1995.

Forman, Joan. *Haunted East Anglia.* Great Britain: Fontana, 1976.

Fortean Times. London: John Brown Publishing Ltd.

Fowke, Edith. *Canadian Folklore.* Toronto: Oxford University Press, 1988.

Gettings, Fred. *Encyclopaedia of the Occult.* London: Guild Publishing, 1986.

Godwin, John. *This Baffling World.* New York City: Hart Publishing Company, 1968.

Graves, Robert. Introduction to *Larousse Encyclopaedia of Mythology.* London: Paul Hamlyn, 1959.

Gribble, Leonard. *Famous Historical Mysteries.* London: Target Books, 1974.

Guerber, H.A. *Myths and Legends of the Middle Ages.* London: Studio editions Ltd., 1994.

Gurdjieff, G.I. *Beelzebub's Tales to his Grandson.* London: Routledge and Kegan Paul, 1974.

Haining, Peter. *The Restless Bones and Other True Mysteries.* London: Armada Books: 1970.

Hancock, Graham. *The Sign and the Seal.* London: Mandarin, 1993.

Hancock, Graham. *Fingerprints of the Gods.* New York: Crown Publishers, 1995.

Hapgood, Charles. *Maps of the Ancient Sea Kings.* USA: Adventure Unlimited Press, 1996.

Heywood, Abel. *Mother Shipton's Prophecies.* U.K. George Mann. 1978.

Hitching, Francis. *The World Atlas of Mysteries.* London: Pan Books, 1979.

Hogarth, Peter and Clery, Val. *Dragons.* London: Penguin Books Ltd., 1979.

Hogue, John. *Nostradamus & The Millennium.* New York: Doubleday Dolphin, 1987.

Knight, Gareth. *The Secret Tradition in Arthurian Legend.* Great Britain: The Aquarian Press, 1983.

Knight, Christopher and Robert Lomas. *The Second Messiah.* London: Arrow Books, 1998.

Lacy, N.J. *The Arthurian Encyclopaedia.* Woodbridge, Suffolk, U.K: Boydell Press, 1986.

Lampitt, L.F. (Ed.). *The World's Strangest Stories.* London: Associated Newspapers Group Ltd., 1955.

MacDougall, Curtis D. *Hoaxes.* New York: Dover Publications, Inc., 1958.

Mack, Lorrie, et al (Ed.). *The Unexplained.* London: Orbis, 1984.

Metcalfe, Leon. *Discovering Ghosts.* U.K.: Shire Publications Ltd., 1974.

Michell, John and Robert J.M. Rickard. *Phenomena: A Book of Wonders.* London: Thames & Hudson, 1977.

Morison, Elizabeth and Frances, Lamont. *An Adventure*. London: Macmillan & Co., Ltd., 1913.

Moss, Peter. *Ghosts Over Britain*. Great Britain: Sphere Books Ltd., 1979.

Newton, Brian. *Monsters and Men*. England: Dunestone Printers Ltd., 1979.

Pohl, Frederick J. *Prince Henry Sinclair*. Halifax: Nimbus Publishing Ltd., 1967.

Poole, Keith B. *Ghosts of Wessex*. Canada. Douglas David & Charles Ltd. 1976

Porter, Enid. *The Folklore of East Anglia*. London: B.T.Batsford Ltd., 1974.

Pott, Mrs. Henry. *Bacon's Promus*. London: Sampson Low, Marston and Company, 1883.

Pott, Mrs. Henry. *Francis Bacon and his Secret Society*. London: Sampson Low, Marston and Company, 1891.

Rawcliffe, D.H. *Illusions and Delusions of the Supernatural and the Occult*. New York: 1959.

Reader's Digest Book. *Folklore, Myths, and Legends of Britain*. London: The Reader's Digest Association Ltd., 1973.

Reader's Digest Book. *Strange Stories, Amazing Facts*. London: The Reader's Digest Association Ltd., 1975.

Ritchie, Anna. *Picts*. Scotland: HMSO, 1993.

Rolleston, T.W. *Celtic Myths and Legends*. London: Studio editions Ltd., 1994.

Russell, Eric Frank. *Great World Mysteries*. London: Mayflower, 1967.

Saltzman, Pauline. *The Strange and the Supernormal*. New York: Paperback Library, Inc., 1968.

Sampson, Chas. *Ghosts of the Broads*. Norwich: Jarrold & Sons Ltd., 1973.

Sharper Knowlson, T. *The Origins of Popular Superstitions and Customs*. London: Studio Editions Ltd., 1995.

Sinclair, Andrew. *The Sword and the Grail*. New York: Crown Publishers, Inc., 1992.

Snow, Edward Rowe. *Strange Tales from Nova Scotia to Cape Hatteras*. USA: Dodd, Mead & Company, 1946.

Spencer, John and Anne. *The Encyclopaedia of the World's Greatest Unsolved Mysteries*. London: Headline Book Publishing, 1995.

Spicer, Stanley, T. *The Saga of the Mary Celeste*. Nova Scotia: Lancelot Press Ltd., 1993.

Strachey, Lytton. *Elizabeth and Essex*. London: Penguin Books, 1950.

Strong, Roy. *Lost Treasures of Britain*. USA: Viking Penguin, 1990.

Tesla, Nikola and David Childress. *The Fantastic Inventions of Nikola Tesla*. USA: Adventures Unlimited Press, 1993.

Tomas, Andrew. *Atlantis: From Legend to Discovery*. London: Sphere Books, 1974.

Toulson, H. David. *Knaresborough: It's Murder, Mystery & Magic*. Leeds: Yorkshire Press Agency, 1991.

Underwood, Peter. *The Ghost Hunter's Guide*. U.K.: Blandford Press, 1987.

Wallis Budge, E. A. *The Book of the Dead*. Secaucus, New Jersey: The Citadel Press, 1984 reprint.

Walters, Terry le Riche. *Who on Earth Am I?* Ringwood, Hants, UK: Amora, 1997.

Whitehead, John. *Guardian of the Grail*. London: Jarrolds, 1959.

Whitehead, Ruth Holmes. *Stories from the Six Worlds*. Nova Scotia: Nimbus Publishing Ltd., 1988.

Williams, Neville. *Francis Drake*. London: Weidenfeld and Nicolson, 1973.

Wilson, Colin and Damon. *Unsolved Mysteries Past and Present*. London: Headline Book Publishing, 1993.

Wilson, Colin, Damon, and Rowan. *World Famous True Ghost Stories*. London: Robinson Publishing, 1996.

Wilson, Colin and Christopher Evans, (Ed.). London: *The Book of Great Mysteries*. Robinson Publishing. 1986

X-Factor. London: Marshall Cavendish Partworks Ltd.,

Young, George. *Ghosts in Nova Scotia*. Halifax: George Young, Nova Scotia, 1991.

Young, George. *Ancient Peoples and Modern Ghosts*. Halifax: George Young, Nova Scotia, 1991.

9 780888 822024